THE HORSEMAN'S MANUAL

E. HARTLEY EDWARDS

THE HORSEMAN'S MANUAL

J.A. ALLEN
London

British Library Cataloguing in Publication Data
Hartley Edwards, Elwyn, *1927*
  The horseman's manual.
  1. Horsemanship
  I. Title
  798.2

ISBN 0–85131–487–2

First published in Great Britain in 1990 by
J. A. Allen & Company Limited
1 Lower Grosvenor Place
London SW1W 0EL

Book production Bill Ireson
Typeset by Waveney Typesetters, Norwich, Norfolk
Printed by St Edmundsbury Press, Bury St Edmunds, Suffolk

This is for: Peterkin, Benjamin,
Max, Bandook, Muffin
and Tara.
There were none better.

Contents

Acknowledgements

I have to acknowledge the help given to me by my friends John and June Abbott, who get all sorts of tunes out of a word-processor and come up with a beautifully presented manuscript. Sian Thomas BHSII, of the Snowdonia Centre, Waunfawr, together with Taurus and Merlin, carried out every sort of movement asked of them with the utmost patience and my old friend Leslie Lane took the pictures. I am grateful to them all and very particularly to Caroline Burt, Editorial Manager of J.A. Allen, my publishers, whose enthusiasm encouraged me to make this revision.

Finally, mention must be made of my dear friend the late Alison McInerney who was responsible for the early training of the Arab Bandook. The grooming, lungeing and long-reining pictures show Alison working with this little horse. Alison died as the result of a riding accident but those who knew her remember her with the greatest affection.

Introduction

When I wrote *The Horseman's Guide*, predecessor to this *Manual*, over 20 years ago, it was for a horse-world which might at first glance have seemed very different to the one with which we are familiar today. In fact, on a closer appraisal, the horse scene of the 1990s differs no more than in details of emphasis and accent.

In 20 years great advances have been made in veterinary science – far more indeed than in the preceding 50–60 years. Much valuable research has been done in the fields of equine nutrition and, indeed, a whole industry has grown up around the keeping of horses. (Interestingly, when *The Guide* was published in 1968, the first horse and pony feed nuts, pellets etc. had been on the market for no more than a decade.)

By 1968 the disciplines of eventing and showjumping were certainly well established; that of dressage was rather less so, being as it were "by schism rent asunder, by heresy distressed", and that of competitive carriage driving had hardly found a footing in Britain.

Since then change has been swift and dramatic in quality. Course-building for horse trials, for example, has developed into an exact science with a touch of artistry. In consequence, the sport has advanced in every respect, not least that riders have acquired the techniques required to solve the problems set by skilled and ingenious course-builders.

Riding safety is now a platform and a powerful lobby to boot – which is surely as it should be when the British Horse Society can report eight horse-related accidents on our roads each day. (I confess that for 30 years I and others of my generation rode in soft caps – I would not do so today.) That Society produces a welter of advisory pamphlets on every sort of subject and awards a multitude of qualifications to the career-minded, whilst the run of instructional literature, informed and less-informed, continues unabated – as, indeed, it has done since Kikkuli and Mittanian inscribed his manual for the Hittite chariot corps in about 1360 B.C. and Xenophon his treatises on cavalry training nearly 1,000 years later.

Whether the *general* standard of riding has improved noticeably in the past 20 years is a subject open to argument, and the same applies to the overall level of horse-management.

Interest in horses and participation in horse activities is certainly greater than ever before, and it is salutary to remember that the greybeards of the late 60s were talking about having reached saturation point in the middle of that swinging decade.

If I was invited to stick my neck out, I would say that the basic principles, whether those relative to riding or management, are no better understood than they were 20 years ago, and in some respects are even less clearly appreciated.

Today, as in the immediate past, there is no shortage of people who *love* horses, and, indeed, make real sacrifices to keep them. But *love*, even with a capital L, is still no substitute for knowledge; nor does it do much to further a soundly-based relationship with the horse based on respect and the acquired ability to communicate with an animal which happens to belong to a different species to our own.

Inevitably, as we approach the 21st century, there is an increasing number of *experts*, either self-appointed or those with initials to support their status (I hope I belong to neither group). These are the Big Brothers who know what is good for us and our horses – how many of them are *horsemen or women* is less certain.

The one constant element in this climate of continual change is the horse, who for all that expert attention runs no faster, jumps no higher and is no more enduring than ever he was.

In all his essentials he remains the same animal as that which galloped across the Asian steppes 5,000 years ago and the horse which, please God, will inhabit the Earth 1,000 years from now will be no different.

What follows is the *Preface* to *The Horseman's Guide*. It is included as something of a period piece, if you like, but is not, I think, entirely irrelevant to the last decade of our century.

E.H.E.   Chwilog, 1990

Preface

There are many, very many, books on horses and it is probable that no other animal has attracted so great a wealth of literature. But then probably no other animal attracts so much devotion, and often controversy, too, or exerts so great an influence on the lives of his admirers.

More and more people each year seem to fall under the strange influence that the horse is able to exert, and more and more of them are fixed with an ardent desire to become his "faithful servant". There are many reasons advanced as to why this should be so.

Some see it as an urgent human need to maintain a relationship with a living creature of another species, before the ability to do so is lost for ever. They see it as a reaction against the advance of automation and urbanisation, and as an escape from a world which accepts the necessity of nuclear armament. The more materially minded regard it as an inevitable result of an affluent society with leisure on its hands and money in its pocket. There are, I believe, people who hold that the ownership of a horse or pony is a form of social snobbery or one-upmanship. And, of course, in 1968, there are bound to be some who relate horse-ownership, horse-riding and even horse-admiration with a form of sexual motivation.

Whatever the truth may be (for myself I just enjoy horses without indulging in an analysis of my reasons for doing so) the cult of the horse goes on increasing and as a result the literature of the horse is enlarged correspondingly.

It is not possible, in my view, to learn to ride or to care for horses from books alone, and certainly not from this one.

Nevertheless, the written word is an important, and even an essential, factor in an equestrian education. However bad the book, there is always something to be learnt from it – even if it is only what not to do. This is, perhaps, part of the fascination of the horse, for even the greatest of horsemen will admit that they are always able to learn something new. For myself the more I know, the more clear it becomes to me how much I have to learn.

Book learning is no substitute for practical experience acquired under a skilled instructor, but once this latter has been established it is a valuable means of enlarging and deepening our understanding and our knowledge.

It is as well, however, for the newcomer to the horse-world to remember that while there are plenty of books (a list of suggested reading appears at the end of this one) they do not, as might be supposed, say much the same thing in slightly different ways. Some of them, in fact, present diametrically opposed views, the mental consumption of which can be reckoned to cause confusion and even dismay in the strongest and most stable of minds.

It is, indeed, more than possible that certain aspects of this book will disagree with statements appearing in others of similar subject matter and, in all probability, written by authors of far greater distinction than myself.

Although more than ready to admit fallibility, such a situation does not necessarily mean that I am wrong and they are right, or vice versa. Providing that a statement or practice is backed by sufficient logic it merely proves that "there are many paths to the top of the hill". The fact that there are a number of ends which can be achieved by varying means is just one more delightful facet in the study of the horse.

What we all have to do, having acquired a basic knowledge of horsemastership and a seat of some security, is to recognise this fact and, while regarding the other fellow's approach with tolerance, decide how far up the hill we wish to go (you don't always get the best view from the top), then choose the path which seems to be most suited to us.

The motives which drive people to commit their thoughts, theories and advice to print are as diverse, and as arguable, as those that prompt people to share their lives with horses.

It would be presumptuous of me to say that this book came into being because I wished to share the happiness and enjoyment I have received from horses with other people, or because I wished to improve the lot of horses and ponies and to help their owners to get more enjoyment from their association. And yet if this book does any one of those things for some horse and some rider, even to the smallest degree, its existence will be amply justified.

I have tried to cover the main aspects of horse management and training in an elementary fashion in the hope that it will be useful to those individuals and families who are just embarking, or have recently embarked, on horse and pony ownership.

There are, therefore, chapters and passages devoted to the handling and training of ponies and the part that grown-ups can play to ensure that the children get the maximum enjoyment from their mount, while the parents enjoy peace of mind in similar proportions.

To enjoy a happy family life is one of the most precious gifts man can receive. When horses and ponies can be brought into that circle then, surely, the cup overflows.

If we establish a proper relationship with the horse we attain something which is both satisfying and rewarding. Through him, who is neither wholly saint nor wholly sinner, we and our children learn patience, tolerance, the exercise of kindness combined with firmness, self-control and unselfishness – even, perhaps, a little harmless guile. There is no room for force, harsh words or actions, temper or anger. These may be somewhat old-fashioned qualities, but then I am old-fashioned enough to think them worthwhile.

CHAPTER 1

First Find Your Horse

Every year, every day, and for all I know every hour, there are a number of people who experience disappointment, sometimes even heartbreak, and certainly financial loss over the purchase of a horse.

This is regrettable and one has every sympathy with the person who has clearly been sold a pup. There are, however, many more cases where the purchaser, through ignorance, has bought a horse or pony quite unsuitable for his or her purpose and suffered in consequence.

Buying an animal is always likely to be something of a gamble, but the odds against one buying a real pig in a poke can be greatly reduced if one sets about the operation with forethought and is armed with a certain elementary knowledge.

Relevant Factors

The first thing to decide is the type of horse you want, and this choice should be governed by factors other than those of personal preference.

Logically your choice must be influenced by the purpose for which the animal is intended, the facilities you have for keeping him and the amount of time you can devote to him, your own equestrian ability and personal conformation and, of the utmost importance, how much you can afford to pay.

If you keep a competent groom, or are able to devote most of your time to a horse, the matter is obviously simplified and your choice, all other things being equal, is less restricted.

If, on the other hand, you intend to ride and care for the horse yourself, with the help of co-operating members of the family, and earn a living as well, it is wise to consider all these factors very carefully.

Much will depend on your circumstances and the facilities you possess. People of average means with jobs to do may find it difficult, if not impossible, to keep a horse stabled in the winter. Stabled horses need a great deal of attention and, of course, considerable exercise. It is more likely, and certainly more advisable, for a person in this situation to decide on keeping the horse out at grass entirely, leaving him unclipped, but with a shelter against prevailing winds, or going in for the so-called *combined method*, entailing stabling the horse at night and turning him out in a New Zealand rug during the day.

Types and Breeds

Either of these two methods precludes the majority of Thoroughbred horses, who rarely winter out well. It is possible to use the combined method with some Thoroughbreds but, in general, a three-quarter or half-bred horse would be a better choice, particularly if there is some native blood in the background.

The ideal *family* horse to live out (and that precludes the smaller native ponies) would be one of the larger native breeds, the Fell, the Highland, Connemara, New Forest or the excellent Welsh Cob, or at any rate, something containing a large percentage of Mountain and Moorland blood. These animals inherit qualities of unsurpassed hardiness and have remarkably robust constitutions. All of them, of course, can be hunter clipped and kept on the combined method if one wished to hunt regularly. The breeds mentioned make ideal hunters in anything but real galloping country and are all up to the weight of the average adult. As an all-round family hrose which can be ridden by parents and older children they are probably unsurpassed. They also go well in harness.

If, however, you are more ambitious and wish to hunt more seriously and perhaps to enter into competitive events, you will need an animal possessing greater scope. You will also, of course, need the time and facilities to care for him properly. If you have these requirements you may consider the Thoroughbred, for whom I confess to having a personal preference. He is the Rolls-Royce of horses, being extremely responsive and having natural balance, good paces and great courage.

There are, however, drawbacks to high breeding when used other than for racing. The Thoroughbred is not always the easiest of rides and it is rare that you will find one who has the necessary temperament for either showjumping or dressage. To enjoy him to the full you need to be an experienced horseman and horsemaster and you must have a secure seat, light hands and an abundance of equestrian tact. His constitution, too, is more delicate and he needs far more care and attention than his humbler brethren. Most people, and certainly those of average ability, will be better suited to the half or three-quarter bred animal. The majority of them, indeed, would be sadly at sea if put on a fit Thoroughbred.

The author's three-quarter bred mare by Good Apple. Her dam was by Damascus out of a Clydesdale mare. The mare is fitted with lungeing tackle.

Mr Keith Luxford's champion cob, Grandstand, a pure Irish Draught.

First Glance, a small riding horse who shows a lot of quality.

An excellent example of a young half-bred hunter. The sort of horse who could fulfil a variety of purposes.

A splendidly made Hannoverian horse. A big, powerful specimen with great presence.

The ideal stamp of young horse likely to make an eventer. This five-year-old is by the Thoroughbred Fourburrow.

The late Marchioness Townshend's pure-bred Arabian, Saffron Sky, one of the most notable pure-bred performers of recent years.

For those who favour the colourful life. A beautifully marked young Appaloosa of exemplary conformation.

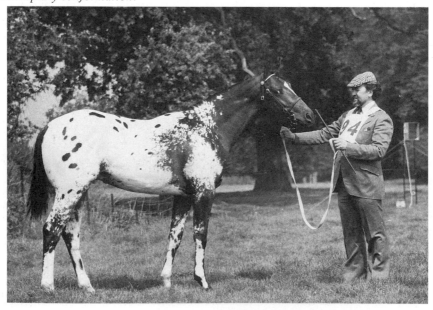

So far as the Arab is concerned, there is no doubt that most of them are delightful and intelligent rides with appealing characters. They are usually exceptionally sound and as long-distance, endurance ride horses they have no equal, for their stamina is boundless. The Arab is also the only breed which can be raced on the Flat under Jockey Club rules by the D.I.Y. owner/trainer/jockey. There is, nonetheless, a prejudice against the breed in Britain and perhaps elsewhere, too. That it exists, one is bound to say, is more the fault of the owners and breeders of Arabian horses than that of the horses themselves.

For too long they have allowed and even encouraged the "poodle" image of "the thing on a string", and whilst paying lip-service to the all-round Arabian riding horse have done little in reality to promote the breed as a practical proposition. All that, however, is changing fast.

There are in this book, for instance, pictures of a little pure-bred Arab given to me by Major and Mrs Hedley of the Briery Close Stud, Windermere, Cumbria. He competed very successfully in showjumping, dressage and one-day events at a good Riding Club level and never put a foot wrong.

Nonetheless, the Arab, probably on account of his size and scope, is rarely seen in competitive events. Indeed, whilst there is no reason why he should not compete successfully in dressage competitions, for instance, it is an unhappy fact that very few dressage judges would have the eye to appreciate his distinctive movement.

The Arab is hunted by enthusiasts of the breed, but his size and perhaps his overall "awareness" may be against him. Or it just may be that a four-foot fence looks very much more formidable from the back of a 14 hh Arab than from a large hunter.

Anglo-Arabs, however, although not sufficiently encouraged in Britain, are bigger and exceptionally good rides. The French Anglo-Arab, for instance, is the toughest and most brilliant of performers.

Increasingly, there are the European (and British) Warm-blood horses to consider; the Dutch, Hannoverian, Holstein and Trakehner, as well as the Selle Française, which may be the best of them in terms of general usage.

These, with the exception perhaps of the latter, are big, strongly-built horses. They are carefully bred to a rigorous selection system, well produced and promoted with great professionalism.

Temperamentally they are ideally suited to the disciplines of the *manège* and they are powerful showjumpers. Most of them are very correct movers to boot. However, with the exception again of the Selle Française and possibly the Trakehner, they are only rarely much good for hunting and cross-country riding – for these last pursuits there is nothing to beat the three-quarter bred who carries a bit of native pony blood.

Assessing Physique and Ability

At this stage it is as well to make an honest assessment of one's own ability. Very few of us are first-class horsemen and some of us will never become anything more than average. In buying a horse, or in dealing with one, nothing is more important than to be able to recognise one's limitations.

There is no more pitiful a sight than a rider obviously over-horsed. You may secretly dream of amazing your friends by appearing on a magnificent Thoroughbred, prancing and cavorting "to witch the world with noble horsemanship". Unless, however, you are sufficiently competent, buy something more suited to your capabilities and let the dream remain but a dream. You will be far happier, safer, and less likely to die of fright, or a broken neck, on something not so spectacular, but more suited to your standard of riding.

It is just as important to recognise the failings of your own temperament. So often a horse is said to have a bad temperament, he is nervy or impetuous, or just down-right bad tempered. There are, of course, horses that are more difficult than others, but nine times out of ten it is man who has made them so. The demeanour and behaviour of a horse, a dog or a child is, I believe, a reflection of the master's or parents' character. The highly strung horse is certainly made more so if his master is cast in the same mould, and conversely the idle animal becomes increasingly dull under a lethargic rider. If, therefore, you are of a hasty, impatient, hot-headed nature, all of which faults you should seek to eradicate if you want to succeed with horses, it is hardly sensible to choose a tearaway sort of animal for a companion. In general, the rule of contrasting opposites, often so successful in human relationships, is a good one to follow in the choice of a horse.

Jorrocks said that as he didn't ride steeplechases his weight was a matter between himself and the horse. Weight, and shape too, is, however, a consideration when looking for an equine partner.

Capacity to Carry Weight

The weight carrying capacity of a horse is not determined by his height but by the size and density of his bone (measured below the knee) and his general proportions. Welsh Cobs and our other native breeds are usually up to very much more weight than the beginner might think, and display wonderful bone and excellent limbs. As a rough guide a horse having 8 inches of bone below the knee should be up to 11–12 stone, 9–10 inches up to 13–14 stone, and 10–11 inches up to 15 stone and over.

Much, however, depends on his proportions and, in fact, the bone of the Thoroughbred, being of greater density, will carry a greater weight, inch for inch, than that of a common-bred horse, where the bone structure is coarser and more open. Bone is in fact constructed like a tube and has a hollow centre, or rather a centre that *would* be hollow if it were not filled with marrow. The strength of the bone depends on the thickness and density of the substances surrounding this central core. The best and strongest structure is obviously that with the smallest core and the greater surrounding area of bone. However large the bone measurement, it is of little value if the central core is wide and encompassed by only a thin wall.

There is, of course, no way of discovering the type of bone structure by external examination, but it is well to remember that 10 inches of common bone may be a weaker structure than 8 inches in a better-bred horse.

Now horses with the ability to carry a heavy weight, particularly when that ability is accompanied by scope and quality, are hard to come by and correspondingly more expensive than the lighter type of horses. It follows, therefore, that it is just as stupid for a person of 11 stone to buy a horse up to 15 stone, as it is for a heavyweight to risk breaking down a horse well below his weight.

The height of a horse in relation to the rider must also be taken into account and so must the rider's physical shape. Big horses, by which I mean the 17 hh gargantuan, may make fences look small and their riders feel big sitting on top of them, but they have disadvantages. Apart from the difficulty of getting on to the animal without a pair of stepladders, his limbs have a greater body mass to carry and, in the case of jumping, to lift over an obstacle. It is true that he may have greater physical strength in proportion, but there are many cases when the weight factor is in excess of the physical effort that can be applied.

Big horses, too, are more liable to go in the wind and seem to be more prone to the throat formation which disposes this failing. They are rarely clever horses, able to get themselves out of trouble, although there are exceptions, and they are usually less intelligent, less responsive and slower on the uptake. Much of this may be attributed to the admixture of cart-blood in their breeding, which may also account for their size.

A smaller horse, closer to the ground, is usually better balanced. He is handier and more responsive, and to my mind always the more receptive.

People with short, round legs will find a broad, roly-backed animal difficult to encompass. I am myself of the short-legged variety and I can testify to the discomfort of sitting on an enormous broad-backed horse which spreads my short legs out, almost at right angles, and makes me feel as secure as the proverbial pea on a drum. A narrow horse is infinitely easier to sit into for those of this conformation.

Incidentally, while long legs and flat thighs look pleasing on a horse, they are no more effective than the short, thick ones. Both Brigadier Lyndon Bolton (*Training the Horse*) and myself are agreed on this point. Both of us, of course, have short legs!

The Price to Pay

Always with us is the problem of cash.

If one has plenty of it there is no problem, and if one requires a potential eventer or showjumper the fact that money is of little object makes the way easier. There are, however, good workmanlike horses, to be obtained at more modest prices. How much depends upon the horse's conformation and appearance, his capacity to carry weight, his age, his soundness, his performance record, stage of training and his manners. A well-bred horse will always command a higher price than a common one.

So if you want a five-year-old horse up to 15 stone, well bred and good looking, who has been trained by an experienced trainer and is completely sound, you will pay a large sum of money for him, after you have spent a very long time looking for him. It follows that those whose pockets are not so deep will have to accept a horse lacking in one or more of these qualities to some degree.

Importance of Conformation

Good conformation is desirable because a well-made horse should, in theory, be able to work better, with less effort and less wear and tear, than one of poor conformation. Nevertheless, I have had horses whose conformation left much to be desired, but who have proved themselves exceptional performers. Very often, in fact, a horse that is deficient in one aspect may be compensated by having particularly good points elsewhere. There is a theory, dependent on related triangles and, indeed, a whole book devoted to the subject, which proves the point pretty well conclusively. I have to confess that my mathematical prowess has never permitted me to understand either.

It is certainly true that although one is unlikely to produce a silk purse from a sow's ear, correct training and management can improve the appearance of any horse and defects, while they cannot be eradicated, can be made much less noticeable.

Lack of conformation, in certain respects and within reason, must, therefore, be acceptable in the cheaper horse and the subject is dealt with more fully later in this section.

Breeding and weight carrying ability have already been discussed and will affect the choice of the individual according to his own make and shape and his circumstances.

The Effect of Age Upon Price

Age has a definite effect upon price and the value of the horse increases up to about seven years. It then decreases slightly until the animal is around twelve years, after which the price falls more rapidly.

At the present time there is a depressing tendency for horses to be broken, sold and ridden at too early an age. It is nonsense to buy a three-year-old with the idea that he will "grow up with the family" or to fall for the dealer's patter, "Well, of course he's got all his life in front of him". He may have, but because he has been used when his bones are unformed and his muscles and organs immature his useful working life has already been shortened.

I used to think that a horse was best broken at three, put away for a year until he was four and then put into work quietly, but now I am not so sure. The late Colonel V.D.S. Williams (father of the late Dorian Williams) for whom I had the highest regard, recommended breaking at four, putting into quiet work at five and hunting at six, and I believe him to be right even though the practice might not in these hard times be commercially viable.

Any young thing should be allowed to develop physically and mentally before being asked to do a serious job of work. In the case of the horse he is immature at three, is still growing at four and even five, and does not reach maturity until six or seven. If he is used too early we run the risk of doing him permanent damage and shortening his working life. Given time to develop, and being properly trained thereafter, he may continue to be active well into his twenties. The

Lipizzaners of the Spanish Riding School, for instance, perform the most demanding exercises at an advanced age. Although the breed is famed for its longevity much of this ability is due to their systematic and unhurried training. (Some of the best of my own horses were working well into their twenties and one, a little skewbald cob, hunted brilliantly up to the age of 32 years.)

Thoroughbreds, as we all know, are raced as two-year-olds, but few thinking horsemen could accept this practice as anything but a necessary evil dictated by economics. The wastage from unsoundness in horses raced at this age is high and, indeed, one only has to visit the Natural History Museum to see the effects of weight having been carried on an immature bone structure. The racehorse is not meant to last and is unlikely to do so while he is worked at so early an age, on the other hand the type of horse I am discussing should have a working life spread over a fairly large number of years.

A good age to buy a horse ready for work is between six and nine, but don't disregard the older horse if price is to be considered and if he is sound. There is many a good tune to be played on an old fiddle, but you must not be surprised if he has developed habits which prove difficult or impossible to correct. If you have the time and the necessary experience an unbroken three-year-old will be less money and is probably the most satisfying horse of all. Unfortunately, people with time and experience to make a horse are rare birds and most of us have to buy horses which may have had a number of owners.

Unsoundness and Blemishes

The one essential I would always insist on is that the horse be sound. An unsound horse will be cheap to buy, but may prove to be an expensive purchase in the long run.

There are minor unsoundnesses which could be overlooked, a horse for example which has suffered a strain of the back tendon and check ligament is quite likely to continue to give good service, but one that has suffered a rupture of the suspensory ligament (the term used to describe this injury is "broken down") will seldom be of much use.

A horse that has been "tubed", or Hobdayed (an operation performed on the larynx for roaring, which is an affection of that organ), is probably a good one, otherwise the operation would not have been carried out, but his price will be lower. Otherwise steer clear of any suspicion of unsoundness.

Blemishes are a different matter, for although they are disfiguring they do not affect either soundness or performance. If one does not wish to show the animal they are of no significance, except in regard to price.

Manners and Temperament

Manners and temperament are important in a horse and must have a bearing on the price. The stage of training is not so essential if one can do a little for oneself, but if you want to buy a nicely schooled horse you must expect to pay for the time and knowledge an expert has expended. One should, however, bear in mind that one's own stage of training and competence must be equal to that of the horse, otherwise the result is likely to end in a confused and spoilt animal and a discouraged rider. In any case it is really much more fun to school your own horse and not really all that difficult if you have taken the trouble to acquire a proper seat and some fundamental knowledge.

If a horse is said to have good manners under saddle and in the box one should be able to take it for granted that he is a safe ride, quiet to handle, and free from all the common vices.

A strong, not a rough, horseman might safely buy at a lower figure a horse known to be nappy, but I would never advise buying a horse that bucks with the determined intention of getting rid of his rider, nor would I touch one that reared persistently. Twenty years ago (alas, that has now to be extended to 40) I quite enjoyed horses of this type and as a result bought some very cheap ones, but they are not to be recommended once the nerve, or foolishness, of youth has passed. Likewise horses that quite suddenly seem to go berserk and take-off for no apparent reason should on no account be considered, even as a gift. Usually the poor animal is suffering from some damage to the brain and it is kinder to put him down before he kills someone.

The one failing I would not accept, unless I lived on a moor and was never likely to ride on a road, is a horse that is traffic shy. It is possible to effect a cure, but it requires experience and, as always, much time. Even then under present day conditions the element of danger, not only to oneself but to other road-users, is too great.

There are, in any case, so many perfectly genuine horses to buy that unless price is a real problem it is just not worth burdening oneself with an animal who is hardly a pleasure to keep.

Having said that I must admit to retaining a personal sympathy for some of these fallen angels. When I see a horse that is difficult my first reaction is one of anger. Not for the horse, but for the men who reduced him to his unhappy state. More often than not he *is* unhappy. Very few horses are born difficult and the great majority are happiest when they can place their trust in man and lead a useful organised life. If they have been abused and ill-treated is it surprising that they should become first bewildered and eventually driven into making resistances which brand them as equine delinquents? Nothing is more satisfying than to be able to regain their trust and it can usually be done if one is prepared to be very patient, and to proceed very slowly. On the other hand, courageous horses of ability, the "tigers" of the game, may be difficult characters until their energy can be channelled to the proper advantage.

Colour and Sex

One last word before considering where and how to buy a horse. This concerns sex and colour, both of which are personal preferences. The female of any species, can be, if not more deadly, certainly less predictable than the male. If one buys a mare it is possible that one has at the back of one's mind that one day she might breed a foal and so her value need never be entirely lost. A mare, however, can be more temperamental than a gelding, and may be touchy when in season. This natural occurrence can take place every three weeks, approximately, between February and June and in some cases the mare will appear a little off-colour and will lose concentration when at work. She may also be inclined to kick in the stable and be generally irritable. This is not so in all cases and in some mares the cycle is hardly noticeable. A gelding, on the other hand, being unaffected sexually, is likely to have a more equable disposition.

As far as colour goes a good horse is never a bad one, but certain skin pigmentations are significant. Washy, ill-defined colours are supposed to denote a weak constitution, strong colours, of whatever sort, denote the opposite quality. Chestnuts, particularly mares, have a reputation for excitability, while greys are sometimes termed "rich men's horses" because of the labour involved in keeping them clean. Where the horn of the foot is white it is often supposed to indicate softness and a poor quality, but while many experts accept this as true there are others who do not hold this opinion. There is also the old adage about "one white sock buy him, two white socks try him . . ." and so on, but there does not seem to be any sound foundation to justify this one or, indeed, anything like universal agreement.

Writers of the 16th and 17th centuries, and even before, did, however, lay great stress on colouring, but I wonder whether this might not have been the result of some personal prejudice which, as it was handed down, gained credence and acceptance. I am sure that if one did happen to have particularly unpleasant experiences with a horse or horses of a certain colouring it would not be difficult to form a prejudice against similarly coloured animals. (My grandfather would never have a black horse. "Time enough for one of those b——", he used to say, "when they draw me to my grave.")

Where to Buy

There are three principal methods of buying horses. They can be bought from a reputable dealer, from private owners or at public sales. Reputable dealers do exist, running horse businesses which are their main source of income. Unfortunately there are also a great number of back-yard dealers (some of them with long-lashes, limpid eyes and curvaceously-filled jumpers) who attract the unwary by a mixture of patter and the prospect (a quite impossible one) of obtaining a good horse for very little money.

With very little justification the term horse-dealer is synonymous, in the minds of many people, with roguery and skulduggery. There may still be horse-dealers of the type described by Surtees in his novels, but I have, fortunately, never made their acquaintance. This is not to say that all horse-dealers are knights in shining armour, but the vast majority are honest business men and it is not in their interest to sell bad horses and lose goodwill by doing so. Indeed, having spent five years touring the horse-show circuit, I can say unequivocally that I made my best friends among the professional showing folk, the horse-dealers. I would trust them implicitly. Which is much more than I would say for the amateurs.

Don't, however, confuse these people, whose wares will in any case be realistically priced, with the back-yard dealer I have mentioned. In spite of the Riding Establishment Act, which makes it illegal to operate a riding school without it being passed as satisfactory and registered with a local council, there are still wretched establishments, claiming to teach riding, run by incompetents who are only too willing to sell their under-fed and possibly unreliable animals.

If you do not know of a good dealer in your area ask around until you find one. If children belong to the Pony Club the District Commissioner is likely to be helpful and, of course, for adults membership of a riding club brings plenty of horse-minded contacts.

Many good riding schools, besides teaching riding, may also operate a dealing side where the beginner, particularly if he is also a client, may obtain a reliable animal. There is an advantage in this method of purchase in that the proprietor or manager will have first-hand knowledge of your capabilities and should be able to find a horse to suit you and them.

A word of warning, however, don't buy a riding school plug for whom, in an ecstasy of enthusiasm for all things equine, you may have formed a strong attachment. In the school, properly fed and receiving an abundance of work, he may plod round as quietly as a lamb. He has become accustomed to the work and to the presence of his companions. Removed from this environment and divorced from his particular herd he can, in combination with an insufficiency of exercise, become a different and even a difficult animal. The quiet hack, who followed dutifully the tails of his preceding brethren at the school, is quite likely to view his new world with some trepidation and to refuse to put one foot in front of the other.

If you have set your heart on a particular breed, an Arab, a Welsh Cob or perhaps a Fell, Highland or Dales pony, it is as well to write to the secretary of the breed society concerned asking for advice as to whom you may approach. A list of up-to-date addresses will be found in *The British Equestrian Directory*, published annually by Equestrian Management Consultants, Wothersome Grange, Bramham, W. Yorks.

Incidentally, should you decide to buy from a riding school make sure it is a properly run one, preferably one approved by the British Horse Society and where qualified instruction is obtainable. If you are in any doubt get hold of the B.H.S. publication *Where To Ride*, which gives a complete list of registered schools together with the facilities and standards of instruction available.

If you decide on going to a dealer you will expect him to be honest with you. Meet him halfway and be honest with him in return. Tell him what you want the horse for, how good you are and how much, exactly how much, you want to pay. It is no use to make out that you are an experienced horseman, capable of riding anything, if you are really something of a rabbit. Nor is it sensible, or even reasonable, to suggest that you might consider paying a higher price than you can afford. It may seem rather silly when seen in print, but this is exactly what people do. If they then get an unsuitable horse they will blame the dealer when the fault is really their own.

You may, of course, prefer to buy privately, in which case it is no bad plan to confine your activities to the area in which you live. In this way you will be able to make local enquiries about the horse and there is the additional point that few people are so thick-skinned as to sell a bad one on their own doorstep.

The Welsh Mountain Pony, arguably the most beautiful of all the pony breeds.

An example of a Highland Pony who is very difficult to fault.

The Welsh Cob – enduring, hardy, up to weight and a performer under saddle or in harness.

The New Forest Pony – docile, intelligent and a first-class performer.

Ireland's Connemara is acknowledged as one of the world's best performers across country.

The Fell Pony is the North of England's all-rounder.

A working hunter pony, possibly having a Welsh background, who has scope, substance and quality.

Native pony crosses will have greater scope and speed than the pure-breds. This Highland cross would be a good choice for all sorts of activities

Hundreds of horses, most of them perfectly genuine, are sold each week through the columns of *Horse and Hound*, but again, if only for reasons of economy, it is as well to keep within reasonable distance of home, unless the horse is one you know.

Advertisements for horses are rather like those inserted by house agents – they can be a tribute to the power of the pen. Most people have suffered disappointment, if nothing worse, from taking the effusions of house agents too literally. The same can apply where horses are concerned.

A further point to remember when buying privately is that all of us tend to regard our geese as swans to some degree, and that many of us, unaware, possibly, of general price levels, see our horses as being of greater value than they really are.

Lastly, you may try your hand at a public sale, but there is a very definite chance of your paying dearly for the experience. At some sales you will be able to try the animal, but at many more you will not, although where horses are advertised previously as being entered for a particular sale there may be a line or two saying "these horses may be ridden at Blank Stables by appointment". In general, however, you will be confined to looking at him in his box or at best having him run up outside for you. If he is a good and well-known horse other people will have noticed him too and bidding is likely to be brisk. On the other hand it is by no means the crocks who fill a sale catalogue. Many people prefer to sell this way and a number of Hunt establishments sell their horses regularly each year at places like Leicester. Every so often, in fact, it is possible to pick up a bargain, but you must remember that you are taking a gamble on an untried and very much unknown quantity.

Descriptions and Warranties

The principal auction sales are well conducted and respectable affairs and the buyer, by reading the conditions of sale which the auctioneers print on their catalogues (and these may vary from one to another), will find that he is well protected from any outright dishonesty. In addition a number of words or phrases will appear in the descriptions accorded to individual entries, some of which, in law, are a good deal more binding than, for instance, the so-called guarantees one gets with a motor car. One does, however, need to understand the implications of some of these expressions and what constitutes a complete warranty and what does not.

Among the most common descriptions is "Good Hunter". This is a complete warranty that the horse is sound in every respect, is quiet to ride and is capable of hunting. A horse described as a "Hunter" must be quiet to ride and capable of being hunted, he must also be sound in wind and eye. But you will notice that there is no mention of the last member of the trio, action. This does not, therefore, constitute so complete a warranty and some inherent weakness may be suspected. When the description "Hack" is applied to a horse it may be taken to mean that the animal is sound in action and quiet to ride – again an incomplete warranty if unsupported by any other statement.

The phrase "a Good Performer" is almost as complete as "a Good Hunter", but not quite. It only means that the horse is sound in action at the time of sale and admits, therefore, to there being some doubt as to how long he remains so. The words "Believed Sound" are a warranty of soundness in all respects. A veterinary surgeon's certificate is usually "lodged in the office" and can, or should be, inspected by the intended purchaser. Even so such a certificate is subsidiary to any warranty of soundness as it appears in the catalogue.

Certain faults must accompany the description of any entry suffering from them, and are three in number. They are crib-biting, wind-sucking, and any operation for unsoundness of the wind that the horse may have undergone.

Despite these safeguards should you buy a horse which does not fulfil his warranty you are at liberty to return him, providing you adhere to the ruling laid down by the auctioneers in this respect and which is printed on the catalogue.

For anyone with a legal turn of mind who wishes to study the intricacies of the law of warranty I would recommend the purchase of T.J. Sophian's *A Guide to the Law Relating to Horses, Riders and Riding Establishments* (J.A. Allen and Co.). It is really quite enlightening to see how much legislation there is concerning the horse.

As a last word on warranties I will quote a very relevant passage from Mr Sophian's book. It does not, of course, apply to horses purchased at a sale where the warranty is implicit in the description given, but rather to buying a horse from a private person.

"The General rule of Common Law is *caveat emptor*, let the buyer beware. There will be no implied warranty or condition on the sale of a horse, and it is up to the purchaser to protect himself by taking adequate warranties and the like. Unless he does so he must accept the animal as he finds it, and he cannot be heard to complain afterwards if the animal happens to be unsound or vicious, or unsatisfactory in any other way."

Nevertheless, we may still take heart, for the law says also, and again I quote Mr Sophian:

"Certain warranties and conditions are implied and read into every contract for the sale of goods (and therefore of horses) by the Sale of Goods Act 1893, unless such warranties are expressly, or by necessary implication, excluded or modified." Mr Sophian then quotes sections of the Act among which, under Section 14, the law states, "where the buyer makes known to the seller the particular purpose for which he requires the goods, so that he shows that he relies on the seller's skill or judgment, and the goods are of a description which it is in the course of the seller's business to supply, then there is an implied condition that the goods are reasonably fit for the purpose."

In other words, if you asked Mr A, the dealer, to supply you with a showjumper and that animal refused outright to enter the ring, let alone participate, then you have a case against Mr A who did not supply you goods "reasonably fit for the purpose".

As the man said, "*Caveat emptor*". You may think it advisable to beware of the law, too!

One last word of warning. When I talk of sales I mean those such as are held at Leicester, Ascot and Hereford and run by properly established auctioneers with experience in this field. Affairs held in the market square of your local town or behind the pub are best avoided. Prices are undoubtedly lower, but so is the quality of the animals brought there. Nothing makes me so angry, and at the same time so sad, as to see a fond parent, with a shining-eyed daughter, buying some virtually unbroken youngster, too weak to display any spirit, in the mistaken belief that they have acquired an ideal pony (young too) for a minimal outlay.

There is more abuse of young, immature animals in this way than in any other and I know only too well how much trouble can be caused, not only to the pony or horse, but to the buyer as well.

Now for a few general remarks before we consider what you should look for in a horse when you have decided on the type and from what source you intend to buy.

Strangely enough, in view of the preceding paragraphs, you need not take your lawyer with you when you go to look at a horse. You can take your vet., but you must not expect him, unless he is a personal friend, to make your mind up for you. He will rightly confine himself to giving his opinion on the conformation of the horse, his age, and his soundness or otherwise.

If you do not have your own vet. with you *insist* upon purchase subject to veterinary examination. Anyone who is not prepared to have their animal vetted must expect to be suspected of having something to hide.

If you have a really knowledgeable friend who will accompany you by all means take him or her along. But do make sure that the friend is, in fact, knowledgeable and experienced, otherwise it will be a case of the blind leading the blind. Some "young girl" who has "ridden all her life" (she may be 20 or 50) is not necessarily an experienced person. Even young ladies with letters after their name, beautifully though they may ride, are not always so skilled when it comes to deciding what is, or is not, a suitable horse. Try to find someone who is properly qualified to advise you – if you can't you are probably better on your own, having spent the preceding evening reading this chapter over and over again.

The Hunt Horse

Many people on seeing that a hunt horse is for sale take it for granted that it must be a good one and off they go to see him with their minds full of images of well-mannered horses standing quietly at covert-side, and performing thereafter with urbane and almost super-cilious expertise. It is true that he probably is a good horse and he may well be nicely mannered, considering the amount of work he gets through in a season. He will, however, have done a great deal of work and may be quite uncontrollable when asked to wait his turn instead of going in front as was his wont. This is not to say that you should not under any circumstances buy a hunt horse, although some of them, particularly those habitually relegated to carrying the whipper-in, can be very rough customers, but you should do so with your eyes wide open.

Remember, too, that a weak, under-conditioned horse may ride quietly enough in the dealer's yard, but may turn out to be a very different gentleman when he has been fed and is fitter and stronger.

If you can get a horse on a week's trial, or if you are offered a day's hunting on him, accept with alacrity. You will have an opportunity of finding out something about him before committing yourself. Don't, however, *expect* such offers. They are occasionally made, but it is by no means a regular rule, and there are not many people who will entrust a horse to a stranger for a week or for a day's hunting.

Whatever else you do you must ride the horse, for you cannot come to a decision without sitting on him. No private seller or a dealer will refuse you this right.

What to Look For

Having got as far as the box of your intended purchase you should have in your mind what points you are particularly going to look for and also those which need not weigh so heavily. The ability to size up a horse, or as it is known "having an eye for a horse", is not acquired from books nor is it gained overnight. Some people have an instinctive ability to sum up a horse's points, but you may rest assured that they have spent many years developing their gift.

Nonetheless, most of us can improve ourselves in this respect if we are prepared to learn what to look for and then to spend as much time as we can watching the well-known judges dealing with a top flight show class.

It is possible that you may at first be puzzled by the selections made, but gradually you will begin to see what the judge is looking for as to type, conformation and action, and in time you may even find yourself disagreeing with their decisions on occasions. When this happens,

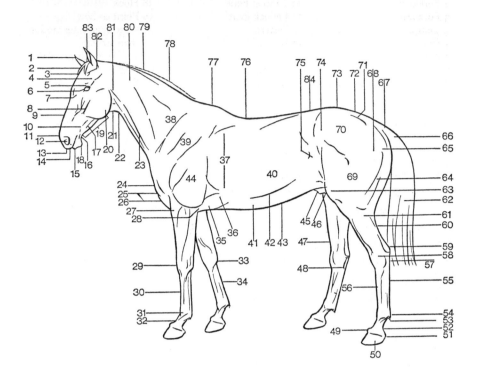

Points of the horse (key on opposite page).

providing your disagreement can be based on sound argument, you are *beginning* to develop an eye for a horse.

Long before this happens, however, you should have been able to fix in your mind's eye a picture of a well-made horse; it is this picture you must hold onto when your intending purchase comes out of his box.

Conformation

Compare his make and shape and his general appearance with that perfect model in your head and make a mental note of points which do not measure up to the ideal. Now stand back and take a really good look at him. At this point the seller will usually begin to enumerate the

1 Ear	29 Knee	57 Seat of curb
2 Forelock	30 Cannon bone	58 Hock
3 Forehead	31 Fetlock joint	59 Point of hock
4 Temple	32 Pastern	60 Gastrocnernius tendon
5 Haw	33 Back of knee (pisiform	(hamstring)
6 Eye	bone)	61 Gaskin (second thigh)
7 Face	34 Tendons	62 Tail
8 Cheek bone (zygomatic	35 Brisket	63 Patella
ridge)	36 Spur vein	64 Buttocks
9 Nasal bones	37 Girth	65 Point of buttocks
10 Lower jaw	38 Base of neck	(tuberischii, seat-bone)
11 Nasal peak	39 Spine of scapula (or	66 Dock
12 Nostril	shoulder)	67 Root of tail
13 Muzzle	40 Ribs	68 Hip joint
14 Upper lip	41 Belly	69 Thigh
15 Lower lip	42 Groove formed by rib	70 Quarter
16 Chin	cartilages	71 'Poverty' mark
17 Chin groove (or curb	43 Barrel	72 Croup
groove)	44 Triceps muscle	73 Point of croup
18 Bars of jaw	45 Sheath	74 Point of hip (haunch
19 Sub-maxillary groove	46 Stifle	bone or angle of haunch)
20 Cheek (overlying	47 Shin	75 Flank
masseter muscle)	48 Chestnut	76 Back (saddle)
21 Throat (gullet)	49 Coronet	77 Withers
22 Trachea (windpipe)	50 Hoof (wall of foot)	78 Mane
23 Jugular groove	51 Heel	79 Crest
24 Point of shoulder	52 Hollow of heel	80 Axis
25 Breast	53 Ergot	81 Wing of atlas
26 Pectoral muscle	54 Fetlock	82 Supra-orbital fossa
27 Forearm	55 Back tendons	83 Poll
28 Elbow	56 Shank	84 Loins

animal's good points, studiously avoiding those that are not so good. Do not allow yourself to be distracted. My own defence in this instance is to interrupt the eulogistic flow with a request to "stand him up, will you please", and pretend that I am so lost in contemplation that I haven't heard.

Good conformation is a matter of proportion, no one aspect of the horse impressing itself more than, or to the exclusion, of another. If the head is too large or the limbs too long they are immediately noticeable because they are disproportionate to the rest of the body. The horse of perfect conformation is perfectly proportioned, and is yet to be foaled, while those of near perfect conformation do not come within the range of anything but the deepest pocket.

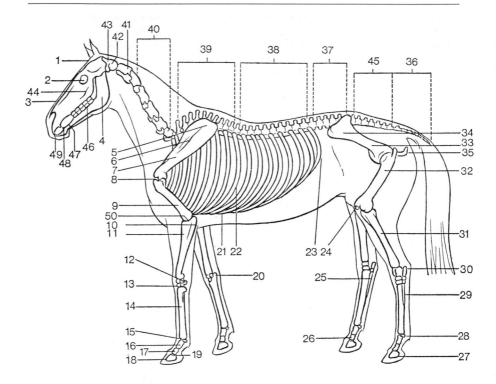

Skeleton of the horse (key on opposite page).

Nevertheless, we must try to buy a horse whose deficiencies in conformation are not over exaggerated and one of as good a make and shape as our resources allow. All things being equal, as I have mentioned before, good conformation should mean greater, and longer lasting, working efficiency.

The Head

Having taken your good, long look now concentrate on the individual points of the animal and I suggest you start with the HEAD.

The head and eye by their shape, size and general appearance can tell us a great deal.

It is not very difficult to make an assessment of the character and intelligence in the extremes of the human head, although the intermediate appearances may present more of a problem. In a general way if we see an unattractive, coarse-featured individual, low browed with close set, piggy eyes and a generally dull look about him we are likely to hazard a

1 Parietal ⎤	17 Short pastern	34 Trochanter ⎤ Pelvic
2 Eye socket ⎟ skull	18 Os pedis (coffin bone)	35 Ischium ⎦ girdle
3 Nasal bone ⎟	19 Navicular	36 Caudal (tail or
4 Lower jaw ⎦	20 Trapezium	coccygeal vertebrae)
5 Supra-scapula cartilage	21 Rib cartilages (or costal	37 Lumbar vertebrae
6 Spine of scapula	cartilages)	38 Dorsal vertebrae
7 Scapula	22 Ribs (23 – last rib)	39 Anterior vertebrae
8 Shoulder joint (point of	24 Patella	40 Cervical vertebrae
shoulder)	25 Inner splint bone	41 Axis
9 Humerus	26 Os coronae	42 Atlas
10 Ulna	27 Heel	43 Occipital
11 Radius (forearm)	28 Sesamoid bones	44 Malar bone
12 Pisiform	29 Outer splint bone	45 Sacral vertebrae (or
13 Knee joint (or carpus)	30 Os calcis (point of	sacrum)
14 Cannon or metatarsal	hock)	46 Molars
bone	31 Tibia and fibula	47 The bars
15 Fetlock joint	32 Femur	48 Canines
16 Suffraginis (long	33 Ilium	49 Incisors
pastern)		50 Elbow joint

guess that he is not likely to be of a high level of intelligence. We may also think that he is not a very pleasant individual. It is possible that we may be maligning a perfectly good citizen, but without knowing him intimately this is the only way open to us to make an assessment of his character. Conversely, we associate a man with refined, clearly cut features and the alert look with intelligence. Again we may not be correct in the assumption, but this is the impression we receive. It is, also, not too difficult to recognise the genial, jolly, honest sort of fellow by his face, or by the same means the miserable, perpetually disgruntled one. I am sure that human characters, although more complicated than those of animals, are portrayed in the face, particularly when the character of the individual contains the extremes of human failings and virtues.

In the same way as we do not have a close acquaintance with the horse we are thinking of buying, it is only by an examination of his head and the general impression it creates that we can make a judgment of his character and temperament. We may be able to add to our impression later by noting his reactions to our handling of him, but initially we shall have to form our opinion by studying that part of him which is most capable of expression.

The Eye

The impression one should gain is of alertness, interest and kindness. The eyes should be calm and large and placed well to the front, with the intervening space of the forehead wide, but not *too* much so. On the width of the forehead depends the ability to see objects directly in front more or less accurately. Horses with a high percentage of blood have narrower foreheads than the more common bred ones who, like the cart-horse, have their eyes placed more to the side; a position which gives greater facility of lateral vision, but entails making more exaggerated movements of the head when the eyes wish to focus on objects in front of them.

The theory is often held that great width between the eyes allows room for a larger brain. This, however, is a fallacy.

The brain of the horse, which is not very large, is contained within the cranium which is placed beneath the temporal muscles and between the ears. The width between the *eyes* can, therefore, have little effect upon either the size or capabilities of the brain.

The Arab horse often shows considerable width between the eyes, but somehow manages to avoid having the exaggerated lateral type of vision associated with cart-breeds. Nonetheless, the position of the Arab's eyes, which are characteristically large and very beautiful, may very well account for the "awareness" of the breed and be responsible for a certain reluctance to leave the ground in *some* Arabians.

Sunken, pig eyes seem to go with sulky dispositions and a mean temper and most people avoid horses who do not have a good eye. A pit above the eye, almost a hole, is a sign of advanced age or poor condition, or it may occur in the progeny of an elderly dam.

A clean-cut, chiselled head, lean and fine with a thin skin covering is indicative of breeding, a heavy, coarse head shows common blood. A bump between the eyes is generally taken to be a sign of a stubborn disposition and a surly, mean nature. Nearly every horseman will tell you this, although there is no real explanation or foundation for the assumption. It does, nevertheless, give a rather unpleasant look to the head and I would not wish to argue the significance of a point that so many eminent horsemen have made.

A dished, concave face is a characteristic of the Arab and much prized by his admirers. A Roman nose belongs to more plebeian stock, but is ideally formed for looking down.

Looking at the head in detail the formation and action of the ears is also worth a glance, they should be responsive and mobile. They will be neat, not unduly large or hairy in the better class of horse and easily and frequently pricked. The movements of the ears in a commoner are less active, and the ears themselves coarser. Ears laid back, accompanied with a wild eye showing white are a means of expressing temper.

Lop ears are unsightly, but many good horses have them and they are thought to be found in horses of stamina. Their disadvantage is that they are unable to give the rider any signal of the horse's intention.

The nostrils in a horse (who does *all* his breathing through them) should be wide and well developed if he is to be able to breathe effectively, particularly in moments of physical stress.

Probably the most important thing about the head is that it should be proportionate to the shape and size of the neck and be properly connected ("set-on" is the horsy term) to that part of the horse.

This really is important because the head and neck is the agency by which the horse balances himself. His neck is used like a pendulum with the head as a weight on the end of it. A heavy head on a weak neck throws his balance on the forehand and is bound to make the horse heavy on the hand. Where the head is heavy, and it is in many weight carriers, it must have a correspondingly strong neck, even though it be rather shorter than a judge would think ideal. In perfection we shall have a fairly fine, small head on a graceful, muscled neck forming an elegant curve from the withers to the head.

The angle at which the head and neck should meet is between 90 and 100 degrees, a more acute angle than this makes the horse more liable to unsoundness in the wind and he is likely to become overbent when ridden.

The opposite is always associated with weak muscular development and will again make bridling difficult and the horse unpleasant to ride. Stargazers, who carry their heads excessively high, appearing to have the head pushed onto the neck almost vertically, are likely to make control something of a problem.

A further consideration affecting the horse's ability to bridle correctly is the width between the lower jaws under the neck. You should be able to fit your fist between them. Thick jowled horses also find it difficult to flex the head, from the poll, and accept the bit easily.

The Mouth and Age

Now a look at the mouth. This is something one is expected to do and certainly there is no other way of finding out the approximate age, or whether the seller was telling the truth when he said the horse was a five-year-old. Not very long ago I heard of a case where a child's parents had bought a pony as a six-year-old. They did not have the pony vetted and later, when its condition began to deteriorate and a vet. was at last called in, it was found to be the best part of 15 years older than that.

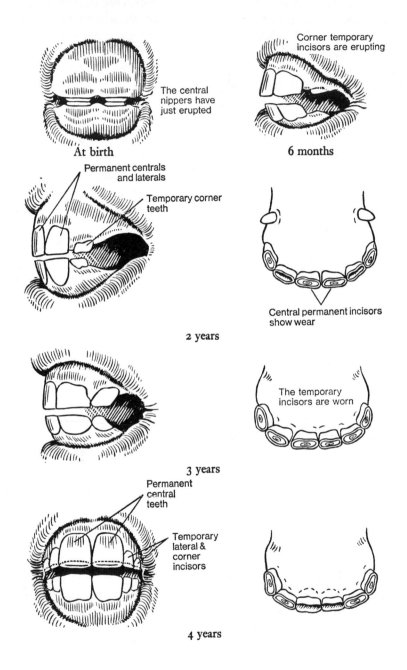

The central nippers have just erupted

At birth

Corner temporary incisors are erupting

6 months

Permanent centrals and laterals

Temporary corner teeth

2 years

Central permanent incisors show wear

The temporary incisors are worn

3 years

Permanent central teeth

Temporary lateral & corner incisors

4 years

Ageing (this, and next two pages) *as shown by the teeth.*

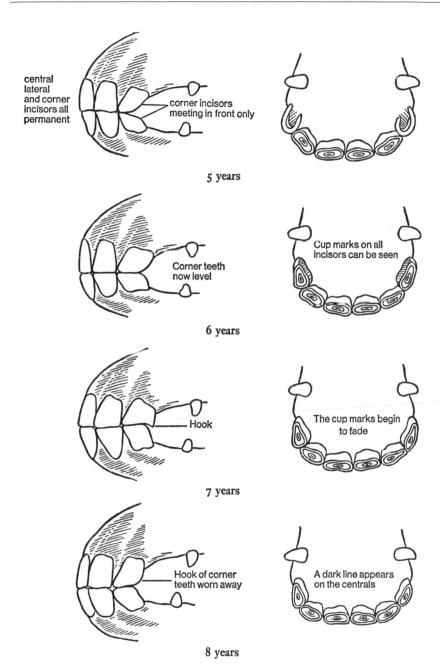

central
lateral
and corner
incisors all
permanent

corner incisors
meeting in front only

5 years

Corner teeth
now level

Cup marks on all
incisors can be seen

6 years

Hook

The cup marks begin
to fade

7 years

Hook of corner
teeth worn away

A dark line appears
on the centrals

8 years

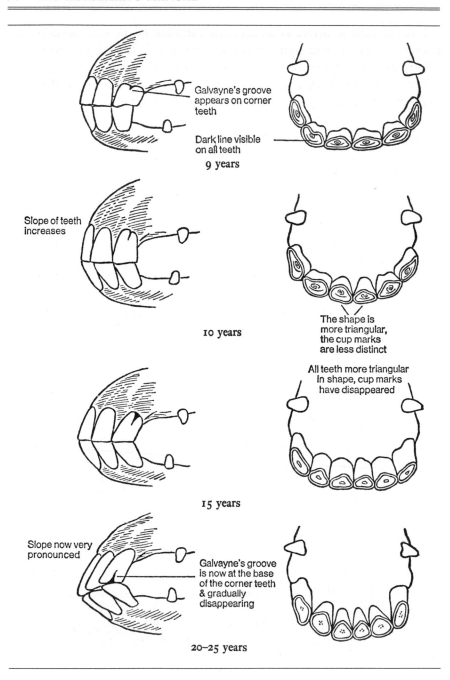

Galvayne's groove appears on corner teeth

Dark line visible on all teeth

9 years

Slope of teeth increases

10 years

The shape is more triangular, the cup marks are less distinct

All teeth more triangular in shape, cup marks have disappeared

15 years

Slope now very pronounced

Galvayne's groove is now at the base of the corner teeth & gradually disappearing

20–25 years

It is not easy to arrive at an accurate estimate of the age, particularly when the horse is over eight or so years, but a little basic knowledge will help to avoid errors or occurrences of the dimensions I have quoted.

The horse has both *incisor* teeth, the biters, at the front, and *molar* teeth, the grinders, at the rear. It is from the former that the age can be estimated. Up to the age of five the horse is in the process of shedding the milk teeth – a process which is completed at five years when he is said to have a "full" mouth of permanent teeth. Thereafter one must rely on other indications of ageing.

The diagrams which accompany this section will help to make the stages easier to understand.

The foal at birth has no teeth, although it is possible to see the central incisors through the gum. These are cut at 10 days and are followed by the lateral incisors, somewhere between four and six weeks, and the corner incisors at six to nine months, giving him his full complement of six milk incisors. Milk teeth are easily recognisable by their shape, which is one coming to a definite point at the base. Codrington (*Know Your Horse*) describes the tooth as having a "distinct neck". They are also white in colour, rather than yellow as is the case with permanent teeth.

It is not until three years are reached that some of the temporary or milk teeth are clearly replaced by permanent incisors, and the animal will then show two central permanent incisors in each jaw, flanked on either side by two milk teeth. At two years "marks" or "cups" are clearly apparent on the tables of the milk teeth, but the permanent central incisors appearing at three years will not show these marks. At four years the temporary lateral incisors are replaced by permanent ones, leaving only two milk teeth, the corner incisors. By this time the central incisors will have developed cups on the tables while the two new laterals will be unmarked. In the male horse the tushes situated behind the incisor teeth are now visible. Mares do not grow tushes except in one or two rare cases.

At five years the remaining corner incisors are replaced by permanent teeth and again all, with the exception of these, display cups on the tables.

Because the newly erupted teeth are immature and have as yet received no wear, these corner incisors will only meet at the front in the five-year-old mouth. The horse now has a mouth of permanent teeth and, as our American cousins would say, from here-on-in the task of assessing the age will be beset with more difficulty, and considerations of wear and changing shapes, among others, must be taken into account.

By six years the corner teeth will be worn level, meeting along the complete surface of the tables and the cups on all teeth will be clearly visible. The tushes, too, are now fully prominent. Now the cups, which have so far been helpful in their regular appearance, begin to change their form. At seven years their distinct outline begins to fade and to lose the formerly hard outline. In addition the upper corner incisor develops a hook overlapping the rear of its opposite number.

The appearance of the cups alters again at eight, becoming very indistinct in the central incisors, but at this time a dark line appears at the forward edge of the table in these teeth. The hook on the corner incisor has worn away at eight years.

The dark line is noticeable on all the incisors at nine years and all the cups have disappeared, although those on the corner incisors can still be seen in outline. At this age another hook begins to appear on the corner incisor as the direct result of wear. The most significant change at this age, and one that presents a sound guide, is the appearance of a dark groove, Galvayne's groove, on the upper corner incisors. This groove extends down the tooth as the horse gets older. In general terms it will have reached halfway at around 15 years and will have reached the bottom of the tooth at 20 years.

The teeth become longer and project forwards at a greater angle by the time the horse is 10, altering their shape and becoming more triangular. As the years advance the slope of the teeth becomes more apparent and any faint outlines of the cups on the tables will disappear altogether.

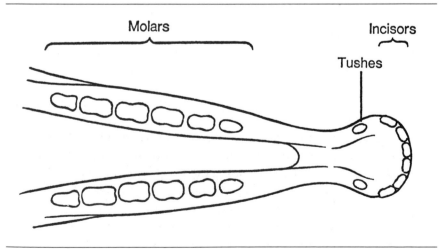

The lower jaw.

The incisors become more and more triangular in shape and our estimate of the age must be based increasingly on experience and on the position of Galvayne's groove. At 10 the groove may be ¼ inch long and from then on it will proceed down the teeth at a rate of approximately ⅛ inch each year.

An important feature to be noted when examining the mouth is that it is neither parrrot shaped, the upper jaw and teeth overlapping the lower, nor undershot, when the opposite structure will be seen. In either case the horse is best rejected. These mouth formations make the proper fitting of the bit difficult, and in the case of a double bridle almost impossible.

To examine the mouth part the lips gently, using a hand for each lip. To open the mouth insert the thumb and forefinger, held on either side, onto the bars of the lower jaw, i.e. between the incisors and the molars. There is no need to take the jaw in a vice-like grip, the insertion of the fingers is usually enough to secure the horse's co-operation.

The Neck

From our examination of the head we naturally pass on to a consideration of the neck to which it is attached.

Obviously it should be strong, but it should not be of the very short, thick cresty sort. If it is this shape the horse is more inclined to be stiff in his neck. This type of neck is also frequently associated with animals who tuck their chins in and "motor-on" quite regardless of the indications or wishes of their riders. If the thickness of the neck continues into the junction with the head the horse may still "motor-on", but with his nose poked out in front of him. There is very little that can be done to rectify this sort of conformation.

If the neck is too long and too weak it becomes difficult for the horse to carry his head correctly for any period of time. The neck is, in fact, overweighted by the head and for practical purposes is an inefficient piece of machinery which overburdens the forehand and must produce a faulty balance.

Although, again, proportion in relation to the size and set-on of the head is all important, the way in which the neck is joined to the shoulders, which in turn affects the joining of shoulder and trunk, is an equally vital point. The base of the neck must be of sufficient width and very well formed. Too low a junction with the shoulders, often found when the latter are inclined to be straight, will have the effect of overloading the front end and any sort of practical head carriage will be almost impossible to achieve.

The ideal appearance is when the neck, broad at the base, blends itself without interruption into the shoulders. Such a neck, neither too long nor too short, when accompanied by a well-connected head of proportionate size, will enable the head to be carried fairly high. In this position the balance is properly placed and there is greater control over the forehand.

There are two types of neck to be avoided according to all the authorities. First the *swan-neck*, where there is a pronounced upward curve in the upper third of the neck with the head looking as though it were dropped on vertically. Any horse with a head and neck of this shape just cannot bridle. R.H. Smythe, however, perhaps one of the greatest equine authorities in the matter of make and shape and the mental processes of the horse, while condemning the type, remarks that the animal "usually sees well and may be a good ride over jumps . . ."

Secondly the *ewe-neck*, more often found in mares than in geldings. This is where the neck is definitely concave along the upper edge. Smythe admits that it is possible to see some quite adequate performers with necks of this shape, but I feel he would join with every other expert in condemning it.

I would not be so rash as to disregard the advice of these authorities or to advise people to buy ewe-necked horses, but I do believe that much can be done to overcome this defect by intelligent schooling.

Although the conformation is due, basically, to an incorrect structure, many animals are made worse than they need be by bad riding. Quite recently I bought a mare (or rather my wife saw something attractive in a very unattractive creature) in weak condition and with this fault among a host of others.

Having got over the initial shock of seeing so misshapen an animal in my stables I decided, as I could certainly make matters no worse, that it would be interesting to see what a horseman of no more than average ability could do to improve her.

To start with the mare was rather like a ship without a rudder, and our progress down the road resembled that of a drunken man. Gradually, as she began to make up, I started to school her, first on the lunge and then from the saddle. For three months it was impossible to carry out a sitting trot and I concentrated on riding her in our sand school allowing her a long rein and with the minimum of contact. In time she learnt to find her own balance and would circle quite happily stretching her neck downwards and outwards. After six months, which included mounted and dismounted work over cavalletti, the muscles on the top of her neck had begun to develop, a process encouraged by much hand massage, whilst those on the underside of the neck began to fall away. The defects in her conformation are not eradicated, but their effect has been decreased, and she is now a fairly well-balanced, pleasant and safe ride. She was, incidentally, a cheap horse to buy, and while much time and effort have been expended on her she has increased my knowledge in corresponding measure.

To sum up this question of necks, a longish neck with a well set-on light head contributes towards speed with a long length of stride. A short neck, though stronger, shortens the stride and, therefore, in theory, the speed; where then speed is not a factor of great necessity a slightly shorter neck is not unacceptable.

The Withers

Before examining the shoulder in detail it is necessary to look at the withers, the formation of which are of the greatest importance in the saddle horse. Unless the wither is well formed it is unlikely that the upper part of the shoulder, or the scapula, will be long and laid back, necessary for maximum efficiency in the free movement of the fore-limbs.

The withers should be fairly prominent and well covered with muscle. Very fine, very high withers are not so good, being deficient in muscle. A horse having them will ride well, but the construction will not have the strength of those normally formed.

Low or flat withers are *usually*, but not always, found in conjunction with straight shoulders, which result in a short stride and greater concussion, and therefore wear, on the legs.

Flat withers, too, make saddle fitting difficult and in the case of ponies, especially, who are often very deficient in this respect, can give rise to the saddle riding forwards.

The Shoulder

I imagine that everybody knows that the ideal shoulder should be long and well sloped. This is applicable to all horses if the fore-limbs are to be efficient and if undue wear and tear is to be avoided. Obviously the conformation also gives a more comfortable and balanced ride, the potential speed will be greater, as will the freedom of the action and the ability to extend.

Smythe gives the desirable measurements of a good, well laid-back, shoulder as follows: "It should have", he writes: "a degree of inclination, measured from the point of the shoulder to the junction of neck and withers, of approximately 60 degrees. From the point of the shoulder to the centre of the withers, their highest point, should give a reading of 43 degrees. From the point of the shoulder to the junction of withers and back, the reading should be 40 degrees."

There has always been controversy about the position and length of the humerus, the bone connecting the scapula with the fusion of the radius and ulna of the foreleg. It is largely upon the length and position of the humerus that the position of the foreleg will depend. The more horizontal and the longer this bone the further back under the body will the leg be placed. In consequence it is argued with some justification that the action will be correspondingly restricted. Whereas if the humerus is more upright and fairly long the leg is placed further forward, which gives greater freedom and extension. But, say the critics of this view, the leg is subject to more jarring.

The simplest way out is to avoid a horse displaying either of these extremes.

The Foreleg

There is very much less argument over the foreleg. From the top, the elbow must be free from the body and should not look as though it was "tied in". If in doubt turn the horse round when the elbow should turn out naturally. The forearm should be long, with good muscle development and the knee set low to the ground.

A knee high off the ground means a long, and therefore weak, cannon bone. A short, strong and straight cannon is what is required. The knee itself, viewed from the front, must be flat; from behind the pisiform bone should be prominent, so that there is sufficient width for the flexor tendons to pass downwards.

Some horses will appear to be a little "over at the knee", that is they appear to have a forward inclined bend to the knee. This may be a matter of individual conformation or the result of hard work, but it does not seem to produce any ill effect upon action or soundness. A horse that is "back at the knee" is so termed when the leg below the knee curves inwards. It is a definite weakness to be avoided.

Horses that are "tied in below the knee" are an abomination. This is where the measurement immediately below the knee is less than the measurement taken lower down towards the fetlock joint. It denotes weakness and a certain chance of future unsoundness. Too light a bone under the knee is also hardly advisable. The bone present should be in proportion to the animal and the weight it is to carry, bearing in mind

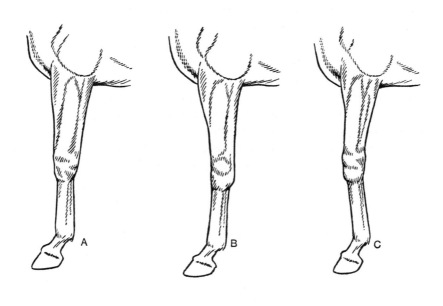

Conformation defects of the limbs: A. Tied in below knee. B. Back-at-the-knee or calf-knee. C. Over-at-the-knee.

the differences in bone structure between the Thoroughbred and the common horse which have already been mentioned.

In every case the ligaments and tendons, running downwards below the knee, should feel hard and firm, there should be no puffiness apparent anywhere. In a horse that is light of bone, ligaments and tendons will be correspondingly small and weak.

The fetlock joint must be flat on all sides, never fleshy and never round.

The pastern is the shock absorber *par excellence*. If it is short and upright there will be undue concussion to the foot and leg, resulting in unsoundness. Overlong pasterns put a greater strain on the suspensory ligament and the tendons which run down the rear of the foreleg. How great a strain is placed on these can be seen from photographs of horses landing over a fence when, on occasion, the rear of the fetlock joint is touching the ground.

A good pastern should have a gentle slope to it, being neither too upright nor too much the other way. The hind pasterns, because of the compensating flexing action of the hock, are a little shorter than those of the forelegs.

The Foot

The foot is a subject in itself and is dealt with in some detail in the chapter on shoeing. There is no truer saying than "no foot – no 'oss". A horse is as good as his feet and if they are bad then no other aspect of conformation can compensate for them.

Look carefully at them and make quite sure that the two pairs, fore and hind, are as near a perfect match in shape and size as is possible.

If one foot is smaller than its companion we may deduce with some certainty that the horse has a record of lameness. If a horse is lame he naturally puts less weight on to the foot which is causing him pain and as a result the foot shrinks because it is not subject to the same spreading pressure as its fellow.

Small, boxy feet which appear to be too small in proportion to the size of the horse are best avoided. They usually *are* too small.

Heels must be open, deep and never contracted. In order for this to be so the bars of the foot must also be deep and well-turned.

The soles of the feet should be thick and strong and not give when pressure is applied with the fingers. The shape of the sole in a healthy foot is slightly concave in the forefeet and more so in the hind ones. Avoid feet with dropped soles. The frog is an anti-concussion and anti-slip device for the foot and a healthy one will be large, well formed and coming well down to the ground. Shrivelled looking frogs not coming into contact with the ground are bad, as in this condition they cannot perform their proper function.

The wall of the hoof must be strong and show no signs of breakage or longitudinal cracks.

The wall is usually dark grey in colour; white walls, usually found in horses with white legs or coronets, are considered to be of softer horn and are, therefore, more prone to wear. However, opinions differ on this point and providing the feet are otherwise good there is no need to worry.

The coronary band secretes a protective, waterproof oil (the periople) over the hoof wall and healthy feet (those that have not had the wall rasped by the smith or polished with blacking) should show evidence of this secretion.

Feet that turn out or turn in will affect the action. Those that are turned out presenting the more serious fault, as brushing is then almost inevitable. Turned-in toes are not as bad a fault and many authorities will say that a horse will go better in the deep. This may be so, personally I prefer feet that point straight to the front in any sort of going.

The weight bearing parts of the foot are the frog, the wall, the bars and the outer edges of the sole. If these are properly formed and healthy there will be nothing much wrong with the foot.

At this point I was about to suggest the most desirable angle of slope in a healthy, well-shod foot. I had always understood that the correct angle of the forefeet was about 50 degrees and that of the hindfeet between 55 and 60 degrees. On checking this, however, I found the experts, including three veterinary surgeons, at some variance. The consensus of opinion is around these figures, but it is surprising to find differences involving 10 and more degrees. Nevertheless, feet displaying slopes approximating to these figures can, I think, be considered correct. What is certain is that if the proper Foot/Pastern/Axis, discussed in the later chapter on shoeing, is to be maintained the slope of the forefeet should approximately closely to the slope of the shoulder.

The Chest

Viewed from the front, should be wide to allow for expansion of the lungs. The shape of the chest depends upon the curvature of the ribs. If the ribs are not well sprung, the horse will be flat sided and the chest cramped and narrow. Under these circumstances the forelegs will be set too close together, "both legs coming out of the same hole", and there will also be a predisposition to brushing and a generally inhibited action. Too heavy and wide a chest, often found with heavy shoulders, is not likely to produce a turn of speed in the animal concerned. Horsy people talk about *heart* room when they should talk of *lung* room. The heart does not need an enormous amount of space, the lungs do.

The Girth

To correspond with a good chest, the girth must be deep and ribs well sprung. The latter should come well back to the loins and one should not have the impression that the horse could do with another rib. Any slackness here is an indication of want of stamina.

The Back

Requires careful examination – after all it is the part you sit on and deficiencies in this department have a great influence on the ability of the horse to perform under saddle, and upon the comfort of the ride you will receive.

The back is that portion of the horse between the withers and the quarters and is bounded on each side by the ribs.

A back, like any other part, cannot be judged on its own. However good in itself it must be supported by good withers at one end and good loins and quarters at the other.

As it is the only convenient part of the horse upon which we can inflict the presence of our bodies it must, necessarily, be shaped to carry a saddle, Further, as it is easily damaged (and when it is the horse will not be able to give of his best), it must be so constructed as to be protected as well as it may be from its principal enemy, the saddle plus the rider's weight.

Any back which does not carry a saddle well must be a serious fault in any horse whose purpose is to do just this. Abnormalities, such as a pronounced hollow-back, or its opposite, the roach back, make saddle fitting difficult and increase the danger of damage to the structure. Roach backs are also uncomfortable rides and encourage faulty action.

Excessively short backs may be strong, but restrict the freedom of the hind limbs and are uncomfortable for the rider, who receives the full force of the propulsive thrust. A very long back is equally bad and must be regarded as being potentially weak.

For speed, however, and for comfort, a longer rather than a shorter back is desirable. Mares, by virtue of their sex, may have somewhat longer backs than geldings.

The Engine of the Horse

Supplying the necessary forward propulsion, is contained in the loins, quarters and hindlegs. Obviously, therefore, the "back end" must give an appearance of power and should never look mean.

The Loins

Which rise from the last rib to the croup, should be somewhat elevated and always muscular. Any tendency to an overlong loin results in slackness and the structure will be a weak one and consequently defective in performance.

The Croup

Is the highest point behind the saddle. In the young horse it will be higher than the withers, while in the mature horse the latter will have developed, ideally, to be on a line with the croup, or even a little higher.

A high croup, giving a sloping effect to the quarters is often termed a "goose-rump". It may be somewhat unsightly, but authorities argue that it displays a good bone development, which is advantageous for the attachment of muscle, and may indicate a horse having considerable jumping ability.

Animals possessing a large proportion of Arab blood (the pure-bred Arabian frequently has 19 ribs as opposed to 18 in other breeds and five lumbar bones instead of six) often have a straight croup, resulting in their characteristic high tail position.

Otherwise the quarters should appear well rounded over the top when viewed from behind, filling out on both sides as the eye travels downwards.

The Gaskin

The gaskin, or second thigh, between the stifle and the hock, supplies much of the power. In general, and for speed, most people would prefer it to be long and muscular, a development usually associated with a low hock, rather than a shorter, and possibly stronger, second thigh which will be found with a longer cannon bone. There are perfectly cogent arguments advanced on behalf of both formations, but for most of us the important thing to remember is that whatever the shape it is most necessary for a horse to show strong development in this area.

Again looked at from the rear, a pronounced lack of muscular development between the thighs, resulting in a horse being "split up behind", is bad, as is a pair of very heavy thighs, joined very low down and appearing to force the animal to move wide behind.

The Hocks

Possibly the point of greatest importance in judging the efficiency of the back end is the position and shape of the hocks. Ideally to achieve maximum efficiency and true proportion the point of the hock should be level with the chestnut which lies above the knee in the foreleg, and, in conjunction with a long second thigh, should be set low.

In perfection a line drawn from the point of the buttock to the

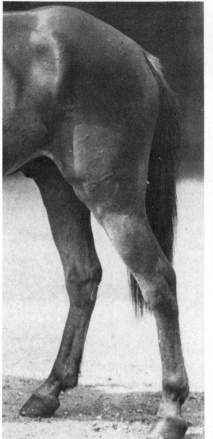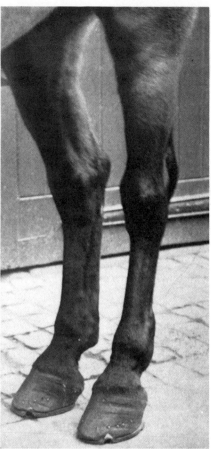

(Left) *Bad and mean quarters without power. The tail is badly set on and there is a notable absence of a second thigh;* (right) *a pair of very objectionable "cow-hocks".*

ground coincides with the point of the hock and the cannon bone should not deviate from the vertical.

In practice a number of good hunters and jumpers will be found to carry the hock a little to the front of this line and the cannon bone, too, will be slightly in advance of the perpendicular and rather more under the horse. This position may not contribute to speed, but it has strength and supplies the necessary jumping thrust.

Where the hock is carried well to the rear of the line dropped from the point of the buttock there will be a loss in propulsion and a greater risk of damage to the joint. Hocks which are too straight and are in advance of the vertical are likewise a source of weakness.

Sickle hocks, those which are too overbent, or curved on the front surface, subject the joint and ligament to greater strain and are frequently disposed to disease.

Hocks out of true, that is either turned out (bowed) or turned in (cow-hocked) must be less efficient than those that are truly symmetrical. Both result in a loss of speed and possibly contribute to uneven wear in the mechanism of the joint and greater strain on the connecting ligaments. Here again there is a confusing divergence of views among expert opinion. I have, for instance, found one authority stating categorically that cow-hocks are a sign of weakness, whereas bowed ones are an indication of strength, and an equally eminent source saying exactly the opposite. They are both talking rubbish.

My own, by no means expert, opinion, is that anything which is very much out of true, any extreme malformation, is bound to prove less effective whatever the shape it takes.

The Perfect Shape

I have included a diagram which is of assistance in giving us a picture of the proportionate horse. With the help of a tape-measure hours of innocent amusement can be obtained comparing the measurements of one's own animals with this perfect horse.

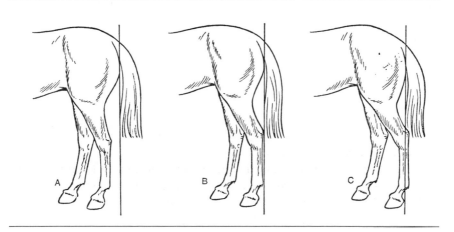

Hocks: A. Straight hocks in front of vertical line. B. Good. Hocks in line with seat-bone. C. Sickle hocks projecting behind the vertical line.

I have dealt with the subject of conformation in some detail, and in doing so I have tried to give some idea of the reasons why one structure is preferred to another and why it is possible to overlook certain differences according to the type of work the animal is asked to perform.

There is no such thing as the perfectly made horse. There are general rules which apply to all riding horses, but it is not possible to lay down rigid requirements to cover every activity to which the horse is put. The

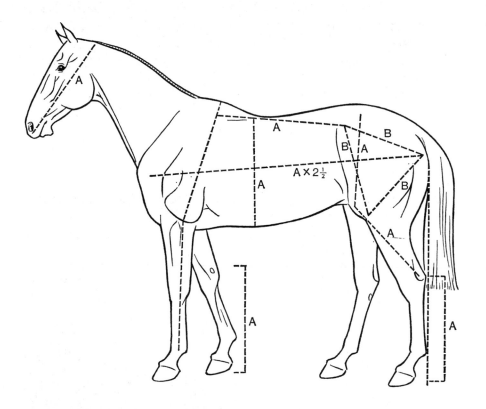

The perfect shape.
A=1 Length of head, 2 Point of hock to ground, 3 Point of hock to fold of stifle, 4 Chestnut to base of foot, 5 Depth of body at girth, 6 Fold of stifle to croup, 7 Posterior angle of scapula to point of hip.
Length from point of shoulder to seat bone=2½ times length of head.
Height from fetlock to elbow=approximately height of elbow – wither.
B=1 Seat bone – point of hip, 2 Seat bone – stifle, 3 Stifle to point of hip.
   A line dropped from the seat bone meets the point of the hock and continues down the back of the cannon bone.

Two of the best: (above) *the author's pure-bred Arabian Bandook, a very successful horse in showjumping, one-day events and dressage,* (below) *the author's dearly-loved skewbald cob, Max, 14.3 h.h. and a phenomenal performer. This picture was taken in his last season when he was over 30 years of age.*

ideal conformation of the racehorse is not necessarily that of the showjumper, and in the former case there will indeed be a difference in conformation between sprinters and stayers.

What is important is that we should try to buy as well-proportioned a horse as our pocket permits, and that when we are compelled to buy one with a fault in make and shape we should appreciate the significance of the particular deficiency in relation to the work we intend to ask of the horse.

A horse of good conformation, if sound, must be of better balance than a badly made one, and, therefore, more easily trained and more pleasant to ride. The more ambitious our aims, the greater, therefore, will be the need for our possessing a horse of good conformation and balance.

As in all things there will always be the exception to prove the general rule, horses that appear to exhibit nearly every fault and are yet outstanding performers. The point to remember is that these *are* the exceptions and that the majority of badly made horses are poor performers.

As it is unlikely that one would knowingly buy an unsound horse and it is hoped that no-one will try to sell you one that is clearly unsound, I do not propose to go to deeply into the subject (which is dealt with more fully in a later section) at this point. If you are wise you will not under any circumstance buy an animal before you have had a satisfactory report from a veterinary surgeon.

Running Him Out

You must, of course, before riding the horse have him run up for you so that you have a chance of assessing the trueness of his action. If he is abundantly lame it is unlikely that even a person of little experience will fail to see that this is the case. If he is just a trifle uneven, or going the tiniest bit short, it is rather more difficult to detect, unless one has great experience or is a competent veterinary surgeon carrying out a thorough examination for soundness.

Providing the horse seems to go sound, concentrate on watching the action. Have him walked away from you and then trotted towards you.

The Action

Deficiencies in action are, in nine cases out of ten, as we have seen, due to faulty conformation.

The action should be true and straight. Watch for any irregularities such as "dishing", i.e. turning the toe of the foreleg, followed by a throwing out of the foot in an outward circling movement.

It may not be of vital importance, but because it is out of true the affected limb receives undue strain and, of course, the ability to gallop is reduced. Plaiting, or crossing the forelegs one over the other when in movement, is rather more serious. Not only does it seriously restrict the freedom of movement, but there is a likelihood of the horse coming down. Animals that turn the toes out have a tendency to knock their legs about, as will one who goes too close in front or behind. This latter practice, called "brushing", can be alleviated by special shoeing, but it is a constant nuisance and may mean that the horse always has to wear protective boots.

At the walk, which should be free and long striding, the hindlegs should be brought well under the body, coming down in advance of the hoofmark made by the foreleg. A horse with a good walk is rarely bad in any of his other paces and should be able to gallop.

At the trot watch the action of the knee, if it is high much of the energy which should be expended in going forward is dissipated. The faster paces will, therefore, lack speed and extension and the ride will not be so comfortable. In addition, of course, the limbs are subjected to greater concussion.

The Horse under Saddle

Now have him saddled up. This is an opportunity to judge his behaviour in the stable. Watch him being bridled and note whether he accepts what can be a little uncomfortable with equanimity.

His reactions to the saddle are also a useful pointer to the condition of the back. If he humps his back and looks generally unhappy and uncomfortable it may just be a habit and mean nothing. On the other hand it could be indicative of some derangement or damage to the kidneys or to the spine itself. There are horses who are termed "cold-backed", and it is suggested that they resent the cold surface of the saddle in much the same way as a person might dislike the feel of a cold shirt first thing in the morning. This is possible, but it is far more likely that these horses are suffering from an arthritic condition between some of the lumbar vertebrae. It is, in fact, quite surprising to learn that very many horses, even if they do not exhibit these signs, suffer more or less constantly from back pain of this nature. All the more reason, of course, why young animals should not be asked to carry weight before they are reasonably mature.

Many so-called "cold-backed" horses are perfectly all right once they have had a few minutes exercise, although they may be more inclined to buck than others.

Avoid, however, the horse who almost sits down when saddled or when the rider comes to mount. He is undoubtedly suffering from one of the conditions described. After all, the object of our keeping a horse is to ride him and in order to do so we must first be able to get on. Before getting on the horse yourself watch him being ridden by either the vendor or his/her assistant. It is only reasonable that the horse should be shown to you *before* you get on and put *your* neck at risk.

Once you are up, without we hope any objections from the horse, ask him to walk on and get the feel of him. Some horses give one an immediate feeling of security, these are usually the well-made, nicely balanced ones; others, with little "front" to them, may give just the opposite feeling.

Try the horse at walk, trot and canter *and on both reins.* You will soon see whether he favours one side or the other and by how much.

If you have the opportunity to jump over a low fence, do so – you want to find out as much about the horse in the short time at your disposal as you possibly can.

Now take him away from his home surroundings, turning him away from home. If he is going to be nappy he will try it at this point. If possible ride him down a road where there is some traffic and make sure that he is all he is claimed to be in this respect. If you can possibly find a gentle slope trot the horse down it and see whether his action shortens uncomfortably.

It is unlikely you will uncover any definite tricks he may possess, but you will have gained a fairly good impression of the sort of horse he is and whether he measures up to your requirements.

Handle him in his box, putting on his rugs, lifting his feet and rubbing his ears. Ask him to move over and note his reactions to these things.

A horse that appears nervy in the box, is fussy about his head or lays his ears back when you adjust his rugs is not necessarily vicious, but to be forewarned is to be forearmed.

If at the end of it all you decide that the horse fulfils the majority of the conditions you have in mind – it is unlikely that he will fulfil them all – then buy him, *but subject to his being passed sound in every way by the veterinary surgeon.*

BUYING A CHILD'S PONY

The purchase of a child's pony is, to my mind, a far more difficult thing to accomplish satisfactorily. If one wishes to risk one's own neck that is, within reason, one's own affair. One should not, however, risk the limbs and maybe the lives of small children.

It is an unfortunate fact that the standard of pony breaking (and it is often *breaking* and not *making*) is appallingly low. I think this is due to the deplorable tendency, which I have already mentioned, of selling and buying ponies at too young an age.

I have seen with my own eyes, as well as having hundreds of instances brought to my notice, young ponies, two-and three-year-old babies, sold to inexperienced homes – often with the most frightful results. I have before me now a letter from a ten-year-old child desperately asking for advice about her pony. She says, "My pony is three. We bought him at a sale last autumn and he was very quiet. Now when I ride him on the road he whips round and bucks, and if I try to make him go on he rears up. He is also very bad in traffic. My father gets very cross with him and hits him, but it does no good and makes him worse. Now I dread riding him because he frightens me so much. Please can you help me."

You may well ask, what sort of parent would expose his child to such danger? But there really are people who do just this sort of thing.

This is a bad example, but it is by no means a solitary one. It is typical of a large number of letters that editors of magazines receive every week. All they can do is to reply immediately, urging the parents to get rid of the pony before it maims or kills their child.

We may blame the person who sold the pony, we may blame the parents for their ignorance, what we cannot do is blame the poor, wretched pony.

The fact is that the pony, in spite of the father's treatment, was not properly broken for riding and was certainly not an animal suitable for a beginner to handle on her own.

Anyone with a modicum of knowledge can break a weak, immature animal incapable of resistance. I have no doubt, and God forgive me if I ever should, that had I a two-year-old, unbroken pony I could within three days have accustomed it to wearing a bit and to accepting a child on its back. I would not, however, have a made pony at the end of the operation. At best he is half-broken, and *broken* is the word, and that badly.

Sold in poor condition he may initially appear to be quiet enough, but when he begins to feel better and stronger, because he cannot understand what his rider wants him to do, and she cannot tell him, he becomes confused. Then he becomes nervous, then angry and resentful. Add to these feelings that of fear, fear of noises and sights with which he is totally unfamiliar, and then, because he shows he is frightened, terrify him by beating him until all his instincts urge him to flee, to get away anywhere and anyhow and what have you left? You have no longer an animal willing and happy to put its trust in man, it is now an animal which has reverted to its wild state, only because of its contact with humans it is doubly distrustful, doubly unreliable. Man is now associated with pain and terror.

A beginner's pony, a first pony, should be bought with the object of giving the child confidence. Any old pony just will not do.

A first pony must be quiet, he must not move like quicksilver and if he has little ambition beyond a modest trot he will be none the worse for it. He need not necessarily be very, very old, for it is not so much his age which is important, but his temperament. There are lots of seasoned old reprobates at 20 and many very nicely mannered ponies of nine or ten. The young pony of four or five may turn out to be perfectly satisfactory, but you run more risk of his getting a little above himself than you do with an older and more experienced one.

Here again, Pony Club District Commissioners are usually prepared to be helpful and may know of a suitable outgrown pony in the district.

Failing this go to some reliable person who specialises in providing ponies for children. Don't buy them at sales. Otherwise write to one of the horse magazines, or even to me, and ask advice as to whom you should approach.

Conformation in a first pony is not so great a consideration, providing that it is not the type of pony that is so broad as to make the child both uncomfortable and insecure. Avoid if you can, however, the really badly made pony who just cannot carry a saddle without shooting it up its neck.

Sound it certainly should be, although there are many first ponies that would be as lame as dogs with three legs if worked hard, but who are quite able to do the quiet work demanded of them without becoming unsound.

Do not grudge a little extra money if it buys you peace of mind – it is cheap at the price.

For slightly more experienced children a brighter sort of pony can be bought, but his temperament must be good and he must be 100% safe in traffic. In these cases more account should be taken of conformation. Don't buy a great, heavy-necked, cresty sort of pony, he will always be too strong and will ruin even the most sensitive young hands.

In this country we are fortunate to have our indigenous pony breeds and these, or crosses with them, make ideal young people's mounts.

Unless you are set upon showing the pony it is as well not to have one of the miniature Thoroughbred types. They are not nearly so tough and take far more looking after. They may also be too much for the average child rider to cope with comfortably.

There are nine native breeds, all of which vary considerably in appearance, but all of which are hardy and often have lovely temperaments and a high degree of intelligence (although some might call it downright cunning).

My own particular favourite is the Welsh – but then I am a Welshman. There are four principal sections in the Welsh Stud Book, the Welsh Mountain pony, who is a little fellow not exceeding 12 hh; his brother the larger Welsh pony up to 13.2 hh, who is definitely a riding pony; then the Welsh pony of cob type and the larger Welsh Cob. To my mind no pony is more beautiful than the Welsh Mountain – but, as I said, I'm prejudiced. All of them are sure-footed, narrow enough, have substance and are capable of giving a lovely ride and, of course, the bigger ones can carry an adult too. There is also a part-bred section in the Welsh Stud Book in which there are some very nice animals.

The Connemara comes from Ireland and may exceed 14 hh. He is an excellent riding pony and has a reputation of being a "lepper".

A first cross of this breed with the Thoroughbred is an excellent combination and is often bigger.

The Highland varies between 13.2–14.2 hh. They are gentle, docile ponies of great strength and very sure-footed. They will jump and are quite fast enough for most purposes. These ponies are quite capable of carrying adults as well as children.

The Shetland is the smallest of the native breeds. Exceptionally strong in relation to their size, most do not stand more than 40 inches at the wither, these ponies are only really suitable for small children. Even though the Shetland is a delightful "cuddly" person it has to be remembered that he can exhibit a particular independence of spirit.

The New Forest, like the Connemara, has the scope and the freedom of action to make a top-class competition pony in any field and at 14.2 hh can also be ridden very satisfactorily by lightweight adults.

Dartmoors and Exmoors are smaller, around 12 hh, but they can be wonderful riding ponies. The Exmoor, however, a real strong "toughie" is perhaps better suited to the competent, thrusting sort of boy rider.

From the North come the Fell (13.2 hh) and the Dales pony, who may be a little heavier and larger. Both can give splendid rides, the Fell possibly having the better riding action, and both are able to carry any member of the family.

There are, of course, part-breds of all these breeds who may exceed the heights I have given and yet still retain the essential type. With this enormous variety to choose from I often wonder why so many unsuitable and nondescript ponies are about, and why people bother to buy such animals.

I am the last person to discourage a child owning a pony, or parents buying one, and I am only too aware how insistent the young can be when they contract "ponyitis".

Even so, the expense connected with a pony does not end when the purchase cheque is made out. It goes on, month in month out, for as long as the pony is owned. Too many ponies are bought by ignorant and indulgent, or perhaps exasperated and exhausted, parents under the mistaken impression that so long as there is a bit of rough grass a pony costs no more than his purchase price.

"Lives out" does not mean lives on air. He must be fed in winter and properly cared for, he needs a shelter and his feet must be regularly attended to, and if grazing is hired it must be paid for.

All of which means additional and continued expenditure which must be considered before, and not after, the pony is bought.

The totally unhorsy parent is also well advised to view his offspring's assumed expertise in matters equine with some scepticism.

Little girls, and boys if they are interested, are not qualified to look after and manage a large animal on the strength of their having traipsed round the lanes on a quiet pony once a week for a year. At least not without some adult help or supervision. If parents are not able or willing to give this then the child is better off continuing with his or her weekly rides at the local riding school.

These are important considerations to be taken into account before acquiring a pony.

If, on the other hand, the parents are keen, prepared to learn and to accept advice, and are determined that their pony shall not suffer through ignorance, or lack of means or proper facilities, then go ahead and buy one.

It is more than well worth the expense and effort.

CHAPTER 2

Horse-keeping – Which Method?

Well before a horse is purchased plans must have been made for his accommodation and a method of keeping him decided upon.

The final arrangement will depend largely upon the time one has available; for horse-keeping, whatever method is adopted, makes heavy demands on time. It will also, of course, depend upon the work the horse is to do and the facilities that are available.

Keeping at Livery

The easiest way to keep a horse, and the most expensive, is to get someone else to keep it for you at livery. There will be horse-owners who have no alternative but to employ this method but, expense apart, it seems to me to take much of the fun and interest out of horse-owning. It may be very nice to drive up to the stables and have your horse, saddled and bridled, waiting for you, but it is somewhat impersonal and the arrangement denies to the owner the opportunity, and the undoubted satisfaction, of establishing a really close relationship with the horse.

Full livery is necessarily expensive, but there are stables which will charge much reduced rates if they can use the animal as a school horse. There are two disadvantages to what might otherwise be a convenient arrangement. First, the school would like to make use of the horse at weekends, when they have a greater number of clients, and this is probably the time the owner also wants the animal; secondly, it is very difficult to keep a horse reasonably schooled if half-a-dozen different people, all possibly novices and all endeavouring to communicate in different ways, are allowed to ride him. The horse either gives up the unequal contest and becomes just another unambitious plug, or he may develop a number of annoying resistances and habits which become more deeply ingrained as time goes on. If, of course, his use can be restricted to a qualified member of the stable staff the matter assumes a very different complexion.

Nevertheless, there are, increasingly, many parts of country and suburban areas where livery is the only possible answer and people living there must make the best arrangements they can if they are determined upon horse-ownership.

More popular and more practical today is the D.I.Y. system which overcomes many of the disadvantages of livery and is within the financial reach of most horse-owners.

It is, indeed, far more satisfactory to keep a horse in this way than attempting to manage the animal on a half-acre of rented scrub land situated at an inconvenient distance from one's base.

Apart from the advantage of constant supervision many livery stables will have facilities in the way of schooling areas, fences, etc. which they are willing to make available to their clients.

Obviously, it is prudent to shop around so as to find an establishment best suited to one's requirements, but in these days there are enough businesses of this type for it not to be a problem. (In general terms, it is probably wise to select a school which has some form of official approval either under the British Horse Society or Association of British Riding Schools' schemes.)

A STABLE FOR THE HOME-KEPT HORSE

If, however, one has the necessary space at or near one's own property the most enjoyable way is to look after the animal oneself.

The horse that is going to be in fairly hard work, either hunting or taking part in competitive events, both of which pursuits require him to be maintained in hard condition and in the winter to have his coat removed by clipping, will need a stable of some kind, whether he is to live in entirely, or be kept on the New Zealand rug system. If there are no existing stables or buildings which can be converted to the purpose there is only one solution – the erection of a new stable.

Pre-Fabricated Structures

Fortunely there are a number of obliging firms, specialising in ready-to-erect wooden stabling, which are very willing to submit plans and quotations for either a single box or a range of stable buildings. Most of them are also able to lay the necessary concrete foundation and erect the building for you if you feel this is beyond your ability. Otherwise, of course, a local builder can be called in to do the job for you. All this, however, increases the cost and I am assured, although not convinced, bearing in mind my own ineptitude with a hammer, that any average handyman can put the affair up without too much difficulty. I say I am not convinced because I once witnessed the efforts of six strong men, all useful handymen, two boys, two further directing geniuses and one woman (who may have been the trouble) trying to erect a range of two boxes supplied by a well-known firm. The language, which the presence of the lady did little to ameliorate, was horrific, the whole operation appeared to be highly dangerous, and while they did eventually get the thing up, the cost in time alone was far in excess of what a small builder would have charged.

In fairness, many people do manage the job most satisfactorily, but it is as well to make another honest assessment of one's ability before deciding to "do-it-yourself".

Extremely affluent horse-owners may prefer to build in brick, which is a job for a professional builder.

Planning Permission

For a large stable complex it will in most instances be necessary to apply for planning permission from the local authority. However, if you keep one or two, or even three, horses privately as part of your domestic *messuage* you are entitled to provide accommodation for them, just as you may build runs for rabbits or guinea pigs, without consulting the planning department. *Messuage* refers to "a dwelling-house with its outbuildings and curtilage and the adjacent land assigned to its use". In effect, if you have a front or back garden no one can stop you from erecting a stable thereon under the Act of 1988. The law, whether that prescribed by the Mother of Parliaments or the European Tower of Babel, remains as always "a ass", but in this respect it favours the horse-keeper.

Conversion of Existing Buildings

The conversion of existing buildings allows for more personal ingenuity and is generally far cheaper. In the 1969 edition of *The Horseman's Guide* I wrote "My own stables, although far from exemplary, are very satisfactory, and the cost of conversion amounted to only a few pounds. We had a three-sided Suffolk cart-shed of some age, but it was, within reason, structurally sound. It had a storage loft and a pantiled roof which was made completely water tight, and insulated at the same time, by fastening roof felt on the inside across the roof beams. It was made into two large boxes, about 14 ft square, by means of railway sleepers. The sleepers were set upright in a trench to divide the area into two and to make a front wall, and made secure by means of timber stretchers set along their length.

"Any gap between the sleeper wall and the ceiling level was filled in with some rough, but perfectly adequate timber, and gaps between individual sleepers were sealed with plastic filler. The half-doors were filched from other odd buildings on the place, at least the bottom halves, and were fitted easily enough. The top halves were rather more difficult, so much so, in fact, that in the end they never did get put up. If I had really thought them necessary I would have persevered, but as I never shut the top door, even in the worst weather, it would have been a waste of time anyway. The stables have been in constant use for over 18 months and we have never had a horse with even a suspicion of a runny nose.

"By putting the sleeper wall back from the overhang of the roof we also managed to have a verandah in front of the boxes and, apart from our own convenience, this allows the horses to have their heads out on the wettest day without discomfort."

It is, in fact, quite surprising what can be achieved by the intelligent alteration of the most unpromising buildings. Of course, it is very necessary when converting an existing building to make sure that all projections, old nails, etc., are removed, otherwise one is asking for trouble.

First-class stabling is very nice to have, but it is no substitute for good horsemastership.

Today, were I not possessed of adequate stone-built stabling, I would convert part of the barn for the purpose. I would have my horses within the barn, on the American pattern. The boxes would be divided by walls high enough to prevent the animals from getting over the division but sufficiently low for them to have both visual and tactile contact. Why should we keep horses in what amounts to solitary confinement for the greater part of the 24 hours comprising the day?

Fundamental Requirements – Types and Sizes

Nevertheless, however humble the building, there are certain fundamental and common-sense requirements which it should meet and there are certain forms which are better than others.

Loose boxes are vastly preferable to the more old-fashioned stalls. I

Stabling at the Bombay Amateur Riders' Club, India.

Communal feeding for young remounts at the Remount Depot, Saharanpur, India. Their stables, also communal, are in the background.

can think of nothing more soul destroying and likely to produce a neurotic animal than to make him stand in a confined space, facing an expanse of wall, for the greater part of the 24 hours in a day.

Stalls are all very well for ponies who normally live out and who make use of them for short periods devoted to grooming and such like, but they are hardly ideal for the horse who spends most of his time in the stable, and certainly not so for the animal stabled like this on his own. Where a pony occupies a stall for anything beyond a short period he should be secured by means of a rope passing from his headcollar, through a ring or hole in the manger and then through a manger log which may just rest on the straw. A manger log is not a "log" at all, but a sphere of *lignum vitae* with a hole through the centre. Once the rope is passed through the log it can be tied with a simple quick-release knot, in case the pony ever gets a leg over the rope.

This method allows the pony a certain amount of liberty within the stall, without his being able to turn right round, and also lets him lie down if he wishes to do so.

My own ideal size for a loose box would be no less than 14 ft × 12 ft for a horse and 12 ft × 10 ft for a pony. Many pre-fabricated boxes are, however, somewhat smaller and I would always think it advisable to spend a little extra and have a good size box. There is certainly more freedom for the horse and less chance that he will get himself cast in a bigger box. The fact that you have to use more straw to make a satisfactory bed should not be a consideration.

More important is to have a good airy box and this you will not have if the roof level is too low. I would like a 12 ft minimum eaves height, but I admit this may not always be possible to achieve.

Doors should certainly be high enough to prevent the animal jumping out of the box, but not so high that he has to crane his neck to see over the top. A height of 4 ft 6 in is about right and 4 ft is a good width. Narrow doorways are an abomination against which horses can knock their hips. Horses can suffer considerable damage, even to the extent of bone fractures, by knocking themselves in this way.

Two bolts are necessary on this bottom half of the door, one of the normal pattern at the top and one of the kick-over type at the bottom. This will prevent the crafty fellow who has learnt to undo top bolts from disappearing in the middle of the night and also discourages the gentlemen who kicks the bottom of his door for the sake of hearing the glorious rattle it makes.

Siting

The siting of boxes is of great importance to the well-being and the mental serenity of the horse. Boxes should face to the south, out of the head winds and where they receive as much of the sun as we are likely to get in this particular section of our vale of tears. In addition, they should be sited so that their inmates can see as much of what is going on as possible. Horses, like humans, become bored, but can do less about it than their masters. The horse will be much more alert, interested and happy if he can see people, dogs, children and all the comings and goings of the normal household from his box.

THE ESSENTIAL TRINITY

There are then a further three factors to be considered, whatever the type of stabling. They are *ventilation, insulation and drainage.*

Ventilation

As far as the first of these is concerned we need *ample* ventilation without draughts. Draughts are anathema to horses just as much as they are to human beings. Apart from causing aches and pains they contribute materially to colds and chills and therefore cannot be tolerated. If the box is high enough and the top door left open there should be plenty of ventilation. An additional aid would be a set of louvres high up on the rear wall to take away the upward rising bad air which may accumulate in the box. If there is a window in the box (always placed next to the doorway) it should be of the type which opens inwards from the bottom hinge so that the air enters in an upward direction and not directly on to the horse. The more fresh air we can have in our stables the healthier will be our horses.

In very cold weather it is far better to increase the ration of heating foods, to compensate for the extra used by the horse to keep himself warm, and to put on an extra blanket, rather than to shut the top door. The unclothed parts of the animal, his neck and his buttocks, may look a little rough, but he will remain healthy and free from colds.

Old fashioned grooms and some horse dealers shut the top door, put on plenty of clothing and create a fug worthy of a bar parlour. As a result the owner, or client, can be shown a horse who exhibits a glorious satin-like sheen, but that horse is much more likely to catch cold than his toughened, if not so elegant, brother who enjoys plenty of fresh air whatever the weather.

Insulation

Insulation implies the use of materials which will keep the building relatively warm in cold weather and relatively cool under the opposite condition. In order to achieve this object it is necessary in wooden structures to have the inside lined. Apart from creating an insulating cavity between the outer and inner walls it also contributes to the strength of the structure against the depredations of horses with a propensity to kick at the wall for the sheer hell of it. Older stable buildings are usually well and solidly built, but there is always a temptation when converting less well-constructed buildings to use corrugated iron sheeting for the roof. This material attracts heat, when there is any, and doesn't keep the cold out. It is a bad insulator and not to be recommended. Asbestos sheeting is not over expensive and is far more efficient in these respects, but, of course, is unsuitable for any part of the building other than the roof

Drainage and Floors

The problem of drainage is relatively easy if one is building from scratch. The simpler the system the better is it likely to be. Old fashioned stables had floors of very beautiful (and now very expensive) blue Staffordshire brick which were often ruined by having drains set in the middle. The drains were frequently blocked and the box consequently permeated with unpleasant smells.

The best idea is to have a very slightly sloping concrete floor (1½ to 2 inches slope is enough) and an open drain, which can be swilled and brushed out, *outside* the stable door. If the drain is inside the door it makes it uncomfortable for the horse to stand looking out. Many modern stables in fact, have no drainage system at all and manage very well without. The wet straw is brushed straight out of the door on to the concrete fronting the boxes and that in turn is brushed clean and the refuse transferred to the muck-heap. I doubt, however, whether the council of a suburban area would approve of this method; most of them, up to the horse-people's emancipation Act of 1988, required elaborate, sometimes impossible, drainage systems to be installed. Now we can tell them to jump into the nearest European lake. We should, nonetheless, have consideration for our neighbours if boxes are sited where they might possibly create a nuisance.

In many countries overseas, and I have also seen them in this country, floors of hard-packed earth or clay are employed, quite often having a base of rubble. Obviously they cannot be so effective from the viewpoint of drainage, but they are far less likely to cause injuries than brick or concrete and have greater insulating properties. Providing the floor has a thick covering of straw, much of the water will be absorbed before it makes contact with the earth surface, and while the pundits tend to condemn the system I am by no means persuaded that it is impossible to keep healthy horses this way in Britain.

Far more important from the horse's point of view is that whatever the system employed the box is properly and regularly cleaned and kept sweet.

Fittings and Tools

In all types of stabling certain fittings will be required and a number of simple cleaning tools are also a necessity.

These fittings or tools can be elaborate or simple depending upon what the owner can afford. Elaborate ones may not always contribute to healthier horses, but they often make the stable work a lot easier.

First one requires a manger, or at any rate a receptacle, in which to put the horse's food. In the old type of stabling mangers are often massive, porcelain affairs built into the corner of the box. Obviously they are very durable and are nearly always sufficiently deep to prevent a horse sweeping his food out to either side – a wasteful procedure indulged in by some horses. Their disadvantage is that they are difficult to clean easily and quickly. Horses are fastidious eaters and like us do not appreciate eating, as it were, from a dirty plate.

For newly built boxes galvanised or plastic mangers which fit into a corner are very satisfactory. They are usually fitted with two "anti-waste" bars, one on each side, and can easily be dropped into a wooden framework set across the corner. They have the great advantage of being easily removable and, therefore, very easily cleaned.

A manger is, for the sake of safety, set at breast height. There is a school of thought which holds that as the horse in nature feeds from the ground it is illogical to feed him from manger height when stabled. The answer, of course, is that the *stabled* horse is, as far as he is concerned, in a *natural* state, or at least an accustomed one, and seems to have adapted himself to eating from this position very well. Other advantages which are argued in favour of manger feeding are that the horse cannot, having had his meal, kick the manger about, damaging both it and himself and that he is less likely to deposit his droppings into a manger, possibly spoiling the food, than into a similar feeding receptacle on the floor.

The first point I concede, but it does seem to me that it is just as possible for an animal to put his droppings into a manger as into a feed tin on the floor. Providing the horse is correctly positioned at the moment of lifting his tail the difference in height would not appear to be of any significance.

For the very simple reason that I do not possess mangers I feed my horses from heavy, round feed tins of adequate depth which can be obtained from most ironmongers, particularly those in farming areas. They are cheap, easily removable and, therefore, easily cleaned after every feed. They are placed firmly on the straw in the corner and are removed when the horse has finished feeding. No extra work is involved in this as we make it a rule always to see whether a horse has eaten up within an hour of his being given the feed. Once or twice they have been kicked, but no droppings find their way into them. If hay were left in the box all night they probably would get used as footballs and they might contain droppings in the morning, but they don't get left in the box and so the matter doesn't arise. Neither does the close proximity of the bedding induce the horse to eat it – another theory advanced by the anti-ground faction. In fact, should we have a horse with a tendency towards a muscular development on the underside of the neck, which might lead to a ewe-neck and his being constantly above the bit, we would ensure his being always fed from the floor so as to discourage, if only by a little, that undesirable development.

A cardinal rule of feeding, which appears in the majority of horse manuals, is that horses should be watered before being fed. And in principle this is sound because if the horse had his feed and then immediately drank a bucket of water it would have the effect of washing undigested food out of the stomach. But this in fact would only arise where water was not always available in the box, the horse being watered at fixed times.

Modern opinion says "Keep water in the box at all times", and it is right. At one time much controversy raged as to whether horses should drink hard or soft water. I always considered it to be a somewhat pointless argument and my horses have always drunk water from the tap. Very few horses, however, like very cold water and I always leave water in the buckets for about half-an-hour before putting it in the boxes.

Having digressed a little we must consider how water shall be made freely available, and the simplest way is to keep a filled bucket in the stable.

Oak stable buckets are heavy and so not easily knocked over if put on the ground. They need regular cleaning, however, if they are not to become slimy, and even with an inner rim of iron fitted round the top horses have been known to chew at them. Galvanised buckets are a boon to bored horses, they rattle delightfully when kicked and crumple most satisfactorily when sat upon. Heavy plastic buckets are much better and stand up to more ill usage.

Plastic buckets are also light in weight, which is an important consideration. Oak buckets get even heavier with age and use and when filled are beyond the carrying capacity of a girl or a lightly built woman. They do, of course, look very smart outside the stables, painted in one's colours and filled with geraniums.

To avoid the possibility of buckets being knocked over they can be hung from a hook on the wall, but this must be a hook of proper design with the point turned back, elongated, and presenting no sharp projection on which the horse could injure himself.

If you can afford self-filling water bowls in the stable, which will involve the installation of a permanent water system, this is ideal for the horse and will save hours of time for the owner or groom.

If your stables are old ones they may be fitted with hayracks fairly high up on the wall. Pull them down and sell them for scrap or fix them to the wall and fill them with colourful plants. Horses fed hay from these affairs, apart from having to imitate a giraffe to get it, receive all the dust and seeds in their eyes with consequent ill effect. Feed hay from a haynet. You can then calculate how much hay you are feeding and can be assured of the minimum of waste. Suspend the net from a galvanised ring, either screwed into the wall or bolted through it, and have another ring to which the horse may be tied for grooming or when saddled before going out.

Where the box has a window, of the type already mentioned, it must be protected with an iron bar grille. Electric light switches should be of the type designed for outside use and should be placed *outside* where no horse can play with them. Electric fittings inside the box must be out of the horse's reach and as an extra precaution covered with a wire mesh.

The door, bolted as I have already described, can have the top edge covered with zinc to discourage chewing, and mesh grilles can be purchased to close across the top half.

The reason given for using these grilles, which, of course, prevent a horse standing with his head out of the box, are to prevent a horse biting you as you pass by, to prevent a horse contracting the habit of weaving, and also to prevent him biting his next door neighbour.

My own comments on these points are: my horses are not wild animals: I do not expect them to bite me. Should they forget their manners and nip me hard I bite them back and they don't do it again. (This is not as silly as it sounds and is psychologically a sound practice. Very quickly one takes the muzzle in both hands and inflicts a sharp nip on the tenderest part. The effect is salutary and long lasting, and it is amusing to watch the horse puzzling out the "action-reaction" factor.) Weaving is caused by boredom. If you are unfortunate enough to own a weaver a vee-shaped grille, through which he can put his head, will provide some sort of solution. Don't, however, if you can help it stable him in close proximity to other horses, weaving is a highly contagious trick. If horses bite each other over the top of adjoining doors, let them get on with it. They will soon tire of the habit.

Possession of proper stable tools (apart from grooming kit, which is dealt with elsewhere) contributes to the ease with which the stable can be cleaned out. Absolute essentials are a barrow, a stable shovel, a pitch fork (two prongs with blunt ends), a four tine fork, and a broom. A muck skip (there are very good plastic ones on the market, and if you can run to two of them one can be used for carrying the feed to the manger), or even, a muck-sheet, a piece of strong sacking or canvas, which can be used for the same purpose, is also helpful and, indeed, necessary. You will also need a sack, split open down one side and the bottom to carry straw from the store to the box. Without this inexpensive piece of equipment you will not only find the operation difficult, but you will also leave a trail behind you which will have to be cleared up.

As for the barrow, choose one that is large enough and designed for the purpose – there are plenty on the market.

The rest of this equipment is easily enough obtained and requires little comment, although it is as well when buying broom heads to go for the best, they last so much longer. Best of all are the, admittedly expensive, nylon brooms used for road sweeping by many local authorities. They take a very long time even to show signs of wear.

Bedding and Mucking Out

For most of us the removal and replacement of bedding is the job most deserving of the description, "stable chore". Unfortunately, apart from possessing the necessary tools and planning an intelligent yard lay-out there is not a lot we can do to diminish this necessary labour. Nor, in fact, should we seek to suit our own convenience in this respect, or any other, at the expense of the horse.

Good beds are necessary for the well-being of the horse and our only consideration should be to obtain the best material to provide them. Poor bedding, or an insufficient quantity of bedding, does not induce horses to lie down and can cause injuries from contact with the floor when they do.

Nice, happy contented horses express appreciation of their lot by lying down frequently and for long periods. Not only is it good for their legs, but also for their mental state.

Whatever form of bedding is used one should aim at providing a dry, warm and resilient bed which is absorbent and deodorising. Again, the best quality material will amount to nothing if good stable management is not practised.

Straw Beds

Straw is the most common form of bedding and of the varieties obtainable wheat straw is the most satisfactory. In pre-combine days it was cut long and this property enabled one to make a really good bed with little effort. In some parts of the country it is still possible to obtain wheat straw of a good length, but in many more the shorter variety has to be accepted. Even so it is the most resilient and the least palatable.

Oat straw, which can be used for mixing in chaff, is very much more attractive to equines as a food and most horses will become addicted to bed-eating where it is provided as bedding.

The consumption of straw is bad for the wind, upsets one's calculations of the bulk quantity of food required by the horse and is generally regarded as one of the equine sins. The bed can be made less attractive by spraying with disinfectant. These considerations apart, oat straw can be used, but it flattens easily and one needs a great deal of it to provide a good covering. It is best avoided if possible.

Barley straw in the old days was not considered suitable because the awns on the ears are so prickly as to cause skin irritations and if eaten they give rise to colic. Combined barley straw, however, is almost free of awns and makes a good enough bed.

Rye straw is tough and hard-wearing, but is not generally available.

Straw, used for bedding, has an advantage over other materials in that the resultant box cleanings are sometimes saleable.

The Use of Bracken, Sawdust, Peat Moss, etc.

In some parts bracken (cut when green) is used for bedding, but it is scratchy stuff, non-absorbent and often full of insects. It makes a very poor bed. Sawdust is often used where it is easily available, but requires a deal of labour and management if it is to be satisfactory. If sawdust is considered it should not come from other than seasoned woods. Green woods produce a sawdust which ferments easily and becomes very hot as it gets wet and hard packed. Wet patches and droppings must be removed quickly and the bed needs forking and turning daily.

Wood shavings are better as they are less likely to ferment, but they are not absorbent.

These two materials can be used in conjunction with each other and in this case the sawdust forms the under layer.

Peat moss is in popular use and like sawdust is highly absorbent and is the most efficient deodoriser of all. Whilst it does not get hot, like sawdust, it does, however, need the same attention. Lack of proper management, resulting in soaked patches being left in the box, will cause rotting of the feet and skin disorders on parts of the body coming into contact with the bed.

All absorbent beddings such as those described above are remarkably efficient drain blockers and precautions must be taken accordingly. A further disadvantage is that a muck-heap formed of these materials is unsaleable and may even cause disposal difficulties. (Do not think that the muck heap, whatever its constituents, can be used as a handy fertiliser for the paddock. It can't, and the reason? It will probably contain worms or worm eggs and by spreading it over the pasture one is just encouraging a renewed life-cycle for the parasites.)

The advantage is that horses do not eat these types of bedding – which is, I suppose, something to be thankful for.

Some years ago there was a waterproof plastic covered mattress on the market, originally intended for cows, and there was talk of similar mattresses, suitably strengthened to withstand shod hooves, being produced for stables. The makers claimed that it was warm, resilient and easily washed down although, of course, an area of the box would have to be covered with straw upon which horses could stale, as they have an understandable aversion to staling either on surfaces which they feel might be slippery or where they might get their legs splashed.

It never came to anything, but in the future it is not beyond possibility that something other than natural materials may be found which will do the job as well, or perhaps better, and save us all a lot of work.

In my view straw beds should be cleaned out every day. The soiled straw and droppings go to the muck-heap and the slightly wet stuff, which can be used again, put out to dry. The bed is then remade with fresh straw after the floor has been washed down and sprinkled with disinfectant.

At the risk of repeating myself I would stress that beds should be generous. A thin bed may seem to be economical, but it is an economy made at the expense of the horse's well-being and comfort and is, therefore, a false one. Straw should be laid with the stalks criss-crossed to give greater resilience and should be well banked up round the edges of the box. This practice not only makes a cosy draught-free bed, but prevents, in certain measure, the horse becoming cast, i.e. getting himself turned over against the corner in such a way that he cannot get himself up again.

The Deep-Litter Method

There are people, however, who employ the deep-litter method, removing the droppings, etc. and putting down fresh straw on the top. One is, in fact, making a compost heap within the stable, the whole thing being cleaned out in one go when it becomes inconveniently high or, as I suspect, at the end of the season when the horses go out to grass. Adherents of the method claim a great saving of labour with no ill-effect upon the horse, who, they point out, always has a deep, resilient and warm floor covering.

There are obvious arguments against the practice and while I am all for the saving of labour and am well aware that there are many healthy horses kept in this fashion, it does not commend itself as a system which I would personally employ in its entirety. However, I know of a number of horse-owners who practise the method on a weekly basis, leaving the bulk of the mucking out as a weekend job.

(I wrote this over 20 years ago. I still think I am right but confess to employing a semi-deep-litter system – and I do so with no ill-effects to my horses.)

THE COMBINED SYSTEM

Fortunately, for the many people who cannot always exercise every day and have little time to spare for stable work there is an excellent way of keeping horses which reduces labour in these respects. It is the "so-called" combined system. The horse is given a hunter clip, i.e. the legs and saddle-patch are left unclipped, he is kept in at night and then turned out in a New Zealand rug during the day. As a result stable-work is made less onerous and the horse is able to exercise himself.

The system has almost everything to recommend it, for it allows the use of a fit horse during the winter months without the owner having to spend a disproportionate amount of time looking after it.

More important the horse is, I believe, just that little bit nearer to his natural state. Certainly the method is beneficial to his mental state and he is unlikely to develop tricks due to boredom.

The system, of course, does not preclude labour entirely and the horse must have his regular feeds just as a stabled animal does. The fact that he is out at grass for part of his day, grass which in winter has no nutritional value, does not mean that any economy in feeding can be contemplated. In fact, in cold weather, he will need more heating foods to maintain his body heat.

He will, of course, get dirty and there will be a certain amount more work involved in getting him cleaned up for a hunting day. His coat, too, may not carry quite the same bloom as does that of a stabled horse, but these things must be accepted, and providing he remains fit and healthy, and is as well turned out as possible, the question of appearance is of secondary importance when compared with the obvious merit of the system as a whole.

Obviously the system can be operated with variations. My own mare for instance is "quartered" (i.e. given a quick brush, mane and tail made tidy and feet picked out) after her morning feed and is then exercised. On her return she is put out in her paddock, where she has her mid-day feed, and is then brought in during the early afternoon to be properly groomed and strapped.

If for any reason she does not have her hour or two of freedom she is noticeably fidgety and usually indulges in a fit of sulks.

Alternatively, if the box opens on to the paddock, the horse can be left out during the day, and if the door is left open can come in and out as he wishes.

At the other extreme it is possible to keep the horse out day and night in a New Zealand rug. I think you would then need two rugs per horse as they can get very wet and muddy, but it has been accomplished quite satisfactorily, although I have never tried it myself. In this case an adequate shelter, well strawed, is necessary and the horse will need generous feeding. I would also, I think, carry out only a high trace clip, leaving the coat on the top of the back and the upper side of the neck as well as on the legs.

Horses kept in this fashion will hardly ever appear as the epitome of elegance, but so long as they are never brought in hot and have equable temperaments, they will remain free from colds and chills.

Choice of a New Zealand Rug

The rug itself is an integral part of the system, and, therefore, its purchase and subsequent care demand the closest attention. Surprisingly, for very many are used, the majority of the so-called New Zealand rugs available are very poor in design and sometimes in quality too.

Their greatest failure is in the shaping, and the seeming inability of the manufacturers to relate purpose to design. It is essential that the rug should fit really well, that it will not shift unduly in use, that its fastenings do not chafe or exert constant pressure on any one part of the horse and that the wretched thing is waterproof.

Very few fulfil these requirements. A good rug, which cannot be made cheaply, should give more than ample freedom at the neck and particularly over the shoulder. If it is tight in these places the movement of the horse will cause it to first rub away the hair and ultimately cause a sore place. The only way I know of avoiding shoulder rubbing is by shaping the rug at the shoulder and giving it an extra fullness by means of a dart. The rug must be deep enough at the sides and of sufficient length to cover the dock by some three inches. It should then be darted to fit round the quarters and prevented from blowing up either by a cord, which can be tightened and is inset into the rear end, or a tail or fillet strap passing round the upper thigh below the tail.

There are only a few patterns which I would use and none employs a surcingle to keep the rug in place. Surcingles are a snare and a delusion on a New Zealand rug. In fact when they are fitted the rug is no longer a "New Zealand" pattern, but just a waterproof rug. Either the surcingle is fastened so loosely as to be useless, or so tightly as to cause a sore back because of the constant pressure exerted on the spine.

I use a rug employing what used to be known as Pape's pattern, a simple system of leg straps crossing between the hindlegs, joining at the central ring under the belly and then fastening, through the forelegs, at the chest.

The soft drab canvas is the most preferable of the materials, not that frightful green tarpaulin which becomes board-like after one or two wettings.

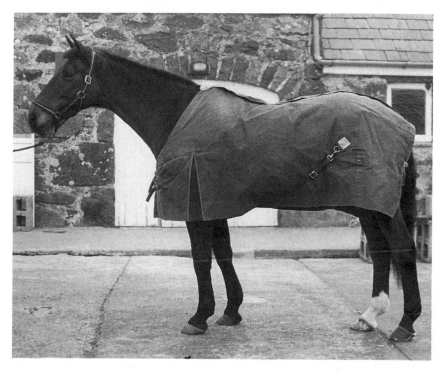

An excellent pattern of New Zealand rug. Note: a) the method of fastening and the absence of surcingles; b) the shaping over the dock; c) the pleat at the shoulder which allows freedom of movement and prevents chafing; d) the "thatching" strip of material laid along the back to ensure that the rug is completely waterproof.

Water penetrates the rug through the back seam and it is impossible to keep out unless the back seam is, as it were, "thatched" by an additional strip of material laid from the wither to the tail part of the rug.

The lining, which should reach only halfway down the flanks to avoid it getting muddied, should be of good, heavy, wool cloth. The check type of collar lining is as good as any. The leg straps, which must be of ample length, need to be of stout, good quality leather. I always think the grey chrome leather, or the very supple red buffalo hide, are the best, and the easiest to keep soft under adverse conditions. Otherwise stout nylon straps are satisfactory. So far as hooks and adjustment buckles are concerned only the best obtainable will do.

The maintenance of the rug is all important. Straps must be kept soft by the continual and liberal application of Kocholine, or some similar preparation, and all hooks and metal fittings always kept covered with a thin layer of grease. Once a year have the cloth re-proofed, and when the rug is in use go and see that it is in place and properly adjusted as frequently as you can.

To prevent chafing and provoking a possible rodeo display loop the leg straps one over the other to keep them away from the tender parts between the hindlegs.

Cleanliness – Next to Godliness

Whether you adopt this system or keep your animal permanently stabled during the winter months, or perhaps during the summer in the case of show jumpers, the maintenance of the stable itself is vital.

The golden rule with the stabled horse is cleanliness in all things.

Most of us are meticulous enough in our own homes and with our own children. Horses are much like children in many ways and require almost as much attention. Babies, in good homes anyway, are not left for long periods in wet and soiled nappies; our families (sometimes under protest) wash regularly and wear clean clothes. We eat clean, untainted food from clean crockery and our living quarters are dusted and kept free from dirt.

The horse asks no more than we give to ourselves, but it is our responsibility to provide for his needs. After all, it is we who put him in a stable for our own convenience and enjoyment. In return that stable must be kept clean. He needs a dry bed, fresh food and water, given in clean receptacles and his body must be kept clean by regular grooming.

There is a school of thought which recommends leaving cobwebs in stables as fly-catchers. Cobwebs are not tolerated in our houses and there is no reason why they should be allowed in a stable. This one of the more stupid horsy maxims which are adhered to only for the convenience of the lazy horse-master. If one is so worried with flies an insecticide spray, "green" of course, is much more efficient.

Sandbaths and Storage

If the layout of the yard permits a small space to be set aside for a sandbath so much the better. All horses seem to appreciate a roll in sand and the cost of this facility is not large.

For the rest of the yard; water supply, feed house and tack room should be within easy reach if time is to be saved. Where it is not possible to store bulk forage, i.e. hay and straw, under cover it should be kept off the ground so that air can circulate underneath. This is easily accomplished by stacking the bales on planks raised from the ground on bricks. A plastic stack cover will prevent the forage becoming wet, but it should be removed and the air allowed to get at the bales as often as possible. If this is not done the condensation, which forms easily on the inner surface of plastic, will encourage mildew.

Siting of Manure

The siting of muck-heaps is even more important. Obviously they do not want to be too far away, but neither must they be placed so close to buildings as to be unhealthy or likely to cause damage to the structure. Wooden buildings, particularly, can be considerably spoilt if they are in too close contact with the ammonia fumes given off by the heap.

Very elaborate manure pits can be constructed with concrete floors, brick or concrete walls, drains and a permanent covering to keep off the rain, but simple and effective ones can be made on a patch of concrete using railway sleepers to encompass the heap.

In either case the manure should be well packed down and the edges tidied up. In a well-packed heap decomposition will be more rapid and the increase in heat produced will discourage fly breeding. Needless to say the heap should be removed regularly.

OUT AT GRASS

We now come to the last method of horse-keeping – the horse kept at grass all the year round.

It is, of course, the natural way for a horse to live. The difference is that in his wild state the horse roamed over extensive areas, feeding and exercising himself as he went. He was not confined to an acre of rough orchard and expected to work during the week and gallop about at rallies and the like at weekends.

Far too many horses and ponies are bought by people who do not realise this fact or its significance, and to whom the phrase "lives out" means "lives on air". The proper management of the grass-kept animal requires as much knowledge and almost as much supervision as that of the stabled horse.

The first essential, of course, is to have an adequate amount of *good* grazing. A requirement that is but rarely fulfilled. Two or three acres per animal, properly managed, and that means rested at intervals, when alternative grazing will be required, is by no means too much, but you can operate on less by the exercise of intelligent management.

In the horse's feral state the problems of horse-sick pastures and red-worm infestation do not arise because of the enormous areas concerned, but in domesticity, where the animal is confined, it becomes a very real problem. The management of grassland is dealt with elsewhere, as it is a subject in its own right and of the greatest importance to the horse-owner; all I would stress at this stage is that adequate grazing is essential and that back gardens and the odd half-acres of waste ground do not constitute *adequate* grazing.

Given that one has sufficient space, or the use of it, there are four prior conditions to be observed, apart from the quality and extent of the herbage. They are (a) proper water supply; (b) shelter from prevailing winds, such as trees, hedges or in their absence a shelter; (c) pasture properly enclosed and free from all bodies which might be a cause of injury, and (d) constant and regular supervision.

If these conditions are fulfilled a pony, particularly one of the native breeds, although not those having a high percentage of Thoroughbred or Arab blood, can be kept out in the worst weather without taking harm, so long as supplementary feeding is practised during the winter months.

To revert to the four conditions mentioned. Water is best supplied by a field pipe to a trough which has no sharp edges and which can be emptied for cleaning. A heavy galvanised tank filled by means of a hosepipe may be pressed into service if a proper trough is not available, but is more difficult to clean. Water is an essential to health and should be clean, so it should not be allowed to collect a covering of scum during the summer, or be positioned where it can become a catchment for falling leaves in the autumn. Stagnant ponds, usually of dirty water, are not suitable as a watering arrangement.

Horses and ponies at grass, even in the bitterest of weather, will, if they are receiving supplementary feed, spurn an artificial shelter, preferring that afforded by trees or thick hedges. During the winter nature creates a film of waterproofing grease beneath the heavy coat which gives adequate protection against rain. Animals kept entirely at grass, and therefore not intended for hard work, do not need a rug, nor should they be clipped and groomed. Cold winds are, however, a different matter and if the paddock does not have natural shelter against the prevailing ones then a field shelter must be provided. This need not be more than a three-sided shelter, but it must be sited to give every possible protection.

In the summer months shelter is equally important to provide shade and a cool place away from the worst attacks of flies.

Safe fencing is a more obvious necessity, although it is often one that is neglected. If the field lacks a good, thick surrounding hedge then it will be necessary to fence it artificially.

Post and rail fencing is obviously good, but is hardly cheap. Plain, heavy gauge wire strung tightly from stout wooden posts is acceptable, cheaper and the next best thing. The lowest strand of wire should not be less than one foot from the ground otherwise there will be a danger of animals getting their feet caught. Barbed wire and chicken mesh fencing are not suitable under any circumstances.

Whatever type of fencing is used it is always advisable to round off the corners of the field. Right angle corners can be a source of danger to galloping horses letting off steam.

All posts will require a thorough soaking in creosote as a preservative measure, and the application should be renewed each year. Creosote will also discourage horses from chewing, a habit many of them contract when bored or when there is insufficient feed in the paddock. Trees can also be treated in this manner for horses and ponies often seem to find the bark quite irresistible. If animals are allowed to chew at the trees they will, of course, soon kill them. Many authorities claim that wood-chewing is an indication of mineral deficiency and can be rectified by supplying large lumps of rock salt for the horses to lick. I am not sure how well-founded a supposition this is – I suspect it may be less accurate than most of us accept – but, as it can do no harm, I like to have rock salt available both in the box and the paddocks.

Foreign bodies in the way of large stones, tins, stakes, etc., must be removed – if they are not it is almost certain that the horse will injure himself on them. Horses at grass are not, in fact, very sensible and if there is any sort of trouble they can get into they invariably do. Therefore, be particularly vigilant in these respects and make a careful examination of the grazing area before putting animals out. Hedges must, of course, come in for the closest scrutiny to see that they contain no poisonous shrubs or trees, such as yew. Ivy, too, should be removed. It is not so poisonous to horses as yew, but its effects are bad enough to be worth avoiding. Ragwort and deadly nightshade should also be removed, as these plants can be fatal if eaten.

These are the plants, etc. possessed of lethal potential: *Buttercup* (indicative of lime deficiency in the land); *Monkshood* or aconite, *Delphinium* and *Columbine* (of these monkshood is the most trouble-some and dangerous); *Hemlock* (the content of the poisoned cup which did for Socrates) and *Cowbane*, which is water hemlock, as is *Water Dropwort*, the yellowish tuber (Dead Men's Fingers) being the poisonous element; *Ragwort*, the baleful yellow flower which is as bad as any of the poisonous plants and shrubs; *Foxglove*, *Horsetails*; *Bracken*, when it is green – if used for bedding it should be left to brown; *White* and *Black Bryony*; *Rhododendron, Privet, Box* and *Laurel*; *Yew*, the most poisonous of our native trees; *Laburnum*, ornamental but nearly as deadly, and then the common *Potato* and the *Acorn*. Potatoes are poisonous when green and so are the potato haulms of the same colour. *Acorns*, which in some years are extraordinarily prolific, will cause acute digestive problems and if ingested in sufficient quantities may result in death.

I have already indicated that horses at grass are the most accident prone of all animals and this faculty for damaging themselves is just one reason why regular supervision is so essential. Horses are at best rather helpless creatures in a domestic state and although the thought of putting stabled horses out at the end of winter may be welcomed with a feeling of relief, it does not mean that the owner can forget them.

At least once a day, preferably twice, and ideally three or four times, they should be visited to ensure that everything is in order.

Water has to be checked for quantity and cleanliness, the animals inspected for injury, fences looked at, and if necessary repaired, and in addition feeds and hay must be given when this is necessary.

Regular visits to the field in any case pay dividends in the saving of time and temper. An animal who is frequently handled, and possibly fed, when at grass is far less likely to become one of those exasperating creatures who refuse to be caught. Once the animal associates the visit with feeding time, which is not necessarily or always followed by work, he is far more likely to be amenable and co-operative in this respect. In addition regular inspections of this kind help to maintain and reinforce the contact between master and horse.

Although the method of keeping horses at grass permanently has advantages in the saving of labour involved one must appreciate that it restricts the owner's usage of the horse.

Living out is the natural existence for the horse, and in a wild or semi-wild state is perfectly satisfactory, but when we confine a horse to a relatively small area this is not much more in accordance with his natural state than is shutting him up in a stable.

Wild horses who have, or had, the freedom of vast areas found sufficient nourishment in the variety of grasses and herbs contained in these areas, a variety that in the domestic state we endeavour to reproduce and to improve in nutrient value by agricultural skills, in a very much smaller space. It is a fact, however, that with the exception of professionally operated stud farms, a great number of horse pastures are of poor quality.

The Feral Versus the Domestic State

It is also a fact, and one conveniently ignored by many owners practising this method of horse-keeping, that in his wild state nature maintains the horse in the condition best suited to the exertions he is likely to make. The wild horse keeps himself in trim by wandering *slowly* many miles in search of grazing, a procedure denied to the animal kept in a small paddock. In addition he does not carry a weight upon his back, he very rarely gallops and except when panicked does not jump.

By domesticating the horse and asking him to do these things for our pleasure we have, over a period of time, imposed upon him a life quite at variance with his natural existence. In consequence we must prepare and condition his body to perform the work we require of it. We achieve this object by feeding him artificially with foods designed to increase his energy and to replace the loss of body tissue which occurs during work. We groom him and in cold weather we remove his coat and his natural protective grease covering, replacing it with rugs while he is in his stable.

Exercised, groomed and shorn of his coat which would prevent him from working hard without losing condition through excessive sweating, and properly fed with a balanced, if artificial, diet, the horse is physically capable of considerable effort.

Despite the fact that man, over many centuries, has produced breeds of horses aimed at perfecting the qualities and characteristics suited to his purpose, the domestic horse cannot be expected to work unless he is conditioned to do so.

In many cases, particularly that of the English Thoroughbred, the breed has become so far removed from the wild horse that they can no longer withstand the rigours of what to them is no longer a natural existence. Our native ponies, on the other hand, are still to some extent bred on the moors, mountains and in the forests and are therefore nearer to their natural environment and less dependent upon man for their well-being. Even so, while they retain the qualities of hardiness, lost by the Thoroughbred, they are not fitted to perform hard work unless physically prepared for it.

Grass alone does not possess the necessary energy and tissue replacing properties needed by the horse in work. In summer, grass is a soft, bulk and laxative food producing a soft condition. Where grazing is lush animals quickly enough run to fat, a condition in which undue strain will be placed on organs and limbs. If, therefore, an animal is to be kept at grass during this period of the year and also subjected to work, then grazing on lush pasture must be restricted and the animal fed artificially in relation to the work he is to do. If this work does not exceed a few hours gentle hacking in a week his additional food requirement will be small and he will come to no harm. If, however, the animal is to be in regular use, carrying an exuberant child to gymkhanas, mock hunts, club rallies and the like, it will be necessary to curtail his grass consumption to a few hours a day and feed him a greater quantity of body-building and energy-producing foods.

In winter, or more correctly from October to April, the grass will contain little nourishment and will do nothing but provide bulk. Much of the horse's food intake will be expended in producing sufficient body heat to maintain health and, indeed, life itself, and the animal will require considerable and regular feeding for this purpose alone if he is not to lose condition. The winter coat will prevent him from indulging in fast work without his becoming distressed. It should not be groomed, other than for the purpose of removing the worst of the mud, lest the protective grease is removed also. It is, however, possible for him to be worked quietly, provided that his intake of heating foods is increased accordingly.

In conditions of snow, or conversely in a very dry summer spell, his inability to obtain sufficient bulk from his pasture will necessitate the feeding of hay.

As I have said elsewhere, the tragedy is that while literature on the subject is by no means sparse and horse-magazines, as well as Pony Club branches and Riding Clubs, continually stress the importance of understanding the fundamental requirements of the animal kept at grass, there are still people who ignore all the proffered advice because it doesn't suit their convenience to act upon it.

Quite recently I wrote an article on conditioning horses for long distance rides. In this I stated that the hard, muscle fit condition, necessary for such exertions, could not be obtained by keeping a horse solely at grass with a minimum of exercise and possibly a few handfuls of horse cubes. Not unexpectedly, I received a number of letters telling me, in hardly more polite terms, that I was talking through my hat or that what I had said could not possibly apply to the writer's pony or horse because they regularly rode 30 miles off a handful of grass.

I do not say that it is impossible to work horses off grass. It is quite possible, and some horses put up with it better than others. What I do say is that it is wrong to do so, because, to suit your own selfish convenience, you are imposing undue and possibly unseen strains on a body not properly prepared to sustain them. Apart from the damage that can be done to ligaments, sinews, bone structures and internal organs which are unprepared for work, muscles are much more likely to be strained.

The results of muscle strain may not be immediately apparent, but there is every chance of a rheumatoid or arthritic condition being set up which will not only cause pain in the future but will incapacitate the horse and prevent him from functioning to his full ability.

In the keeping of horses, love (usually the wrong kind) is no substitute for knowledge, and ignorance is just as much "the devil's trade mark" as it ever was.

CHAPTER 3

Feeding Horses and Ponies

I have tried to make it clear in the preceding sections that by domesticating the horse we have imposed upon him a mode of life which is in contradiction to his basic nature. In his natural state he existed very well on a diet of grass, herbs and the like and can still do so, in some cases, so long as he has a sufficiently large area over which to graze and is not called upon to do more than travel slowly from one grazing ground to another with very occasional short bursts of speed.

In domestication, however, he is made to carry weight, often at speed, and sometimes over obstacles. To do so satisfactorily the efficiency of his organs and the strength of his body and muscle structures must be increased, and he has to expend a great deal more energy than it is ever necessary for him to do in nature. It is in fact a basically unnatural procedure for him for which his natural food is unsuited.

If he is to perform his work properly, and without risk of damage to himself, he must, therefore, be fed food other than that which sustained him in his natural state. Unnatural food, in fact, to correspond with the unnatural demands made upon him.

The Four Life Requirements and the Utilisation of Food

The food consumed by the horse in freedom, grass and herbs, is used to fulfil the four fundamental requirements of life and under normal climatic conditions is adequate for the existence led by the wild horse, or, if the acreage is sufficient, for the domestic horse not called upon to do more than very light work. These four requirements are:

(1) To maintain body temperature;

(2) To replace natural wastage of the tissue. (If the food intake is insufficient for the maintenance of these two factors death results);

(3) To build up body condition;

(4) To supply the energy required for movement and for the internal processes of digestion, circulation, etc.

Of these four factors the first two are paramount and in times of scarcity they will be maintained at the expense of the others. To a certain extent the body can lose *condition* (i.e. become thin) and also lose the strength, or *energy*, to move with any speed, without death immediately ensuing.

A condition of this sort will occur in very severe weather when a greater proportion of the food intake will be needed to maintain the *body heat*, and the proportion which would normally be devoted to *building up the body* will be correspondingly reduced, resulting in a loss of weight.

Conversely in the spring and early summer, when feed is more plentiful and the weather warmer, less of the feed will be needed to promote *body heat* and the horse will gain in *condition*. In this natural state only a small proportion of food is used on the expenditure of *energy*.

In the same way it follows that if the horse were to be divorced from a life in which he needs to expend little energy and put into hard work (requiring a high degree of energy output) without compensations being made in his diet, then similar circumstances would obtain.

The *energy* expended by the body would demand a greater share of the total output supplied by the food intake, the requirements of *body temperature* and *tissue replacement*, being prime essentials to life, would continue to take their share, and there would be little left for *body condition*. In other words the food intake would be insufficient to sustain condition as well as supply the energy made necessary by the imposition of work.

If the process were continued, the horse, after becoming very thin, would show increasing signs of weakness, lack of energy and debility. Finally, the process of tissue replacement would cease, the horse's temperature would drop below normal and the animal would die. It would take time for events to run their full cycle, but death would be inevitable.

When, therefore, the horse is put into work which involves an expenditure of energy, the loss must be made good by the introduction of an additional energy producing food if he is to maintain his body condition.

If on the other hand the work is stopped or reduced and the horse is still fed on energy promoting food there will be a surplus in the food intake. This surplus will be used to build *body condition* (the needs of *temperature* and *tissue replacement* will have been met), and the horse will become fat.

If the process were allowed to continue the digestive system, perfectly designed to cope with a natural diet and existence, would become overloaded, the blood heated and so on, with correspondingly unpleasant results.

First Principles

The principle which emerges is that *intake of energy food must equal energy output* and vice versa. In other words feeding of energy foods must correspond to exercise.

The diet of the horse in his feral state was balanced to contain the constituents which are needed to maintain him in the physical condition necessary for his limited requirements. We have already seen that when removed from this environment and required to perform physical work greatly in excess of that which is necessary in nature, it is essential for him to receive additional energy-giving food if he is not to suffer in condition.

It is also, of course, equally essential that his artificial diet should be as balanced as his natural one and contain the same constituents. In addition this artificial diet must be fed to him in a way that as nearly as possible resembles the manner in which he would naturally consume his food. The horse cannot change the digestive system which served him so well in nature, and if we are to maintain him properly we must conform to its requirements and limitations.

Feed Objectives

It may appear unduly elementary to remind ourselves of the objectives involved in horse-feeding, but it is useful to do so if only to remind ourselves again of the basics of management.

(1) To maintain a state of health which will encourage resistance to disease and which in consequence reduces the severity of any contracted illness and allows for more rapid recovery.

(Under-nourishment acts in the opposite fashion. It reduces resistance, delays recovery and makes it more likely that the horse will develop secondary infections and/or suffer permanent damage from illness.)

(2) To produce, in conjunction with *exercise, grooming and strapping,* a physical condition compatible with the work being done.

(3) To feed so as to avoid a stressful mental outlook at whatever the level of fitness required.

(Some individuals suffer stress on high energy producing diets, sometimes when oats are the main constituent but the condition can just as easily be caused by mixes, pellets, etc. which are too high in protein for the metabolism of the horse concerned.

Stress certainly occurs as a result of too rich a diet – given, one suspects, by the well-meaning but less than well-informed. Such diets may well produce physical symptoms such as lymphangitis and may also result in overweight – another condition causing unnecessary stress.

Dietary imbalance is a probable cause of the increasingly common tying-up syndrome, whilst the sufferer from COPD (chronic obstructive pulmonary disease), as a result of dust-laden fodder, will hardly view the world through rose-coloured spectacles.)

Diet Constituents

The constituents comprising a balanced diet are six. They are PROTEIN – FATS, STARCHES and SUGAR – WATER – FIBROUS ROUGHAGE – MINERALS – VITAMINS.

Proteins – perform three main functions: (a) replacement of muscular wastage; (b) formation of body tissues; (c) production of energy and heat.

Fats, starches, etc. – in simple terms, can be regarded as producers of energy and heat and it is, therefore, easy to see that while foods containing these elements in concentration are necessary to the working horse, those foods supplying protein are essential. No food, in fact, consists entirely of protein or entirely of fats, starches and sugar, but too large a proportion of starch and sugar makes the protein element difficult to digest and all three elements are valueless as producers of energy unless protein is also present. (Fats produce $2\frac{1}{3}$ times more heat and energy than starch and sugar. The desirable ratio between protein/fats, starches, sugars is $1:10$ in a horse not in work but will rise dramatically by four times or more when the animal is in full work. The proportion of fat/protein is in the area of $1:2\frac{1}{2}$.

Too much protein, as well as contributing to mental stress, produces excess fat which is neither economic nor conducive to athleticism.

A large protein surplus overloads the system to the point of breakdown, affecting circulation and the liver and often causing diarrhoea.

Make sure, however, that protein is provided from more than one source. During digestion protein breaks down into the particular pattern of amino-acids of which it is composed. For that reason protein must be made available in a variety of feed elements.)

Water – is as essential to life as solid food, in fact more so, as can be appreciated when we realise the horse's body consists of 80 per cent water. The horse, we are told, can do without food for thirty days, but without water he cannot live much more than a quarter of that time. The maintenance of a proper and sufficient water supply is, therefore, all-important. Without it the natural processes of the body and of digestion (all foods to be fully utilised pass into the system in solution) must break down.

Water is present even in dry foods. Oats, barley, etc. contain between 10–12 per cent whilst roots, carrots, swedes, etc., may have as much as 70 per cent content.

Fibrous Roughage – exists to a degree in all vegetable foods and is an essential element in the diet. It provides the *bulk* necessary to herbivores and, very importantly, it assists in breaking up the concentrates in the diet and assisting their absorption into the system.

Minerals – The essential minerals are largely concerned with compounds of lime, soda and potash and they occur throughout the body. In the most general terms, they control the constant changes which take place in the body and if they were absent death would ensue. Continual replacement of minerals, which are constantly excreted, has to be made through the agency of the feed given.

Minerals occur in plant growth and the mineral content reflects the minerals available in the soil in which they were grown. Poor quality hay, grown in mineral deficient ground, will therefore be lacking seriously in these essential elements, and the same applies, of course, to poor quality grazing pasture. In general, the percentage of minerals in hay will be higher than in cereals.

The essential elements are those which are necessary to the horse's metabolism, the so-called trace or non-essential elements are found throughout the body in small amounts.

These are the major elements: CALCIUM (bone structure, blood, heart, nerves, muscles); PHOSPHORUS (bones – adaption for body use of carbohydrates and fats); SODIUM, SODIUM CHLORIDE (common salt); POTASSIUM (regulation of body fluid and muscle function); SULPHUR (connected with amino-acids and therefore a deficency which can only occur in a diet too low in protein);

MAGNESIUM (muscle, bone building. It is closely associated with calcium and phosphorus and is an essential constituent of bones and teeth.)

Calcium/Phosphorus Ratio – In relatively recent years the significance of an imbalance of calcium and phosphorus has been emphasised by nutritional experts but even now many horse-owners do not appreciate the importance of their ensuring that the proper ratio is observed in the diet.

In brief, horses cannot tolerate an imbalance between the two minerals, particularly when there is an excess of phosphorus. High levels of phosphorus can, for instance, cause the disease "big head" in youngstock, a condition which produces enlargement of the lower jaw bones as well as lameness. Deficiencies of either mineral may cause bone disease and an excess acts to increase the deficiency.

It is more usual for phosphorus to be over-fed. An excess of calcium is unusual and even when it occurs has no bad effects. Most plant material is high in phosphorus and it is therefore necessary to counteract this by feeding a calcium supplement, such as limestone flour.

In fact, it is always advisable to include a calcium supplement in the diet, particularly in that of the stabled horse, together with *common salt*, which provides sodium chlorate, minerals which do not appear in any quantity in plant growth. Two ounces of common salt per day is not too much for horses in ordinary work, whilst those working hard may require a little more so as to replace the salt lost through heavy sweating caused by fast work or prolonged effort.

The recommended ratio between calcium and phosphorus is quoted as being as much as 5:1 and if the proportion of calcium is higher than that it will do no harm.

Adverse calcium/phosphorus ratios are said to be common in diets based on hay, cereals and bran. The latter, very high in phosphorus and low in calcium, is frequently cast as the villain of the piece.

Oats, with other cereals, are today considered to have an adverse calcium/phosphorus ratio of around 1:3 and hay is also deficient in calcium.

The trace elements are these: COBALT (a component of Vitamin B_{12}. Growth/replacement of red blood cells); IRON and COPPER (formation of haemoglobin, formation of red blood cells); MANGANESE (normal growth, lactation, reproduction); MAGNESIUM (muscle, bone building); ZINC (general growth); IODINE (general growth/thyroid gland).

Vitamins – exercise an enormous influence on every aspect of the system and are found in minute quantities in most natural foods. They can, however, be destroyed when food is subjected to prolonged heating and it is probable that they do not exist in boiled foods. The principal vitamins are A, B_1, B_2, B_6, D and E and their absence in the diet will result in pronounced disorders of bones, nervous affections, rickets, sterility, low resistance levels, etc.

However, mineral and vitamin supplements should be regarded with great care. Unwise feeding of supplements can easily result in an overdose (hypervitaminosis) which creates just as many problems. In fact, *before embarking on any course of vitamin/mineral supplement other than the salt and calcium mentioned, it is advisable and much safer to obtain veterinary advise.*

A recent supplement which seems to have had good results is based on the discovery of the value of Vitamin E and its inter-reaction with the trace element selenium.

It is claimed that this type of supplement increases stamina and that the chemical reaction on muscles is most advantageous in the treatment of azoturia (tying-up).

A Balanced Diet – for the horse in work, which will provide the necessary constituents, can be conveniently divided into three categories: BULK FOODS – ENERGY FOODS – AUXILIARIES.

Bulk Foods – consist of hay, chaff (a mixture of chopped hay and oat straw), and the various proprietary brands of nuts and mixes. To a degree we may also regard bran and green food as performing some of the functions required of bulk feed. Grass is a bulk food and, when of good quality and properly managed, provides a balanced feed for the horse not in work during the summer when its growth and nutrient value is at its highest.

While all these foods contain proportions, in varying degrees, of the essential constituents of a balanced diet, they are the principal source of fibrous roughage, hay containing between 25–35 per cent woody fibre. They may also contain relatively high percentages of proteins, but do not on their own supply energy for hard work, although nuts and mixes may replace oats and other heating foods satisfactorily.

Energy Foods – those containing a high percentage of starches and fat (starch is, of course, converted to sugar by the action of saliva and the gastric juice) are, for practical purposes, oats, barley, maize, beans and peas and the nuts and mixes which are formed from those ingredients. They do, however, vary considerably in protein value and the proportions of *digestible* protein to starch (the protein/starch equivalent) they contain.

Oats, for instance, which are the best energy providing food, contain 11 per cent protein and 57 per cent starch equivalent. Although, therefore, the heating and energising element is high the *proportion* of digestible protein is low in comparison, say, to best quality hay which may contain 19 per cent and 37 per cent starch equivalent. These figures reinforce the necessity of feeding in balance and the impossibility of feeding energy foods alone without providing sufficient protein in conjunction with them.

Auxiliary Foods – are those such as bran, containing a high percentage of salts; linseed, which is a fattening food, and the various forms of green food from grass to carrots and other suitable roots. In addition there are the feed-additives and vitamin supplements mentioned.

Cod-liver oil is an excellent condition builder and molasses or molassine meal is also good for the coat and is a means of providing easily assimilated energy food. Shy feeders can often be tempted with molasses and horses are very fond of them. Glucose can be used for horses being prepared for hard work, and seaweed, in powder form, is claimed to supply minerals and trace elements and to improve condition.

Feed Sources

Principal amongst all sources of food is grass, consumed either in its natural state by horses living out or at rest or as HAY by stabled horses. It is of prime importance in the diet as the essential bulk constituent forming between one-half and two-thirds of the stabled horse's diet.

Hay – of good quality provides a high level of digestible protein and a mineral content of between 6–7 per cent. It is also a principal source of fibrous roughage.

In days gone by we bought hay by the tonne. Today, matters are different, it is sold and bought by the bale, which is hardly conducive to the maintenance of a consistent quality, and neither grower nor purchaser are very knowledgeable about its finer points.

Nonetheless, hay still falls into two groups, as it always did.

There is *meadow* hay, made from fields laid permanently to grass, and *seed* hay, from arable land, of which it is one of a rotation of crops. The former has a greater variety of grasses and the latter a higher percentage of clovers. Of the two, the latter is preferable for horses in fairly hard work. It is more nutritious if properly saved but more expensive. It is not, however, so digestible as the softer meadow hay and should be fed with discretion lest it cause digestive troubles. Indeed, it is often worthwhile to mix a strong sample of seed hay with some of the meadow sort.

Meadow hay, which is softer, is, nonetheless, perfectly satisfactory in most instances.

The quality of both types of hay depends upon the quality of the land on which it is grown and how the hay was made.

Ideally, hay should be cut when the grasses are in flower, usually in early June, since much of the nourishment is contained in the flower and the seed. If the hay is cut too late the flower will have gone to seed and the seeds will have scattered.

Hay which has been rained on after turning is not much good for horses since the wet encourages mould growth. Wet conditions always cause problems. Nourishment in the hay is reduced and the subsequent drying process can cause loss of seed and flower.

"Mow-burnt" hay, which has been stacked too soon, heats and can be so badly browned as to be useless as horse feed.

Musty hay, caused by stacking or baling before the hay is dry, is absolutely uneconomical. Most horses will sensibly refuse it and those that do eat it suffer as a result from distended bellies and colic. Good hay is greenish in colour. It should not be dusty nor show any evidence of mould. The grasses should be in flower and when the bale is opened the hay should feel springy. Hay from poor land will be coarse and woody and is of no great nutrient value.

A good mixture of red clover and rye grasses contains around 12 per cent protein and a protein/starch ratio of 1:4.

Much store used to be set on the buying of "old" hay as opposed to "new". Old hay was reckoned to be between 6–18 months old, at which time it was thought to be in the best condition. Before six months it was held to be too soft to promote hard condition and after 18 months it was well past its best. In the forage trade, however, hay becomes old after Michaelmas Day, September 29.

Today, we have to buy the best hay available and avoid as far as possible feeding it before that date whilst it is still too soft.

Modern methods can now produce packaged hay marketed in vacuum-sealed polythene bags. It is, in fact, grass which has been allowed to undergo a small amount of "cold" fermentation within the bag.

It is highly nutritious, indeed it is claimed that horses can be hunted on nothing else and it certainly allows a considerable reduction in concentrate feeds. It is also dust-free and thus very suitable for horses suffering from COPD. It is, however, expensive, and it is not, because of its high protein and nutrient quality, suitable for animals disposed to tying-up.

Lucerne – hay, known as *alfalfa* in America, where it is widely used, is not easily come by in Britain, or in Europe, although it is the most valuable nutritionally. It is, however, available in a convenient nut/pellet form.

Chaff – is either hay cut in a chaff-cutter or a mixture of hay and oat straw. It is useful in that its addition prevents an animal bolting its food and a mixture of oat straw with hay, though reducing the protein content, is obviously a financial saving. A proprietary brand of chaff with the addition of molasses is available and is very palatable. However, it is relatively expensive and if one has a chaff-cutter a similar mix can easily be made up.

The conventional supports to the hay ration are the "natural" cereals which may be fed as individual components of the diet or are incorporated in varying ratios in the feed pellets, coarse mixes and so on.

Oats – Without any doubt oats are supreme amongst the foods supplying energy.

In relative terms they are easily digested. They contain a high percentage of fats and starches and have a protein content of 11 per cent. Admittedly the mineral level is relatively low, but in a balanced diet that is easily enough made up from hay and other sources. Oats, however, are an excellent source of Vitamin B_1.

They are best fed *bruised*. Oats which are *crushed* are a snare and a delusion since most of the nutrient value is lost in the crushing process. It is better to feed oats dry rather than too much dampened and in this state they are more easily digested.

It is important to remember that too much water in a feed hastens the passage of the constituents through the stomach. It discourages the secretion of saliva, the first agent in the digestive process, and by diluting the digestive juices hinders the digestion of food.

Oats should be dry when bought, plump and with no signs of must or mildew. The best are thought to be Scotch oats, but oats of Canadian origin are often as good, although more expensive. (When buying oats do not be shy about asking the feed merchant to open the bag for you to inspect the contents. You have every right to assure yourself about the quality of the goods you are buying.)

Bran – is a by-product of wheat after the flour has been extracted. It is much denigrated as a food by some nutritional experts, largely on account of its very low calcium content and high phosphorus percentage. Broad bran, which is still obtainable, is the best of the millings, the middlings or thirds being nothing more than dust, but it should not be fed in excess. A ration of 2 lb per day is quite sufficient and one should include the 2 oz of limestone flour in the feed.

A good sample will have a mineral content of 5·8 and a useful percentage of fibre. An additional value, other than as the principal constituent of the bran mash, is that it serves as a useful regulator of the bowels. Fed dampened it acts as a laxative, fed dry it has the opposite effect. It should not be bought in other than small quantities as it absorbs moisture very readily and quickly becomes sour and unpalatable.

Barley – in many countries is the horse's staple grain. It is less heating than oats and if introduced to the diet gradually, not more than a ½ lb per day initially, and bruised it is a very good feed. It is estimated that ¾ lb of barley equals 1 lb of oats. Barley is often used in micronised form, a process which cooks the cereal exactly to maximise starch gelatinisation without loss of protein. In this form barley is very digestible. When boiled, barley is even more digestible and is good for putting condition on a horse. It is not used for horses in hard work.

Maize – usually bought as flaked maize, is not very digestible and is lacking in protein. It is, however, a high energy food containing 84 per cent starch. Possibly the best way to feed maize is to use it in a mixture with beans to compensate for the protein deficiency. When two parts of maize is mixed with one part of beans it is claimed that 7¾ lb of the mixture has the feed value of 10 lb oats.

Beans and Peas – are *protein* foods which have to be fed split or crushed. They contain a higher protein/starch equivalent than any other food (25·5/48·5 and 22·5/53·5 respectively). They form a very heating food (hence the term "full of beans") and are to be fed with discretion.

Grain, particularly oats and barley, should not be fed as "new". Current season oats should not be fed before Christmas because they are not sufficiently digestible. Beans and peas should be at least one year old.

Linseed – is very high in protein (26 per cent) with a fat content of 36 per cent. It is a wonderful conditioner but must always be fed boiled.

The highest source of protein is contained in Soya Bean meal which has as much as 45 per cent as well as an oil content of 6 per cent. The maximum amount which can be fed daily is 1 lb and being high in amino-acids it balances the grain ration excellently. It is a valuable source of the essential amino-acid *lysine*, which is necessary in the diet of the performance horse.

Boiled Feeds

Food is boiled to increase digestibility, an important factor when horses have been subject to strenuous exertion or for those in debilitated condition, when the effectiveness of the digestive process is necessarily reduced. Boiled foods, of course, are highly nourishing and excellent conditioners.

Barley when boiled in water swells considerably and 1 lb well-covered with water and boiled slowly for 4–6 hours then mixed with a little bran, hay chaff and 1 oz salt makes a very satisfactory pudding. Linseed is always fed boiled, the process eliminating the poisonous properties of the seeds which when exposed to heat and damp produce hydrogen cyanide.

A linseed mash is made thus: Take 1 lb linseed per horse and soak overnight. Boil the next day over a low heat, stirring frequently, for some three hours. (Be very careful, linseed burns easily and if allowed to boil over makes a terrible mess.) Add to the mixture 1 lb bran and 1 lb oats, cover and allow to stand for 30 minutes, feeding when it is sufficiently cool.

A gruel, which might be given to a tired horse after a hard day's hunting for instance, can be made by omitting the bran and oats and then drawing off the seeds, the mixture being given as a tepid liquid and not being allowed to solidify.

Linseed jelly is made by adding the soaked seed to boiling water (1 lb seed to 2 galls). Cold water is then added and the mixture brought to the boil again and allowed to continue boiling for 20–30 minutes. It can be mixed either with bran or oats, or both, and fed daily to animals in poor condition or to show horses to give increased condition and bloom. However, the daily ration should not exceed more than ½–1 lb.

The traditional bran mash is usually given once a week on the rest day or after hunting. It is laxative in its effect, easily digestible and does not have the heating properties of the usual oat ration. It is also a useful vehicle for the administration of worm powders, etc.

To make a mash allow between 2–3 lb bran per horse, add boiling water and 1 oz household salt. Stir thoroughly until the mash is damp through but *not* too wet. Cover the container with a sack or something similar and let the mash stand to cool. Feed at blood temperature.

Roots/Fruit

Root crops provide variety in the diet and their succulence is much appreciated, whilst they also contain vitamins, minerals and so on. Foremost among the root vegetables are carrots, a source of carotene which is converted to Vitamin A in the liver and the walls of the intestine and encourages growth and well-being as well as being concerned with vision and the tone of the respiratory organs.

Carrots should be fed sliced, to prevent the possibility of the horse choking, and introduced to the diet gradually. Horses unused to roots of this nature will suffer colic if fed too much too quickly. In time up to 1 lb per day can be fed. Carrots are best bought unwashed as they keep better that way and retain their taste.

Horses will often appreciate a turnip or mangold left in the manger for them to gnaw at will and it is a way of keeping them occupied.

Sugar-beet pulp is considered a useful feed for horses in light work. It has a high fibre and sugar content but the protein is of poor quality. However, pulp or nuts have to be well-soaked before feeding for as much as 12 hours. If fed dry they swell alarmingly in the stomach and could cause the horse's death. Sugar-beet can be a helpful addition to feeding at low performance levels but is not suitable when more concentrated work is required.

When apples are fed they, too, should be chopped to prevent choking. Indeed, apples are a good, healthy food. They contain sugar, pectin, amino-acids and an assortment of minerals and vitamins. The ancients used them in the treatment of coughs and they are considered to combat fatigue and microbial infection as well as being good for pulmonary complaints. Not for nothing was it said that "an apple a day keeps the doctor away".

Compound/Mixes

Nuts, cubes or pencils are, one suspects, commonly used as a base for mixed feeds. There is no great harm in this practice but owners should be aware of the nutritional values involved.

To assess the value of nut feeds it is only necessary to look at the bag, on which will be printed the percentages of oil, protein and fibre, the higher the fibre content the lower is the protein value.

The basic nut for horses and ponies in relatively light work has a 17 per cent fibre content, 10 per cent protein and usually 2½ per cent oil.

High performance nuts contain approximately 10 per cent fibre, 14 per cent protein and 3½ per cent oil.

Stud nuts carry a similar oil percentage but are low in fibre, 6 per cent, and high in protein, 15 per cent.

Nuts designed as a complete feed, eliminating all other feedstuffs are formulated with a high fibre content, 20 per cent, and about 10 per cent protein. For reasons already given this is not a very satisfactory method of feeding.

Grass nuts, particularly the alfalfa or lucerne nuts are, on the other hand, a valuable addition to conventional feedstuffs and feeding programmes.

They can be used in conjunction with hay and cereals like oats, etc. and can form 60 per cent of the concentrate feed. They are a good source of protein and energy. The nuts are, however, hard and are not accepted by some horses. They can be made more palatable by soaking them in a little water.

Some care has to be taken when feeding compounds. Horses that bolt their food, for instance, will find nuts difficult to digest and will be uncomfortable as a result. The solution is to put a few large stones in the manger so that the horse is compelled to eat round them, or to mix the feed with chaff.

If a horse having had a full feed of nuts should take a long drink, the water causes the nuts to swell in the stomach causing colic. Horses fed on nuts, which are a very dry food will, of course, drink more water than those on mixed diets containing more moisture.

Mixes

The production of mix feeds has advanced greatly in recent years and a number are now available. The composition varies a little between one and the other but in general mixes comprise coarsely ground conventional feeding stuffs like oats, barley, maize, etc. which are usually combined with bran and other ingredients. The result is a balanced feed which in the middle range gives an analysis of approximately 2 per cent oil, 14 per cent protein and 7 per cent fibre.

The proprietary mixes save the horse-owner from making up feeds himself and they provide a proper balance. Their disadvantage may be in the inevitable lack of flexibility but they are, nonetheless, a valuable innovation and an advance on the average nut feed.

Green Food – is always good for the horse – it is cooling to the blood, a good cleanser of the system and an aid to digestion. Horses always enjoy it, particularly when stabled, and this in itself is sufficient reason for feeding it. In winter, carrots – sliced lengthways to prevent the animal blocking his small gullet, as he might do were he to be fed them cut in circles – turnips, mangolds and swedes, fed whole and left with the horse for him to chew, are all excellent. There may not be any great feed value in roots, as will be understood when we realise the large percentage of water they contain (carrots 87 per cent, swedes 88 per cent and sugar beet 93 per cent), but they are succulent and take the place of fruit in the human diet.

Sugar beet, soaked and pulped, or sugar beet nuts, soaked for at least 12 hours, are good conditioners. Despite, however, the claims sometimes made for sugar beet, it remains a "soft feed" and is not really much good for horses in hard work other than as a variant in the diet.

In addition, seize every opportunity to let the animal have a nibble at fresh, clean grass. Ten minutes a day employed in this fashion is worth all the bottled tonics in the chemist's shop. Do not, however, feed grass clippings during the spring and summer. Some people hold that if fed fresh no harm is done. Possibly this is so, but I would not risk it. Grass cut by a lawn-mower impacts and ferments in the stomach and can cause severe colic.

Herbal Products

There is in the human diet a discernible movement towards "natural" and herbal remedies as well as increasing interest in homoeopathy. Within the horse market a similar movement is taking place and there is a growing range of natural products all the way from seaweed and garlic to cider vinegar and comfrey which can be included legitimately in equine feeding programmes and, of course, with perfect safety.

In some areas there is a paucity of scientific proof or even acceptance but that does not mean that the natural remedies should be disregarded. Many of them have been working well for some 2,000 years. Despite the overall lack of evidence it does seem that long-term natural medication may have a use in the reduction of equine stress, or human stress for that matter.

The development of natural medicine is already under way. Give it a few more years and more specific knowledge about herbal remedies and so on, and perhaps the nutritionists will be including natural supplements in the equine feeding programmes they recommend.

The Digestive Apparatus and Methods of Feeding

The methods and principles of feeding are dependent upon the peculiar digestive apparatus of the horse and the positioning of his relatively small stomach.

In the simplest terms, the stomach, small in relation to his size, is placed behind the diaphragm, a section of muscle separating it from the chest cavity proper. The diaphragm is in contact with the lungs in front and at the back almost touches the stomach and liver.

Immediately following a feed the stomach and the bowels, which will still be digesting the previous feed, will become distended and the stomach will press against the diaphragm.

This will induce no discomfort when the horse is at rest, but should he be saddled and taken out immediately, the effort of moving will cause him to breathe more deeply and to expand his lungs. Now it follows that if the lungs expand they will exert pressure on the elastic structure of the diaphragm, which in turn will press against the now distended stomach. As a result not only is his breathing impaired, but there will be interference with the digestive processes going on in the stomach and the bowels. The outcome will be indigestion which may become so acute as to develop into a severe case of colic. At its worst, that is if fast work were to be carried out on a full stomach, the lungs would become choked with blood and a rupture of the stomach could occur. The general rule, therefore, is *do not work after feeding*. It would be possible to take the horse out if the pace were restricted to a walk, but otherwise do not exercise him within one hour of feeding.

Although the horse has a small stomach its bowel structure (there are two bowels, the small and the large) is capacious. The whole apparatus is designed for the absorption of food consumed slowly and almost continuously over long periods.

At grass the horse passes food via the mouth, where it undergoes the first process of digestion by being broken up by the molars and saturated in saliva, with almost unbroken regularity to the stomach. Once the stomach is filled to about two-thirds of its capacity the food is passed into the bowel at the same speed at which fresh food enters the stomach.

The gastric juice manufactured in the stomach dissolves the food and the stomach muscles move to assist the process. The food, now having the consistency of thick cream, passes into the small bowel where it becomes further liquefied and the unabsorbed pieces of food pass finally into the large bowel where, after a further processing, they are passed out of the body as droppings devoid of all absorbable nourishment.

Ideally the stabled horse should be fed in a similar manner, a handful of food being thrown in his manger every ten minutes, but this is obviously neither convenient nor possible and he must be fed at periodic intervals. As a result he tends to eat rich, not easily digestible foods rapidly, and, if given the opportunity, unwisely. If he were given, to cite an extreme instance, one large feed per day his stomach would be too small to contain it. As a result it would become distended to an extent where the muscles assisting the digestive process became incapable of effort. The process would break down, the food would ferment giving off gases and the animal would suffer such acute digestional pains as might result in a rupture of the stomach.

The capacity of the stomach and that of the digestive system to cope with the food intake is not more than 4 lb in total at one time, of which no more than 3 lb should be grain, and feeds should not exceed this weight. *Feed little and often* is then the second rule and rather than give two big feeds, give the same quantity split between three or four feeds.

Hay, which acts as a digestive aid, may be given in larger quantities because it is eaten more slowly. The bulk of the hay ration is usually given at night when the horse will have a longer period to eat and digest it.

The need to water before feeding is not relevant as the horse should have water constantly available, for reasons already explained.

Inspection of the Teeth

A further lesson does, however, emerge which is connected with the mouth, or rather the teeth. If the horse's teeth are not properly cared for, that is if they are allowed through uneven wear to become sharp, then they will lacerate the mouth and possibly the tongue, mastication will be discouraged and the digestion of food affected.

In extreme cases *quidding* will occur, when, through diseased teeth, the food is partially chewed and then dropped from the mouth – in which case the digestive system doesn't even get under way.

Care of the teeth is, therefore, an elementary duty incumbent upon the horse-keeper and they should be attended to at least once every six months.

Proportions of the Food Intake

Full assimilation of the food given will depend very largely on the horse receiving a proper quantity, particularly in regard to bulk, which is correctly combined with other foods to give a balanced diet, in which there is neither a notable deficiency nor excess. Good, clean food is more easily digested than that of inferior quality. To feed tainted food causes particular trouble due to the horse's inability to vomit. Digestion cannot take place without water being present. Overworked horses, and those in poor bodily health, will have digestions in a similar condition and will be unable to assimilate food properly.

There is now the very important question to consider as to how much food the horse needs, in what proportions and at what intervals.

In these respects there can be no hard-and-fast rules since horses are individuals and vary enormously in their requirements. There will be some animals who thrive on practically nothing and others who need an awful lot of feeding to keep in anything approaching condition. Formulating the correct diet for the individual is the art of the good feeder and the job of every horse-owner.

It is possible, however, to give a general guide to the quantities of food which various horses will require. In theory the amount of foodstuffs required by an animal is dependent, not upon height or weight, but upon the skin surface area. A large skin surface suffers a correspondingly large loss of heat, and, as the maintenance of body heat is a prime need of life, it must be replaced by food.

It can easily be seen that a heavily-built, 15 hh cob, presenting a large surface area, will need a greater food intake than a lightly-built hack of the same height. In the same way a pony weighing perhaps half the weight of a hunter will need more food in comparison because the surface area is greater per pound body weight.

The only real indication of an animal's needs is his bodily condition.

Feed Proportions

There may be differences of opinion which arise out of the more detailed studies of equine nutrition but there is no disagreement about the long established rule relating to the bulk/concentrate ratio.

Horses in light work should be fed in the proportion of two-thirds hay (bulk) to one-third "short" or concentrate feed.

For horses in moderate work the proportion is altered to a 50–50 basis.

Horses in hard work may have the hay ration reduced to as little as one-third of the whole and the concentrate intake increased accordingly.

It is not advisable to reduce the hay ration beyond this level in any circumstances.

Quantities/Weight Estimation

The quantity of food to be fed daily to a horse depends upon the individual. Some horses, like some people, need a lot of food, others, again like people, need far less to perform the same work. Ponies, for instance, to complicate the matter, are better food converters than horses and need less in comparison. Some breeds are notably frugal in their requirements, Welsh Cobs and Irish Draughts, for instance.

There are numerous charts based on height, but for the most part they have in common a lack of unanimity, although the differences are rarely significant.

This one appears to meet the average requirement pretty well but is obviously not entirely accurate in every respect:

Height – hh	Under 12	12–13	13–14	14–15	15–16	Over 16
Aprox. daily bulk food intake – lb	14–16	16–18	20–22	22–24	24–26	26–28

Since the estimation of surface area in relation to food intake is impractical, food intakes can be calculated more precisely by weight. This figure can be arrived at by the use of a calibrated tape (usually wildly inaccurate) or by putting the horse on a weigh-bridge, which is entirely accurate but for most of us impractical.

The following is the most reliable formula I know:

$$\frac{\text{Girth}^2 \times \text{Length}}{300} = \text{Weight in lbs}$$

Take the girth measure in inches round the *largest* part of the barrel. The square of the girth, i.e. girth^2, is found by multiplying the figure by itself (i.e. 78 in × 78 in). Length, also taken in inches, is from the point of the shoulder *upwards* to the point of the buttock.

If the weight is required in kilograms use this formula:

$$\frac{\text{Girth (cm)}^2 \times \text{Length}}{8,700} = \text{Weight in Kg}$$

For metric non-friendly persons like myself it is much easier to do the thing in inches and then convert to Kg using one of those ubiquitous pocket calculators.

The total food intake is reckoned as being between 2–2½ per cent of the total body weight of the mature horse and 3 per cent in the case of youngstock.

Of course, everything depends upon the horse being neither under nor overweight at the start. Once the desirable weight is established, regular measurements, taken at the same time of day with the horse always being made to stand in the same position so far as possible, will show whether the level of feeding needs to be adjusted.

By far the best way of arriving at the ideal weight is by practical experience. The skilful horsemaster will arrive at the ideal weight by careful observation of his horse and by the "feel" the horse gives in performance. He will assess the horse's well-being and fitness level by the same means. There is no scientific formula which can replace the eye and the intuitive feel of the master.

Nonetheless science can provide a guideline. It is a method called Condition Scoring, which takes the horsemaster's long-established practical observations and puts them into a formula.

The areas assessed in condition scoring are the quarters; the saddle area of the back and the base of the neck. The latter, I believe, is somewhat fallacious. A better estimate of condition can be made lower down on either side.

This is how it works:

(1) Standing behind the horse, note the covering of flesh over the pelvis and quarters.

Poor condition reveals the bone structure quite clearly. The flanks are hollow, there is a deep cavity under the tail and no muscle between the hindlegs. "Cut up behind" in fact. Tight skin completes the picture and the score is 0. Award 1 if the skin is loose.

If the pelvis can be felt but the quarters are otherwise rounded and the bones well covered the horse is in good condition if the presence of fatty tissue under the skin is perceptible. Score 2 or 3.

If you can't feel the bone structure and the quarters are fat with a distinct channel dividing the back through the quarters to the dock, the horse is too fat. Any exaggeration of that condition qualifies him as being grossly fat. Score 4 or 5.

(2) Apply the same process to the back area. If at one extreme the backbone is visible, the horse is poor. At the other extreme there will be a channel in the centre of the back and fleshy, flat tables on either side.

(3) Feel the amount of muscle at the base of the neck and search for fat, or the absence of it, lower down on either side. A horse in poor condition feels narrow and slack. Good condition is denoted by a firm, wide base. Crests, except in male horses, indicate over-weight. Ewe necks indicate the opposite but could be a conformational fault.

In both instances score as previously.

The following *adjustment* has to be made to arrive at the final score. Adjust the pelvis score up or down half a point if it is different from the back or neck score. There is no need to alter the pelvis score if the back and neck scores differ by an equal amount on either side of the former. *The Adjusted Pelvis Score is the Condition Score.* The weight can then be adjusted to the optimum condition score by exercise and/or feed intake.

Methods of Feeding

The methods of feeding depend upon the peculiarities of the equine digestive apparatus and the positioning of the relatively small stomach (the latter has a capacity of 20 litres in comparison with 140 litres of the cow).

As an example the following authentic feed chart, applicable to a 15 hh hunter weighing 1,300 lb is appended. The horse was exercised daily and hunted once a week. He received a bran/linseed mash as his final concentrate feed on hunting days. Additionally, he received 2 oz common salt and 2–3 oz limestone flour each day.

Time	Oats	Bran	Alfalfa nuts	Carrots Apples	Hay
7 am	2 lb	½ lb	½ lb		
8.30–10 am	Exercise after quartering				
10 am	Mucking out				3 lb
11–12 noon	Grooming				
12.30 pm	2 lb	½ lb	1 lb	½ lb	
4 pm	2 lb	½ lb	1 lb		3 lb
7.30 pm	2 lb	½ lb	1 lb	½ lb	
10 pm					8 lb

An event horse of 16·1 hh in peak performance condition weighing 1,400 lb received the following ration to which was added 3 oz limestone flour and 3 oz salt, a daily seaweed supplement and 2 tbs of cider vinegar.

A bran/linseed mash was fed once a week.

Time	Oats	Bran	Alfalfa nuts	Carrots Apples	Hay
7 am	2 lb	½ lb	½ lb		
8.30–10.30 am	Exercise after quartering				
10.30 am	2 lb	½ lb	1 lb		
11.30 am–1 pm	Put out in exercise paddock				
1 pm	2 lb	½ lb	1 lb	½ lb	
2.15 pm	Grooming				2 lb
3.15–4.15 pm	Schooling				
4.15 pm	2 lb	½ lb	1 lb		
5 pm	Grooming – strapping				2 lb
6 pm	2 lb	½ lb	1 lb	½ lb	
8.30 pm	2 lb	½ lb	½ lb		
10 pm					5 lb

Both these horses were weighed by formula calculation once a week.

The bulk of the hay has been given at night so that the horse may have plenty of time to digest it and to keep himself occupied through the hours of darkness.

If the horse was inclined to bolt his food 2 lb of the night hay ration could be chopped and divided between the first, third and fourth feeds.

Many people may have to ride before breakfast, or would prefer to do so, in which case one exercises first and feeds afterwards. For my own part I used to concentrate better after breakfast and I see no reason why the horse should not feel the same. Nowadays, I hold the same to be true for the horse – for myself increasing weight precludes the taking of breakfast.

The important thing is that whatever timings are decided upon they should be adhered to most strictly. Horses have a built-in alarm clock in their stomachs and expect their routine to follow a regular pattern.

The hunter quoted hunts on one day a week and this will involve some alteration in the diet. As the horse is going to expend an extra amount of energy on his hunting day it is only reasonable that he should be given the opportunity to store up some extra by being given an increased ration on the *preceding* day. On the actual day he will not have the opportunity to eat his accustomed quantity. Partly for this reason and partly to replace any excess output over intake he may have suffered it is also wise to slightly increase the ration on the day *following* his exertions.

If Saturday was the hunting day the diet sheet for Friday should be altered to show an increase of 1 lb oats in each feed. This addition to the bulk intake would, however, have to be compensated by a corresponding reduction in the bulk foods.

In my own case I would cut out the ½ lb nuts and ½ lb of the carrots in the midday feed and reduce the morning hay ration by 1 lb and the last hay net by 2 lb – a total bulk reduction of 4 lb – to correspond with the increase in corn.

On Saturday the horse would receive his normal first feed, possibly with the addition of a handful of chopped hay. We have already noted that the digestive functions of the tired horse are considerably reduced in efficiency and for this reason the animal on its return from hunting will be given an easily digested feed. I would suggest a linseed mash, and later he may be given his last hay net as usual.

An extra 2 lb of oats over and above his normal ration may be split between the four feeds on the Sunday and the hay ration reduced accordingly. If the horse has had anything like a day's hunting he will not need exercise on Sunday, but he should be walked out for half-an-hour or so and allowed to nibble at some clean grass.

The once-weekly linseed mash should be enough to keep his bowels in order, but if experience shows that he still tends to constipation then a bran mash may need to be introduced once a fortnight, or even more frequently.

In the event of bad weather stopping hunting and making exercise difficult the corn ration must be cut at once and replaced with non-heating auxiliaries, green food and hay.

But what of the horse owned by the working girl who may have neither the means nor the opportunity to hunt during the winter and confines her equestrian activities to Saturday and Sunday, being unable to ride during the week?

The principles, of course, remain unaltered, but the method of application must necessarily change. Let us say that our young lady has trace-clipped her horse and intends turning him out in a New Zealand rug by day and bringing him in at night. As the horse may be doing no more than say a total of six hours work under saddle per week he will not require the same amount of energy food as in the previous case, although he will be using a considerable quantity of his food intake to keep himself warm.

If we take it that his bulk intake is a couple of pounds less than his stabled brother and that the young lady has a member of her family willing to do the feeding while she is at work, the weekly diet sheet could be as follows:

Day	Nuts	Oats	Bran	Carrots	Hay
Tuesday	3 lb	3 lb	2 lb	1 lb	17 lb
Wednesday	3 lb	3 lb	2 lb	1 lb	17 lb
Thursday	3 lb	3 lb	2 lb	1 lb	17 lb
Friday	3 lb	5 lb	2 lb	1 lb	15 lb
Saturday	3 lb	5 lb	2 lb	1 lb	15 lb
Sunday	3 lb	5 lb	Mash* 2 lb	1 lb	15 lb
Monday	3 lb	4 lb	2 lb	1 lb	16 lb

Either Bran or Linseed

The ration could be divided into *three* feeds a day with the greater portion of the hay ration being given, as usual, at night. The fact that the horse may consume some additional bulk in the form of grass, which will be sparse and devoid of nourishment during the winter months, would not under normal circumstances be material. Additional additives can be given without altering the diet, as in the previous instance.

Corn Control

A good, old-fashioned rule of thumb applied to the quantity of corn to be consumed by any one animal is to calculate 1 lb of corn per 1 mile of exercise. My own way is to start on a low corn ration and gradually increase it to the point where the horse is getting somewhat above himself. Then one cuts it back until his behaviour is once more acceptable.

An over-fresh horse is not a co-operative one, and if the rider is fighting to control him for the greater part of the exercise period it is hardly conducive to the attainment of the *entente cordiale* which should exist between the two. A couple of light-hearted bucks and a squeal or two on a cold morning can be regarded as a spot of fun between the two partners and is forgivable in any horse.

If, however, the horse has not settled in ten minutes or so then I would suggest he is getting too big an energy ration in relation to his energy output.

Feeding and Care at Grass

At this juncture let us consider the needs of the horse at grass, either doing no work or doing a limited amount.

During the optimum growth and nutritional period, between May and August, a horse doing no work manages very well on *good and ample* grazing without additional feed. In very dry spells, particularly on poor quality grazing, additional feeding will be necessary to maintain the horse in condition.

Ponies are, however, something of a law unto themselves, in this as in other things. The average pony of native ancestry is tough and hardy and is able to get a living from poor land and still keep in surprisingly good condition. This is not to say that I condone the practice of putting two or three ponies on an acre of scrubland. I do not by any means, but there is a most certain danger in going to the opposite extreme and putting them out on really lush grazing.

Susceptibility to Laminitis and Grass Restriction

Horses at grass, using little energy, put on condition and become fat and soft, but ponies, always greedy feeders, the most efficient converters of food and by nature unused to such high living, rapidly attain a rotundity which is past belief. Now this is bad for the pony, particularly if he is being ridden. He is firstly over weight and, therefore, his legs are overburdened as well as his soft and out of tone internal organs. What is even more important is that he might develop *laminitis* under these conditions. Laminitis is a very serious and painful disease of the feet (usually the fore-feet). The sensitive laminae encased by the non-elastic horn of the foot are subject to intense inflammation and as the foot cannot expand the pain is very great. There are a number of factors which cause laminitis, but in ponies too great an intake of rich grass is the most prevalent.

Fat ponies are also a cause of much frustration in the matter of saddle fitting. Saddles were made to fit backs having at least some outline of the conventional and expected shape, not for billiard tables.

Ponies should not, therefore, be allowed lush grazing. It is far better to restrict their intake by bringing them in for specified periods and giving no food at all than to allow them to get over fat.

The Working Pony

Ponies are often worked far harder during the summer than most people realise. One has only to go to a small gymkhana to see how much work they get through in a day. I did this very thing to satisfy myself on the point, choosing a group of children who had a five-mile hack to get to the gymkhana ground. Their ponies were brushed and cleaned from their field by 9 o'clock and they arrived at the ground at 10 am. They spent the morning cantering and galloping about with occasional rest periods, taken while the riders ate ice lollies and lunch, usually still sitting on the pony.

During the afternoon they took part in at least six gymkhana events, leaving the ground at 5 pm and arriving home at 6 pm. Now that is a very fair day's work for any horse, and, in my book, too much work for a pony. I would not advocate the feeding of oats to ponies, but if they are to work they must be fed accordingly.

I would suggest that a pony kept at grass during the summer and worked every day in the holidays should be kept in the following way.

If the grazing is sparse and poorish he may stay out for the whole 24 hours, but should be given *at least* one feed a day consisting of 3 lb nuts and 1 lb bran as well as the occasional carrot. On this diet he will not become too wild for the child, as he most certainly would be if he were fed on oats. Oats and ponies are not a good combination.

On lush grazing the pony must be brought in during a part of the day to prevent him getting too fat. This must be carried out whether he is in work or not. Alternatively he can spend periods on very poor pasture if this is available. If he is being ridden it is probably wise to bring him in for the whole day, giving him the feed mentioned above split into two, and turning him out at night.

In every case common sense must be exercised and the pony allowed grass and feed in relation to the work he is to do.

In winter ponies will lose condition if kept on small acreages (or even large ones) without additional feed. A hay ration of 10 lb or, if he will eat more, in excess of that figure, is not too much and at least one feed of 3 lb nuts and 1 lb bran is necessary per day.

If the pony is worked during the winter at weekends, the energy ration should be increased on Friday, Saturday, Sunday and Monday, and it may be necessary to feed the pony twice a day. As an example I give a suggested diet for a 13 hh pony out at grass during the winter and worked for a total of four hours on Saturday and Sunday.

Day	Nuts	Bran	Carrots	Bruised Barley	Hay	Total
Tuesday	3 lb	1 lb			14 lb	18 lb
Wednesday	3 lb	1 lb	One or		14 lb	18 lb
Thursday	3 lb	1 lb	two		14 lb	18 lb
Friday	4 lb	1½ lb	sliced	½ lb In two	12 lb	18 lb
Saturday	4 lb	1½ lb	in each	½ lb feeds	12 lb	18 lb
Sunday	4 lb	1½ lb	feed	½ lb per day	12 lb	18 lb
Monday	4 lb	1 lb			13 lb	18 lb

As before the largest part of the hay should be fed as the last feed.

It should be remembered that summer grass is a soft food producing soft condition. Horses kept at grass during the summer are fit for nothing more than very slow work. If the horse is to do hard work he is better kept in on a hard diet and restricted to an hour or two at grass each day. To work soft horses is to impose severe strain on the heart and other organs and upon the legs.

Summary

Horse-owners should be aware and take advantage of scientific research into equine nutrition, but without abdicating their own responsibility. The onus for producing a horse fit for the purpose required is fairly and squarely with the owner and with none other. Similarly the onus for acquiring knowledge and experience is also with the owner.

"There is no secret so close as that between horse and rider."

Finally, it is no bad thing to consider this definition, which appears in the War Office manual of *Animal Management* 1933:

"The good horsemaster is one who can get the maximum amount of work out of his horses at the minimum cost without the animals losing condition." Nothing could be more practical than that.

CHAPTER 4

The Importance of Worm-Control

However well horses are fed and cared for the efforts of the horsemaster will be of little avail unless he also appreciates the susceptibility of his charges to parasitic infestation.

Worm infestation, to the point when debility or even death can ensue, is a direct result of domestication and its control is of just as much importance to the well-being of the horse as is the correct relationship of food to work. One would think that so much effort and ink had already been expended on this subject that no horse-owner could possibly fail to understand its importance.

Surprisingly, however, this is not the case, for there is still a large number of horse-keepers who have little, or no, knowledge of worms or of the need to control them. There are even more (those with the ability to swallow lumps of undigested fact) who know a great deal in *theory*, but never get beyond that stage – an all too prevalent state of affairs.

All domestic horses harbour parasites which, in general, use pasture as a main vehicle in their life cycle. Much can be done by proper grass management to combat the danger but, as yet, there is no sure way of eliminating parasites entirely without possessing an unlimited acreage and incurring enormous expense. At present, therefore, the main area of attack must be confined to the horse itself, although it is more than prudent if one has limited grazing to practise the removal of droppings from the paddock on a regular basis.

There are three common types of worms met with in horses: *White worms*, *Whip* or *Seat worms* and the *Red worm*. In addition there is the *Stomach Bot*, which is not a true worm, but can be conveniently dealt with in company with the others.

The White Worm *(Ascaris)*

The most common in horses. Because of its size and colour (it is white and can be up to a foot long and as thick as a pencil) it is easily discernible in droppings.

In small numbers it will cause no harm in the adult horse, but if it is allowed to increase the horse will lose condition, the coat will stare and there is a possibility of intermittent colic. In severe cases a stoppage or even a rupture of the gut may occur. By the time the worms can be seen in the droppings the infestation is becoming established and should be dealt with at once. If proper worm prevention is carried out this stage should never be reached.

The eggs of this worm are laid in the gut and passed out in the droppings. They hatch on pasture, or in badly managed bedding, and in the former case re-enter the animal with the grass he eats, or in the latter make their way into the manger or the hay.

The small worms having entered the gut penetrate the intestinal wall and move through the internal organs until they return to their starting point, and the whole cycle commences once more.

Whip or Seat Worms *(Oxyuris)*

Very thin and can measure nearly two inches long, occur in the rectum and are not harmful in their effect as far as general condition is concerned. They do, however, cause intense irritation which is manifested by rubbing the tail and a discharge around the anus.

It is not necessary to call in a veterinary surgeon to effect a cure as the treatment is quite simple. An enema consisting of a handful of salt in a gallon of warm water, given after the dock has been thoroughly sponged, is usually effective.

The treatment should be carried out three times with an interval of three days between treatment. Cloths or sponges which are used should be thoroughly disinfected afterwards to prevent re-infestation.

Stomach Bots

Caused by the bot-fly laying its eggs on the legs of the horse at grass. The eggs are carried to the stomach, where they hatch, by the horse licking at the affected part.

The brownish-yellow eggs can be seen adhering to the hair of the leg and are easily enough removed by clipping the hair away. Bots are not dangerous unless they occur in very large quantities when a horse, despite feeding well, will display loss of condition together with a dry and staring coat.

The Red Worm *(Strongyle)*

Common and is by far the most dangerous. There are two types, the Large (up to one inch) and the Small strongyle (about a quarter of an inch). In cases of severe infestation death will ensue. The adult horse in good health develops a certain resistance to the red worm, but young animals are particularly susceptible to the attacks of this parasite and have rarely developed sufficient resistance to their attacks.

Strongyles live and breed in the intestines. In similar fashion to the white worm the eggs are passed out in the droppings and, developing on pasture or soiled bedding, gain re-entry to the system. The large strongyle larvae pass through the organs and blood vessels, and in sufficient numbers will cause stoppages of the blood stream. Eventually they regain the intestine and recommence the cycle.

The small strongyle develops in the gut wall where a percentage remain, together with the adult, large strongyle, and feed on blood. The result of a heavy infestation is anaemia, pronounced loss of condition and diarrhoea, having a very strong and unpleasant smell. The stomach will be distended, the skin tight, the coat stary and the membrane of the eye pale in colour.

In neglected cases the worm may penetrate and close a main artery, cutting the blood supply to the bowel, when death will be almost inevitable.

Clearly the need to keep small or large pastures clear of droppings and not to graze them with horses indefinitely and entirely is of paramount importance, but even if this is done red worm can still be regarded as an almost permanent parasite, whose potential danger will be increased if the host, i.e. the horse himself, is in poor condition.

In the case of red worm and of the less dangerous white worm, effective control can only be exercised by regular treatment.

In the past it was considered sufficient to dose the horse against worms twice a year. This is not, however, nearly frequent enough, particularly where the horse is exposed to recurrent infection, as he will be when allowed access to pasture. It has now been proved that the horse can acquire a new red worm egg burden within six weeks and it follows that to keep the animal free from infestation suitable medication will have to be administered at comparable intervals.

Fortunately, today's proprietary worming treatments, if administered regularly, will be effective against all known parasites. They are also easily administered and so there is no excuse for worm-ridden horses, other than that old "Devil's Trademark", ignorance, combined possibly with indolence.

A word of warning, however. In accordance with the modern packaging phobia, some of the best wormers are in paste form contained in a syringe. In theory, the latter is inserted in the mouth and the contents ejected therein by operating the plunger. In practice, it is quite possible to lose half the dose. All in all it is more satisfactory to put the paste into a feed mixing it well with various succulent morsels.

While worm control is essential for the horse at grass, or for one having even restricted access to pasture, it is equally necessary for the stabled horse. As we have seen it is still possible for the worm cycle to be maintained under stable conditions, although extreme cases of infestation are unlikely if stable management is of a high order. It should be remembered that hay made from worm infected land is capable of red worm transmission and that the practice of piling bedding beneath the manger facilitates the movement of the worm from the soiled straw to the manger.

The absence of discernible red worm in the droppings does not imply that the horse is worm free.

The importance of control cannot be over-emphasised and preventive measures, or at any rate egg counts, under veterinary supervision, should be as regular a part of horse management as are the visits of the blacksmith.

CHAPTER 5

Conditioning and Managing the Stabled Horse

Horses are either stabled or kept on the New Zealand rug principle in order that they may be more easily and effectively conditioned for a particular purpose, such as hunting. (Conditioning a horse for hunting provides a sound basis for preparing horses for other forms of competition.)

Animals kept entirely at grass cannot be properly conditioned for anything more than very moderate work. In winter the grass-kept animal is not clipped, for obvious reasons, and his heavy coat makes it impossible for him to work at anything but very slow paces. In summer, unless he was kept on very sparse grazing and adequately fed and exercised, he would probably be too fat and too soft. To work him in this state would be to run the risk of overstraining his legs and internal organs.

To get a horse physically fit is not, however, achieved just by putting him in a stable, clipping off his winter coat and stuffing him with food a week or two before the opening meet. It is a long, slow process, the length of which depends on the initial physical state of the horse.

In the past, and the practice is still carried out today, it was customary for hunters to be put out to grass after the season, usually in April or early May, depending upon the weather, and not worked until they were brought up again towards the middle of August or the beginning of September. Today, there are many people who use their horses all the year round and this more flexible approach has advantages. A horse kept in moderate work during the summer, with probably three or four weeks holiday at grass, will never get into the gross, soft condition of the animal who is out for the entire summer season. As a result his muscles never entirely lose their tone and he will be more easily brought into hard condition.

If, of course, a horse has had a very hard hunting season, as a hunt servant's horse might have, then there is a case for putting him out for a good, long rest which will allow him to unwind both mentally and physically. Otherwise, if a horse finishes the season in good condition, having not done an excessive amount of work, there is no reason why, after a short rest period, he should not spend the summer hacking or competing in the various events which are available.

Nevertheless, whatever his state and circumstances, a horse must obviously be sound before he can be made fit, and he must be carrying plenty of flesh. It is no use trying to work on a thin horse, he will just go on getting thinner. Therefore, if one's horse is not carrying enough weight he must first be given an opportunity to put the matter right before one thinks of setting him a conditioning programme.

In getting a horse fit, as in most things connected with the equine race, or the human one for that matter, it is advisable to define the objective and then to plan (to the extent of committing the programme to paper) the methods by which the objective is to be achieved.

The objective in this case, as we have taken hunting as an example, is to produce on 1 November, or thereabouts, a hard, muscle-fit horse, big, but without carrying more than a covering of surplus fat.

Within a week or two of the opening meet he will then be hunting fit. There is a deal of difference between this and a horse who is racing fit. The latter will be lean and trained to a very high peak of fitness – the ultimate fitness, in fact. To achieve this sort of fitness requires great skill, and to maintain a horse at this peak for even short periods demands both skill and experience. For the purpose of racing it is a necessary physical state, but not for hunting or anything outside the racecourse. Racing demands maximum effort, of limited duration, over short distances. Hunting, eventing or long-distance riding calls for sustained effort, with occasional bursts of speed, over long distances for an extended period.

A horse that is racing fit at the beginning of the season will be like a toast-rack half way through, that is if he and his rider survive the first day. Conversely, a hunting fit horse would be unlikely to make much of a showing in a fast run two-mile 'chase. The condition, therefore, must fit the purpose.

We shall condition the horse by the intelligent combination of three factors:

Feeding, Exercising and Grooming

Feeding will build up his body and supply the material required for the making of muscle as well as producing the necessary energy.

Exercise will develop, strengthen, and tone the muscles and will remove the burden of surplus fat. Fat, incidentally, is not converted into muscle. Muscle is muscle and fat is fat; there is no question of the latter being changed into the former. By exercise, too, the legs, the sinews and tendons, etc., are hardened, the wind is made clear and the horse is accustomed to carrying weight.

Grooming and strapping not only develop and tone the muscles, but clean the body so that it can work to maximum effect. A dirty, pore-blocked skin is no aid to efficient body function. Feeding has already been dealt with at some length and the importance of it being regulated according to the amount of exercise has been stressed.

Nevertheless, at the risk of being repetitious and for the sake of the horse, I will emphasise the need for a gradual increase in the feeding of hard food. A horse that has been having additional feeds during the summer and has been doing exercise can have his ration increased *slowly* – in proportion to the extra work expected of him. The horse that has been at grass for some months must be taken even more slowly, otherwise his digestive capacity will become overloaded. Ideally, he should have at least two weeks of very light work, possibly lungeing, and one or two small feeds per day to get his digestive system in something like working order. He can also be stabled for a few hours a day before being brought up entirely.

I am not much in favour of the old practice of "physicking" a horse (the administration of a pretty drastic laxative) up from grass in order to clear him out before starting hard feeds. In many cases the shock to the system does a lot more harm than good, and as I wouldn't like it myself I don't see why the horse should either.

The average horse occasionally gets too much *exercise*, but more often too little.

It is impossible to lay down the exact amount of exercise a horse should take at any one time during the process of conditioning, because it depends entirely upon the mental and physical characteristics of the individual. The following factors, however, will always apply: Exercise will be progressive in speed and duration and must always be related to physical condition and the intake of energy foods.

Many people will appreciate the necessity of observing these fundamentals and will conscientiously enough endeavour to carry them out. Unfortunately there are far too many owners who consider only the physical well-being of the horse and neglect, or even overlook entirely, the importance of his mental state. Horses, like children, are easily bored and idle minds are just as much a source of mischief as are bodies in a similar state of lethargy.

The aim in training the horse, and the skill, is in the two-fold development of *mind* and *body*, and in recognising that the full value of exercise lies not only in quantity, but also in quality.

Exercise should be an enjoyable and an instructive business for the horse and these two requirements will not be met by trotting round the same convenient route each day. Variety in the programme is essential, and for this reason, as well as others, it is advisable to have one's conditioning programme planned out well in advance of its commencement. Obviously the programme must be flexible to some degree to allow for the "best laid plans of mice and men" being upset, but the very fact that one has a programme makes it easier to achieve the objectives.

Lungeing, loose schooling and work in the *manège* or jumping ring can all be combined with road work and hacking over broken country, negotiating small obstacles as they present themselves.

The greatest ally in preparing horses for work is time. Condition is achieved by slow processes which cannot be hurried and the more time that can be devoted to the programme the more satisfactory will be the result. Slow work is always beneficial, fast work is rarely so.

Riding exercise require just as much attention to detail as does feeding. The first essential, to my mind, is that when it is planned to give the horse a specified period of exercise, i.e. one hour, he should receive one hour and not 40 minutes. If it takes 10 minutes to saddle up, and another 10 to unsaddle and put the horse to rights on returning to the stable, then one needs to devote one hour 20 minutes to the exercise period.

It is as well, if one is to do the job properly, to find out the speed of the horse's paces in relation to the distance covered. On average a horse walks one mile in sixteen minutes, trots one mile in eight minutes and canters one mile in five minutes. These times, of course, vary slightly with individuals and can be verified by timing over a measured distance if it is considered necessary. Armed with this knowledge routes can be planned to coincide, roughly, with the time available.

Walking and trotting are the two paces from which the greatest benefit is derived. At neither should the horse be allowed to slop along, but on the other hand he does not want to be over restricted.

The walk can be relaxed and swinging but the horse must nonetheless be asked to work within a frame imposed by the leg and hand and with his quarters actively engaged. There is no point in creating bad habits and ultimately resistances by lazy riding. If the horse is allowed to go along anyhow, with his nose poked out and his feet dragging behind, he will not understand what is wanted when later on he is asked to bring himself together and come on the bit. Not surprisingly he will become resentful if the rider insists on his attempts to obtain that sort of carriage.

Occasionally, of course, the horse can be allowed to relax and enjoy a short period of rest on the long rein.

The trot, too, must be similarly positive. Slow, certainly, but very active and rhythmical.

Roadwork, at an intelligent combination of the two paces, will harden the legs and slow trotting uphill is excellent for the wind. Trotting over broken ground and negotiating grids along road verges is an excellent balancing exercise for both horse and rider. When going downhill proceed at a walk.

At the trot the rider should change the diagonal frequently in order that the horse should develop his muscles equally. Changing the diagonal is a very simple process and a commonsense practice.

The trot is a two-time pace, that is the horse moves the two diagonal pairs of legs alternately with a short interval of suspension as he springs from one to the other. The right diagonal is the off-fore and near-hind, and the left diagonal the opposite pair. A rider, when rising to the trot, is said to be on the right diagonal when his seat touches the saddle as the off-fore and near-hind strike the ground. The rider changes the diagonal by remaining in the saddle for an extra beat before rising again. In other words he bumps once. Conversely, of course, the rider will still change the diagonal if he keeps his seat out of the saddle for two successive beats.

The first method is usually preferred because it is held that the rider does not lose contact with the horse. Having decided long ago that the horse was not specifically designed to carry weight on his back, and having the greatest sympathy and respect for that part of the equine anatomy, I do not, personally, carry out this method of changing the diagonal, preferring to have my seat momentarily raised for the extra beat. I do not think I lose contact, as my legs are still available, and even if I do it is hardly a matter of great import. From the horse's viewpoint I am sure it must be more comfortable not to have an extra twelve stone bump (which is what in many cases the average rider's change amounts to) and I am equally convinced he is more relieved than worried by the minimal loss of contact involved. (I have a feeling that in the modern equestrian climate this would be considered a rank heresy. *Author's note.*)

For those who are not very clear as to which diagonal they are riding on a brief glance at the horse's shoulder is informative.

When the left shoulder is to the rear as the seat touches the saddle you are on the right diagonal and vice versa.

When exercising it is good for the horse's concentration as well as for his manners to indulge in a little schooling. On a quiet road ask him to move diagonally from side to side, it is an excellent introduction to moving on two tracks and gets him used to answering to the leg.

If the head is moved slightly in the right direction and, to start with, the action of the outside hand (i.e. the left hand if one is moving from left to right) reinforces the leading inside hand by moving slightly forwards and then pressing intermittently below the withers, the horse will be encouraged to move his shoulders as well. The outside leg acts, again intermittently and gently, behind the girth. (The same effect will be achieved and perhaps more easily for the novice by inclining the head slightly away from the movement to produce "leg-yielding" to one side or the other.)

Make a habit of opening gates, starting with ones that are properly hung and do not have to be lifted out of the mud by brute force.

It is equally valuable to ask for variations in pace and even for very short periods of collection or posture shortening, in so far as the horse is capable. Do not, however, overdo these little requests and always having asked for and received a shortening of the stride and posture, reward the horse by allowing him to work on a long rein.

Above all avoid riding over the same ground day after day and never get into the habit of always cantering over a certain piece of ground. If you do, the horse, in the first case, will become bored and may begin to make resistances from pure devilment, and in the second case will, in time, always canter or gallop when he comes to the spot, whatever his rider's wishes may be.

The introduction of a steady canter and an occasional short burst at speed, apart from getting the itch out of a horse's heels, has the effect of toning the lungs and bronchial tubes. Hence the expression a "pipe-opener".

Never, of course, should a horse be brought into the stable sweating after exercise. He is likely to cach a chill. For this reason it is best to walk the last mile home to give him a chance to cool off. If he is still hot on returning to the stable then one must pay for the sin of omission by walking him round until he has dried off.

The act of grooming removes the natural grease from the coat and, therefore, its waterproofing property. The horse kept at grass and ungroomed suffers not at all from rain, but this is not the case with the stabled horse whose protective grease has been removed and who is, therefore, far more likely to catch cold if he gets wet.

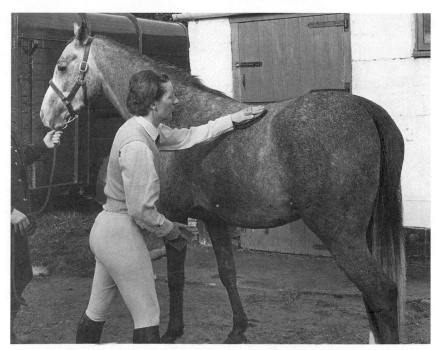

Grooming with the body brush, the curry comb in this instance (since the lady is left-handed) being held in the right hand.

On rainy days, however, the bringing home of a wet horse is unavoidable and under these circumstances it is better to trot briskly home, bringing the horse back warm. Then rub him down with a handful of straw, put a mesh rug on, or alternatively cover his back with straw, and finally throw a top rug, inside out to prevent it getting wet, over the lot. The animal should then dry out quite happily.

Do not, if the horse should be hot, remove the saddle immediately or the cold air on the heated back will either give him a chill or cause other troubles. It is far better to leave the saddle on with the girths loosened and remove it when the animal has had time to dry off completely.

Grooming, the third factor in conditioning, is not only necessary for the sake of appearance, but also for the health of the stabled horse, who is kept under artificial conditions and, by reason of the work he is asked to do, consumes large quantities of artificial foods. As a result of the latter his body has an increased quantity of waste matter for disposal.

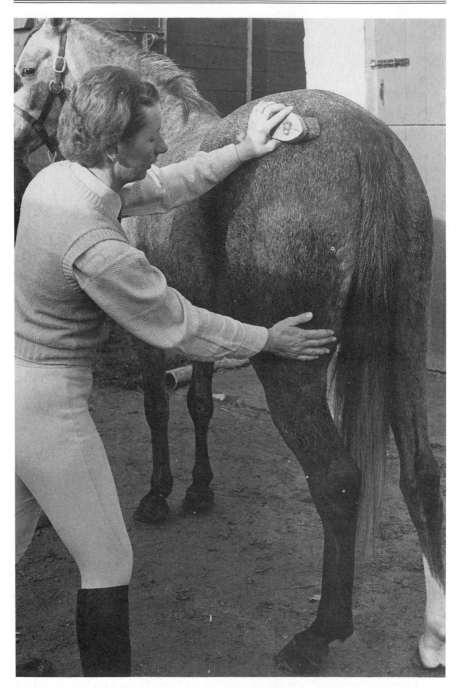

A finish with the water brush, but in safety. Note the restraining hand.

Much of this waste is got rid of through the increased rate of breathing by the lungs and through excrement, but just as great a proportion is possibly dispersed through the skin. In order, therefore, to fulfil this function the skin must be kept clean.

Although the cleanliness and stimulation of the skin is a large part of what is loosely termed "grooming" it is not the whole. Massage, hand rubbing and wisping also play their part in bringing a horse into hard condition. It is these practices which bring the skin to a high peak of functional efficiency and also stimulate circulation and promote the growth and toning of muscle structures.

The items comprising a full grooming kit are as follows:

DANDY BRUSH – a stiff whisk or nylon brush used for removing mud from the legs. It is too stiff and scratchy to use on the body of clipped animals of any but the most common parentage. The brush is not used on the mane or tail as it pulls out the hairs.

BODY BRUSH – a soft bristle brush used on the body and for brushing out the mane and tail.

WATER BRUSH – a soft, boat-shaped brush used damp on the mane and tail and often to put a final shine on the horse.

CURRY COMB – a metal comb of toothed blades set on a metal back and sometimes having a wooden handle or a hand strap. Its purpose is to clean the body brush, not the horse.

TWO SPONGES – one for cleaning the eyes and nose and the other for cleaning the dock.

STABLE RUBBER – a linen cloth used as a final polisher.

MANE COMB – a small metal comb, used usually for trimming.

HOOF-PICK – a good big one is preferable to the rather ineffectual folding ones.

One might also add one or other of the various forms of rubber or plastic curry combs which can be used on the horse and are excellent for stimulating and cleaning the skin. A good chamois leather is also useful to give a final polish and an old dandy or water brush can be helpful when washing out the feet.

The normal procedure for grooming a horse is to start high up on the neck, behind the ears, and work with the body brush from front to rear.

The whole secret lies in placing oneself far enough away from the horse to be able to get one's whole weight behind the brush. If you stand too close this is impossible. Use the body brush in the right hand holding the curry comb in the left. After each three or four strokes clean the bristles on the comb.

Many horses, particularly the well-bred ones, are very ticklish under

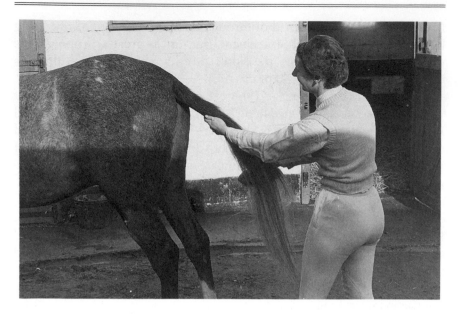

Brushing out the tail.

the tummy and between the hind legs and will object to the brush by either trying to nip their persecutor or by aiming a crafty cow kick with the hind leg. Fortunately the latter is unusual, but if the animal is really ticklish dispense with the brush altogether and use the hand only. If you keep the unoccupied hand against his neck, or even grasp the headcollar, you will prevent his biting you.

Use the body brush for cleaning the head and ears and for Heaven's sake use it gently, being very careful not to bang the bony projections with the wooden back. It is well worth spending time encouraging the horse to drop his head and accept the cleaning quietly. Very many horses become head shy because of rough treatment by some impatient idiot wielding a brush inexpertly. In the stable a horse should come to you of his own accord and allow his head to be touched and the bridle to be put on without fuss.

If you can persuade the horse to accept brushing calmly it is unlikely that you will experience trouble either bridling him or clipping him. However exasperated you become never catch hold of his ear, and certainly don't pull it. If he is nervous about his head it is probable that he was made so by somebody twitching his ear and his fear will only be confirmed by receiving the same treatment again. Never bang the body brush on the horse and be particularly careful not to do so anywhere near his loins, where there is risk of damaging the kidneys.

The legs, if muddy, can be cleaned with the dandy brush, but again be careful not to knock the horse with the edge of the brush lest he retaliate by kicking. Now brush out the mane and tail and then "lay" them with a damp water brush. Clean the dock, eyes and nostrils using both your sponges.

A final polish is attained by wiping the horse over with a damp rubber or chamois leather.

Brushes will require cleaning from time to time and the best way is to place the bristles in a shallow dish, containing a strong solution of soda, overnight. When the grease has been removed wash the bristles only in water and then place the brushes (just the bristle part) in a dish containing salt and water, which will harden them again.

A good brush should have the wooden part made in two pieces which allows the bristles to be wired into the base of the brush. Solid back brushes have the bristles plugged into the base and are cheaper to buy, but lose bristles at an uneconomical rate. No brush lasts for ever, but a good one has three or four times the life of a cheap one.

The feet are usually picked out before one actually commences cleaning the body and the dirt removed can be caught in a skip. To pick up the foreleg, stand alongside the horse facing the tail, and pass your hand down the back of the leg. Nine horses out of ten will oblige by picking up the foot. Hold it firmly in the hand and clean it out using the hoofpick from heel to toe with the point (a blunt one) pointing away from you. The tenth horse may not be so obliging and may even put all his weight on the foot you wish to pick up. If he does not respond to a shove against his shoulder, aimed at getting him to shift his weight to the other side, a pinch on the back of the leg, above the joint, may persuade him to remember his manners, and if this fails a sharp tap behind the knee or a push with the elbow will secure his co-operation.

To pick up the hind leg, face the rear again and run the hand down the quarters to the hock and from thence down the inside front of the cannon bone. As the foot is raised move the joint a little to the rear and let the hand slide round the hoof. Don't ever either pull the leg too far to the rear, to the front or sideways; it is uncomfortable for the horse and makes it difficult for him to keep his balance. Where the feet are particularly dirty they can be washed out either with an old brush or the corner of the water brush.

Washing the hooves should not be overdone as it tends to remove the natural oil secreted from the coronary band. There is, however, no harm

Picking up a hindleg whilst displaying a proper caution.

in helping nature and appearance by regularly oiling the feet with hoof oil (obtainable from saddlers). [For proper use of hoof oil to retain moisture in the foot etc., see "Foot and Shoeing".] Don't, however, use boot polish on the feet, as this only seals the foot and prevents the absorption of oil. After washing a foot out make very certain that the heels are well dried, if they are left wet there is a risk of chapped heels which will cause the horse to go lame.

Geldings will require to have their sheaths washed out periodically and this is best done wearing a domestic rubber glove and using a thin sponge dipped in warm water. Failure to carry out this cleansing of the sheath may result in discomfort for the animal and an accumulation of a scaly substance which forms on the penis may prevent him drawing properly when passing water. When this occurs the urine will be passed directly on to the belly, where it can cause a painful skin condition.

Grooming is best carried out *after* morning exercise when the horse is warm and the skin pores are open, but wisping (strapping) and massage are better left to the later afternoon or even early evening.

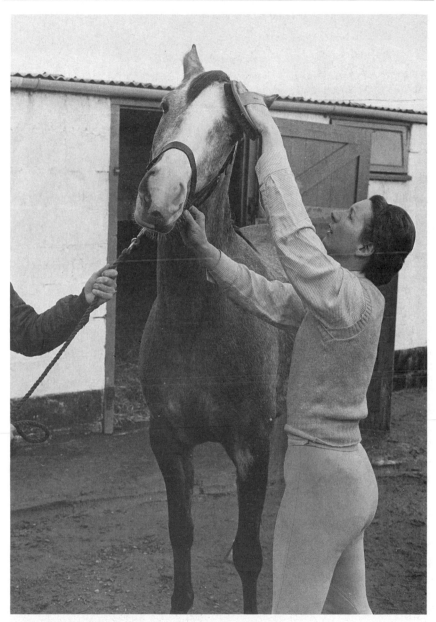

Using a soft body brush to clean the head.

The reason for this is that wisping encourages circulation which will naturally slow down during the night hours.

The purpose of wisping is to (a) develop and harden muscles, and (b) stimulate the skin and circulation. It will also produce a shine or bloom

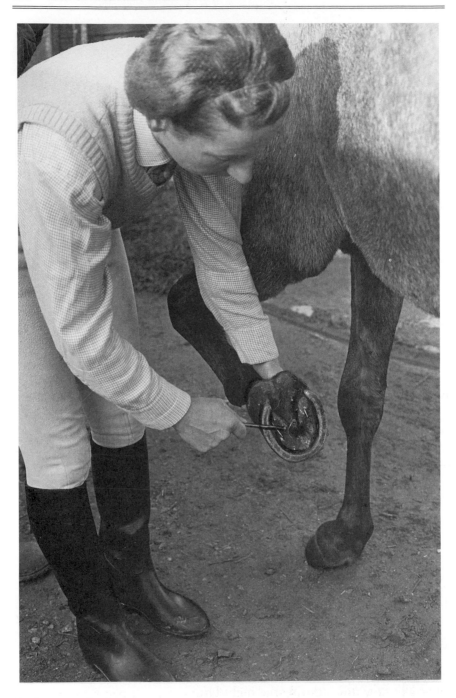

Picking out the foot.

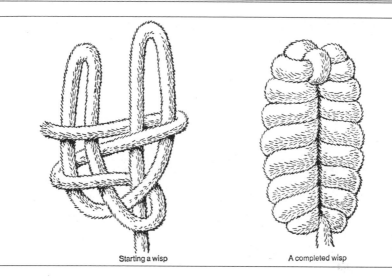

Starting a wisp   A completed wisp

A hay wisp.

on the coat which is caused by releasing the oil from the glands which surround each hair.

A wisp is made from a tightly woven rope of hay, about eight feet long. To make one, open a hay bale and shake it out somewhat, then start twisting a rope, putting your foot on the bulk of the hay. Now make two loops at one end and twist the rope between them. Secure the end of the rope by passing it through each loop and then tuck it in firmly. With a little practise the result should look something like the illustration.

If you find this beyond your accomplishment a chamois leather stitched firmly to make a small bag, and then stuffed with hay until it is firm, is just as satisfactory. Saddlers will also supply a rather more sophisticated article in the form of a hay stuffed leather pad.

To use the wisp, first damp it and then bring it down energetically on to the horse following the lay of the coat. Use it on the quarters, shoulders and neck, but not on the loins, head, belly and legs. Most horses enjoy wisping and when a rhythm has been achieved the muscles will visibly contract and decontract in time to the strokes of the wisp.

Massage Technique

Although I use the wisp a great deal I also carry out a further massage technique with the forearms. This is hard work and one must literally roll up the sleeves, but the result is worthwhile. I am also a believer in a twice weekly muscle rubbing and stretching session. (Today, whilst I remain a "believer" it is the young lady who helps with the horses who "uses the wisp a great deal". *Author's note.*)

I begin by rubbing the body all over with a closed hand, using a small circular motion and quite a lot of pressure. The pressure is increased in that area of the circle nearest to the heart and decreased on the area furthest away from it.

As one becomes more experienced it becomes easier to discover a tightening of the muscles in various places and these areas can then be given more attention until they become relaxed.

The second stage concerns the legs below the knees and hocks, and I begin by alternately squeezing and releasing the bulbs of the heels. From here I work upwards to the coronary band and the pastern, employing stiffened fingers and quite a lot of pressure. The hands are then locked round the leg and worked again *upwards* with the heels of the hands making a small circular motion. This is carried out on all four legs up to the knee in front and the hock behind, and from front and rear. Usually it is combined with an application of Radiol spirit lotion.

To complete this stage each leg is stretched forwards and backwards. Initially the horse may resent this and the limit of the movement will be small. Under no circumstances should the leg be forced to move further than is comfortable, otherwise there is a danger of pulling the muscles. In time, however, the horse will relax and will find it quite easy to stretch his legs in this way.

If he finds continued difficulty in the exercise, however, it is possible that the trouble lies not in the leg itself but in the spine, and one should desist accordingly until the source has been treated.

In the 1990s the extent to which the spine and back muscles can be damaged is more readily appreciated than it was 20 years ago. A great many humans suffer back pains at some time in their lives and it has now, I think, been established that horses experience similar discomfort.

Back pain in the horse is without doubt the source of all kinds of resistances and the cause of faults in the overall carriage.

Much of the trouble begins early in the horse's life, possibly because of carrying weight before the structure is sufficiently developed. It can become confirmed by the use of badly-fitting saddlery which compels the rider to sit out of balance with the movement or, even more frequently one imagines, by plain bad horsemanship, and Heaven knows there is plenty of that.

A very significant factor leading to back problems is the increase in competitive riding and the amount of jumping which is involved. When one considers the concussion sustained through the skeletal frame, and

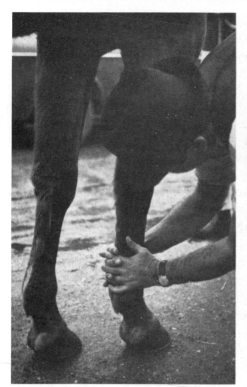
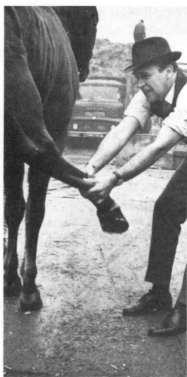

Massage technique: (above left) *the locked finger position used for leg rubbing;* (above right) *leg stretching;* (below) *manipulating the withers.*

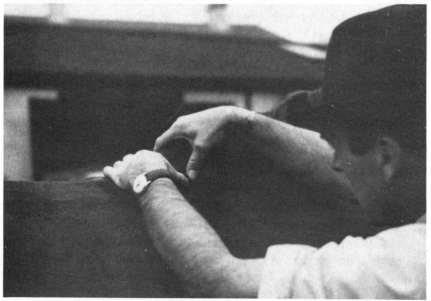

particularly its spinal complex, by a horse landing over drop fences it is not surprising that back injuries are so prevalent.

Examination of the back *by an experienced operator* is now included as part of my regular stable routines in the same way as worming and twice yearly teeth examinations. Should a horse be unfortunate enough to have a fall – and most of them do at some time or another – I always have his back checked over in case it has been damaged.

I would not attempt to treat a back condition nor would I advise anyone other than a properly experienced person to do so, but for many years my massage and manipulative routine has included the neck, back muscles and spine.

I start at the top of the neck, moving down to the withers, kneading the crest with my fingers and rolling it from side to side. I then use the thumbs and the heels of the hand along the spine from the withers to the croup. Quite quickly the horse begins to move under the pressure and to respond to the movements to a noticeable extent. Obviously one must exercise tact and work carefully but it is surprising how frequently one discovers tension and tenderness. Having that knowledge one can then act accordingly so far as exercise goes, or, if the condition persists, call in the expert.

A Programme of Conditioning

Where the horse-owner has carried out the conditioning programme himself he should be as physically fit as his horse and this is an important point. It is no good having a fit horse and an unfit rider, and there is no more distressing a sight than to see a fat, perspiring man trying to cope with a well-conditioned horse. Riding is a partnership between the two and if it is to be successful, or enjoyable to both parties, they must be in equal physical condition.

The form a programme of conditioning takes is dependent upon so many factors, the initial condition of the horse, the purpose, the time available and most importantly, the needs of the individual, that it would be impossible to give a specimen programme which treated the subject anything but generally.

The following programme is, therefore, given only as the roughest guide and to show how the exercise and feed intake should be gradually increased until the horse is in peak condition.

For the purpose of this example we will assume that a 16 hh horse is brought up ten weeks before the commencement of hunting and has been in very light work through the summer.

Week	Feed Intake	Exercise	Grooming
1 & 2	4 lb oats ⎫ 2 lb nuts ⎬ 3 feeds 2 lb bran ⎭ per day 1 lb carrots 18 lb hay 1 Bran Mash per week	1 hour (20 mins lunge, 40 mins slow hacking – walk/trot)	Cleaning 45 mins. Wisping or massage 45 mins. Harden back with surgical spirit
3 & 4	5 lb oats ⎫ 2 lb nuts ⎬ 3 feeds 2 lb bran ⎭ per day 1 lb carrots 17 lb hay 1 Bran Mash per week	1½ hours (15 mins lunge, 45 mins slow hacking, 30 mins school work on the flat)	Cleaning 45 mins. Wisping or massage 45 mins. Harden back with surgical spirit
5	6 lb oats ⎫ 3 lb nuts ⎬ 3 feeds 2 lb bran ⎭ per day 1 lb carrots 15 lb hay 1 Bran Mash per week	1½ hours (15 mins lunge, 45 mins slow hacking, 30 mins school work on the flat)	Cleaning 45 mins. Wisping or massage 45 mins. Harden back with surgical spirit
6	7 lb oats ⎫ 3 lb nuts ⎬ 4 feeds 2 lb bran ⎭ per day 1 lb carrots 14 lb hay 1 Bran Mash per week	1½ hours (30 mins school work incl. cavalletti, 1 hour hacking at approx. 6–7 mph. Include about 3-½ miles canters per week)	Cleaning 45 mins. Wisping or massage 45 mins. Harden back with surgical spirit
7 & 8	8 lb oats ⎫ 3 lb nuts ⎬ 4 feeds 2 lb bran ⎭ per day 1 lb carrots 13 lb hay 1 Bran Mash per week	2 hours (20 mins schooling including a little jumping 1 hr 40 min hacking at approx. 7–8 mph including a steady canter. One 6-furlong gallop per week)	Cleaning 45 mins. Wisping or massage 45 mins. Harden back with surgical spirit
9 & 10	10 lb oats ⎫ 3 lb nuts ⎬ 4 feeds 2 lb bran ⎭ per day 1 lb carrots 11 lb hay 1 Bran Mash per week	As above; if possible increase to 2½ hours	Cleaning 45 mins. Wisping or massage 45 mins. Harden back with surgical spirit

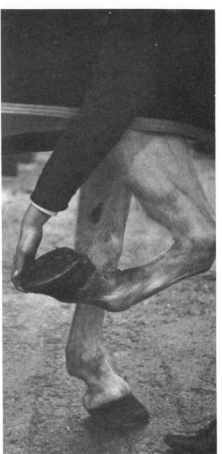

The correct way to pick up a foreleg.

Use of the clippers.

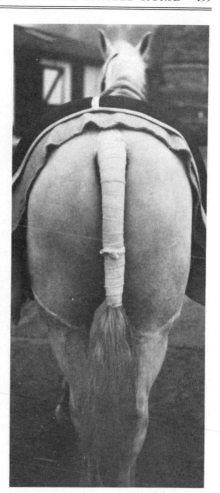

A correctly applied tail bandage.

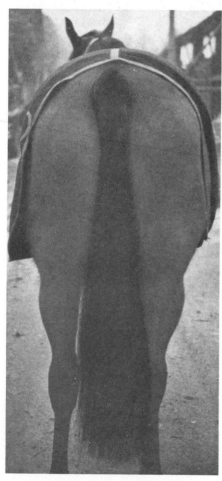

A pulled tail.

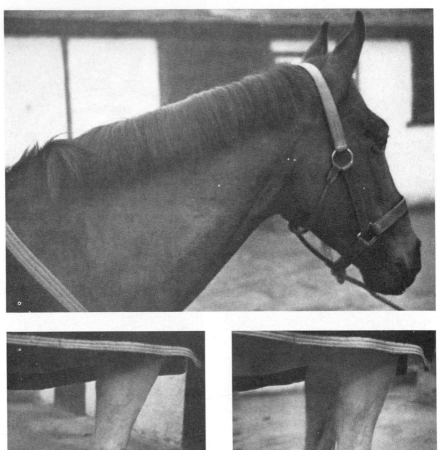

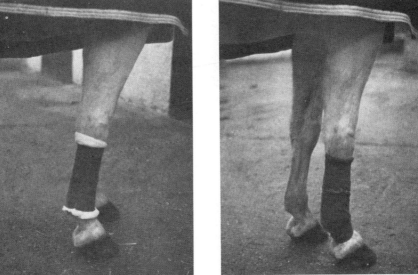

(Above) *a pulled mane;* (left) *an exercise bandage;* (right) *a stable bandage, used to keep the legs warm.*

Part of the hay ration may be given as chaff. Additives such as molasses or Molassine meal, or other proprietary foods can be given as required and variety introduced as necessary. Oats are given bruised and all feeds are dampened.

Throughout the conditioning programme and even when the horse is in regular work it is advisable to let him run out in a rug for an hour or two each day so that he has the opportunity to unwind and at the same time get a nibble of grass. Nothing is more beneficial to the horse's physical well-being and mental equanimity than this daily period at liberty. If he rolls in a patch of sticky mud that is of no consequence. It means more work for the owner but it is a wonderful relaxant for the horse.

Clipping and Trimming

In winter nature provides the horse with a thick winter coat and this, combined with the grease which accumulates on the skin, protects him from cold, wind and rain very effectively. The thick coat is no hindrance to the horse in a natural state, for he does not expend energy to an extent that would make him sweat.

By stabling him, feeding him on energy foods and working him at very much faster paces than nature ever intended we are imposing an unnatural or artificial environment, and, in consequence, we must resort to unnatural methods if the horse is to function properly.

For the stabled horse the winter coat is a positive drawback and if it is not removed the horse will lose condition through heavy sweating during work.

The coat is, therefore, removed by clipping and the operation not only permits the horse to work faster without distress, but makes it easier for horse-keeper to keep him clean. In addition, of course, a clipped horse is dried very much more quickly than one with a coat like a bear. Another reason for clipping is prevention of disease, which should not be applicable in the case of properly kept horses.

The winter coat begins to grow in September and needs to be "set", or established, before clipping. Most horses, but by no means all, can be clipped in early October and will then need a second clipping either just before or after Christmas. This, at any rate, is usually the case with fine-coated Thoroughbreds, but a very common horse may need clipping more frequently.

The type of clip employed depends very much on the type of horse, the work he does and under what conditions. At least it should do, but more often than not it depends upon the ideas the owner has upon the subject. There are two principal clips and two subsidiary ones, with variations between them, all arising from the artistic eye or the inept hand of the machine operator.

The *full* clip involves removing the entire coat. The *hunter* clip leaves a saddle patch on the back, which may vary from a full patch to a three-inch wide strip on either side of the backbone in the saddle area. In addition all four legs are left unclipped. The height to which the unclipped hair is left is roughly governed by measuring, on the hind leg, one stretched hand's breadth from the hock upwards to determine the line at the rear, and one similarly stretched hand from the stifle downwards to obtain a leading edge, which will be some four or five inches higher than the line at the back. On the forelegs the line is obtained by taking one outstretched hand from the elbow down and two from the knee upwards.

The lover of the compromise may, if he wishes, clip his horse completely the first time and give only a hunter clip the second time.

The reasons for carrying out a *hunter* clip are usually given as follows: (a) the saddle patch is left on to prevent galls or scalding; (b) the legs are left unclipped as a protection against thorns, cuts, cracked heels and chills. Whether these reasons hold water is again a matter of opinion and depends very much on the sort of coat one is dealing with.

A fine-skinned horse will, I believe, benefit by having his saddle patch left on, but it is a dubious advantage with a horse carrying a very thick coat. Not only will it encourage excessive sweating under the saddle, often the cause of saddle sores, but it is very difficult indeed to get dry.

As far as the legs go it is more difficult to find thorns and cuts in a mass of hair than without it, and if you miss them they may turn septic. Hairy legs are also not easily dried and wet heels quickly become cracked heels.

Again it depends on the horse. The fine-coated Thoroughbred will probably do better with his legs unclipped and the hairy commoner may benefit from having them clipped out.

Having said this much I will descend from the fence and say that on Thoroughbred horses I use the hunter clip and on anything else I still employ it, only I clip the legs out with the coarser leg blades which do not cut nearly so close as those used on the body.

There is then the *blanket* clip where a patch approximating to the area covered by a galloping sheet is left as well as the legs. It is suitable for Thoroughbreds. Lastly there is the *trace* clip in which the hair is clipped from the belly and flanks and usually up the under side of the

The blanket clip and the trace clip.

neck as well. This is a useful clip for hunting ponies kept at grass and for harness horses.

I believe that horses can be clipped by hand-operated clippers and, indeed, long ago when the practice first commenced they were clipped with scissors and even shaved with a razor. Today, however, most of us will use an electrically-operated machine, of which there are two types. There is a heavy duty machine with a powerful engine, and a smaller hand machine in which the engine lies within the compass of one's hand. The former is suspended from the ceiling and the clipping head is driven by means of a flexible shaft. For stables with more than three or four horses it is undoubtedly the best tool for the job, but otherwise the hand machine is perfectly satisfactory and efficient. Satisfactory and efficient, that is, when properly used and maintained.

The success of the clipping operation depends to a very large degree on the efficiency of the machine and it is well worthwhile reading the manufacturer's instructions and carrying them out.

In 90 per cent of the cases where the machine breaks down, or will not cut, the fault lies with the operator and not the machine. The usual cause is for the tension nut to be screwed down too tightly, which overstrains and overheats the very small engine. During use the machine will get warm and you will have to stop to clean the air vents and give it time to cool. While it is running frequent application to the blades of a thin machine oil assists efficient working.

We will presume, however, that you have your machine in good order with sharp blades (if it is yours I advise you never to lend it, even to your best friend; if you have managed to borrow one you must persuade the lender that I am being unduly fussy).

You will then have two prime requirements. First, a well-lit box (daylight is always preferable), and secondly a clean horse who is cool and absolutely dry. It will be no good clipping after exercise.

A dirty coat will be more difficult to cut and causes the machine to work a great deal harder. There is, in fact, no reason why the horse should not be shampooed with an animal shampoo some few days before you intend to clip. If the weather is not too cold, the horse rinsed well and dried thoroughly he will come to no harm, whatever the diehards say, and it will make the job of clipping very much easier.

Let the horse become accustomed to the noise of the machine before starting to clip. The object is to do the job as quickly as possible, but without upsetting the horse. A horse that is frightened may begin to sweat and then no clipper will cut. When he evinces no apprehension at the noise, turn the machine off, and spend ten minutes running it over his body. Begin clipping on the shoulder, a place that is not unduly sensitive, keeping the blades flat and working against the lay of the coat. Do not *push* the machine or you will be putting additional strain on the engine. The operator's job is to guide the machine, not to do its work.

If you are leaving the saddle patch and the legs unclipped, put the saddle on and trace the outline with a piece of chalk and mark the leg lines in a similar way. The edges can either be trimmed with the clipper or with the scissors.

Do not clip either the mane or tail. If you do they will have the appearance of a shaving brush for months. When you reach the quarters make a V-shape above the dock and not an abrupt, straight line across it.

Clipping the belly and between the hindlegs can be a ticklish business for both operator and horse. It is possible to clip a quiet horse single-handed, but it is usually helpful to have an assistant. When these difficult areas are reached he or she can then pick up a forefoot, holding it by the toe with the tip of the fingers, so that the horse cannot lean his weight upon the raised leg or use it as a prop. In theory the horse should then be unable to move any of the other three feet from the ground. In practise this happy state is not always so easily achieved, but, generally, the method will allow the operator to clip the sensitive parts with comparative ease and safety.

As an additional precaution, when cleaning out between the hindlegs, it is as well for the operator to hold the tail about two-thirds of the way down. It is then possible for him to pull the horse on to the leg nearest to him which will frustrate any attempt to kick.

I have already mentioned the inadvisability of cutting into the mane and tail and if there is any danger of this, as there might be with a fidgety horse, these areas are best done with a small hand clipper. Some people clip the mane at the withers and cut a piece out, just behind the ears, for the bridle. This is an unnecessary practice with a properly pulled mane and once done it has to be clipped at least once a week to keep the mane looking tidy.

Where there are wrinkles in the skin, under the elbows, for example, the skin must be stretched flat and pulled with the hand. It is never very sensible to pick up the skin and cut towards the fingers.

The parts between the forelegs are best dealt with by having the assistant pick up a foreleg and stretch it forwards. The wrinkles that remain are then smoothed as described.

If the legs are left unclipped one is usually advised to trim the heels and the heavy hair on the fetlocks and the back of the tendons with scissors and a comb. This requires some skill and both scissors and comb must work upwards against the hair.

On common horses with a preponderance of coarse hair on the legs many people do, however, trim with the clippers; again, of course, moving upwards. This practice is frequently condemned although the only valid argument against it is that one must be constantly at it throughout the season and the legs do look a little bristly. The best solution to the problem of the hairy-heeled brigade is, in my opinion, to use the clippers with the coarse leg blades, the appearance then is much the same as that obtained with scissors and comb.

Somewhat understandably the clipping of the head is the thing to which many horses object. It should, therefore, be left until last or, possibly, carried out on the preceding day when time is not of the essence.

The most common form of restraint used to persuade the horse to keep his head still whilst the operation is carried out is the twitch. In its simplest form this is a piece of wood about a foot long with a hole bored through one end. Through this hole is threaded a loop of cord, or binder twine, and the loop is then slipped round the upper lip and the wooden shaft twisted until the string is tight. The shaft is then either held by the operator or slipped back under the halter. Alternatively, and quite indefensibly, the twitch is applied to the ear. In both cases the idea is to distract the horse's attention from the work in hand by the use of a stronger counter-irritant.

There may be occasions when this barbaric practice is necessary, but to apply a twitch is always a confession of failure. I am wholeheartedly against its use. Few of us would think of applying a similar restraint on a child who was frightened of the barber's chair and we should not think of doing so with a horse.

It is possible that by using the twitch our purpose will be achieved, but the horse will not forget and each successive clipping will be rendered more difficult and require increasingly severe measures to accomplish satisfactorily. More importantly the basis of trust and respect which should exist between horse and trainer, and which to a large degree is built up in the stable, is broken and will not easily be re-formed. Horses that have been twitched are frequently head-shy thereafter. This is particularly the case if the twitch has been applied to the ear. Patience, quiet handling and the establishment of trust between man and horse are the only satisfactory way in the long run. (I have not changed my opinion very much over the years. I accept the veterinary view that twitching releases substances that act rather like morphine and that the horse may even enjoy being twitched, but in my experience few horses evince much enthusiasm for a repeat performance. However, I say, categorically, that I *would* use a twitch if I considered that by doing so I would reduce the risk of injury to either horse or operator. *Author's note.*)

The ears themselves should not be cleaned out inside, as this will remove the natural protection against wind and rain. It is sufficient to run the clippers along the edges, holding them together so that the hair is removed in one sweep.

Once the clipping has got as far as the back a rug should be thrown on to keep the horse warm. If he is cold he is unlikely to keep still.

However clean the horse seemed to be before clipping commenced, the skin surface, after the first clipping, will be covered with grease and dirt. The easiest way to remove this is to make the horse sweat, which can be done by piling on all the available clothing and giving him a little sharp exercise.

There is no need to gallop him into a muck sweat, give him 20 minutes or so and then bring him home; he will begin to sweat when the clothing is removed. Now take a damp wisp and strap him thoroughly. The wisp, if kept constantly damp, will remove all the surplus grease.

Trimming Manes and Tails

For the sake of appearance manes and tails are thinned by pulling out the hair, which if carefully done does not hurt the horse.

The Arabian horse, who has a mane and tail of very fine hairs, is never trimmed in this way and very often a Thoroughbred horse is left with a full, unpulled tail.

The secret of pulling lies in never doing too much at once, a fortnight is not too long to allow, and always pulling the hairs from underneath and not from the top.

The tail should be kept well brushed out and it is as well to wash it thoroughly before you start tidying it up. In this respect avoid the "whiter than white" detergents and use a medicated horse shampoo. The latter will remove scurf and dirt most effectively, whilst the former can set up irritations of the tender skin on the dock.

Remove the hairs one by one, never pulling too many at a time or you will make the tail sore and the animal may well object unpleasantly. Each day damp the tail with the water brush and put on a tail bandage to encourage it to lie flat.

Tail bandages are made either from stockinette, which is the least satisfactory as they slip, or in a three-inch cotton flex cloth which stays in place very well. Don't leave bandages on for more than an hour or so and certainly not overnight, otherwise the continued pressure kills the hair. It is also neither necessary nor advisable to wet the bandage. If you do it contracts as it dries and becomes too tight.

The tail can either be left as a switch or it can be "banged". A "banged" tail is one that is cut off straight at the bottom and a switch one that is pulled down its entire length and allowed to end in a natural point. Most switch tails resemble the caudal appendage of a rat.

The "banged" tail, which you will gather is my preference, is pulled at the top only and is full at the bottom. To "bang" the tail first get someone to lift it up so that it assumes the position it will occupy in movement. Now calculate a hand's breadth below the point of the hock and with a large pair of scissors, the paper-hanging variety are the best, cut the hair off in a straight line, but holding the scissors inclined slightly upwards from rear to front. The tail when held out will then finish in a straight line. If you neglect to hold the tail up you will end by cutting it too short.

Manes are thinned by again pulling out the surplus hair from the under-side. The way to do this is by laying the mane over to the opposite side (i.e. if the mane normally lies on the off-side brush it over to the near-side) and then pulling the hairs with the aid of the small mane comb. Take about half-a-dozen in the comb, push the comb up to the roots, twist and pull. If too many are pulled at a time, or the hair is broken, instead of coming out at the roots, it will grow in upright spikes and will take months before it lies down properly.

When thinned the length of the mane should be about five inches and anything over this length is best removed with a sharp penknife rather than a pair of scissors.

Manes can, of course, be removed altogether and are then termed "hogged". On a thick-necked, cresty sort of horse this does improve the appearance and it saves the labour involved in plaiting the mane for special occasions. To keep it tidy, however, it wants doing once a week unless the animal is to bear a distinct resemblance to his erect-maned, pre-historic ancestors.

The mane is hogged by first cutting off the hair with scissors as closely as possible. The clippers are then run up each side, from the withers to the poll and then a third cut is made up the centre. The whiskers round a horse's muzzle are, or should be, left untrimmed, they perform a function rather like a radar beam by assisting the horse to gauge the distance of objects from his mouth.

Plaiting

For some reason horsemen feel it incumbent upon them to plait their horse's manes on special occasions. It is a time-consuming operation, but if properly done looks smart and neat.

Most books and manuals lay down the specific number of plaits which is acceptable. With respect, this is nonsense. The number of plaits will depend upon the length of the horse's neck and to some degree what pleases the owner's eye. A long neck looks better with fewer plaits than a short one, a weak neck is improved by plaiting loosely to give a false line, a strong neck can have the plaits made tightly. On a well-proportioned neck I use six plaits and one more on the forelock, on a short one perhaps eight plaits plus one for the forelock.

There are two ways of plaiting manes, first by sewing up the plaits with a needle and thread (a method beloved by the diehards, who often leave someone else to do the plaiting) and secondly with rubber bands. Of the two I must admit the former looks neater, but confess to often using the latter method.

To plait the mane, sewing the plaits, a large-eyed needle is necessary and a reel of linen thread the same colour as the mane. First damp the mane, then divide it into the number of plaits required. Make the first plait and just after half-way down it plait in a 10-inch length of thread doubled over.

When you have completed the plait you will be left with two loose ends of thread, loop the ends round the plait and pull tight. Thread both ends through the needle, double the plait under, and bring the needle through it as close to the crest as possible, pull the thread ends through, remove the needle and tie the plait firmly, cutting off the spare thread ends.

Rubber bands are easier. The band is looped round the bottom, the plait turned under and the same band looped round the whole thing.

Tails, if left untrimmed, can also be plaited at the top, and many are the individual idiosyncrasies manifested in design and execution.

The only way to learn how to do this is to watch an experienced artist at work. As I have never mastered the art myself my instructions are hardly likely to prove of any value.

One thing, however, I do know, is that a tail plaited badly looks frightful and that one plaited too tight is uncomfortable. In the latter instance a horse will display his discomfort by either clamping his tail between his buttocks or by carrying it bent to one side or the other.

Stable Clothing

Before the stabled horse is clipped he should be provided with a light sheet, a linen one is the most suitable, which will keep dust out of the coat and encourage it to lie properly.

After the coat is removed it will be necessary to provide heavier rugs for warmth. The basic requirement will be a canvas or jute top rug, fully lined with blanketing, an under-rug of wool or a large horse blanket, which is usually striped and weighs 8 lb, and, ideally, one of the open-mesh sweat rugs made of cotton. The complement of clothing will be completed by the addition of a set of wool bandages, five inches wide, and a cotton tail bandage.

The mesh sheet is probably the greatest advance ever made in horse-clothing. It acts on the principle of trapping pockets of insulating air between the body and an outer rug, thus acting as an insulator which keeps the body warm in cold weather and cool under the opposite conditions. By the same principle it discourages "breaking-out"; that is the profuse sweating indulged in by some horses after exercise or hard work, or sweating induced by nervousness when travelling.

In reasonably clement weather a horse who is properly and sufficiently fed will be kept warm enough with a mesh rug and a canvas top rug. In very cold weather a blanket can be added and laid between the two.

The great difficulty with stable clothing is to ensure that it is kept in place during the night. The most common method is by using a body roller, made of either webbing or leather, fastened round the barrel of the horse.

Rollers can, however, cause sore backs if not properly maintained, and the reason is usually to be found in the absence of stuffing in the pads on either side of the spine. Rollers should be fitted as carefully as saddles and there should be no area of the pads' surface bearing directly on the backbone.

If they are fastened too tightly, and they usually are, it causes the horse discomfort when he lies down and ends up with the securing straps being burst. The necessity, and the temptation, of girthing too tightly can be overcome by using a breast strap attached to the forward edges of the roller which will then prevent the movement of the latter to the rear.

The best type of roller is that where the two pads are joined by an iron hoop and where each is hinged so that they will conform to any shape of back.

Rollers like these, and also ones with fixed pads separated by an iron hoop, are known as *anti-cast* rollers and are supposed to stop a horse rolling right over and getting into a position where he cannot rise of his own accord.

They will prevent a horse rolling over, although the hoop is likely to get somewhat bent in the process, but their most important advantage lies in their allowing freedom to the backbone.

The method I use is to have the top rug fitted with two web surcingles which are sewn to the canvas. The forward one is padded on either side of the spine for some 18 inches and a loop of web left over the top of the backbone.

No pressure is, therefore, sustained by the spine and this surcingle, combined with the second one, which is set some 15 inches to the rear and fastened quite loosely, keeps the rugs in place admirably. Providing the rear surcingle does not hang down in festoons there is no danger of the horse catching his foot in it. Even more satisfactory are rugs fitted with crossed surcingles on the excellent American pattern.

Most saddlers (*some* saddlers) make well-shaped horse rugs allowing for the protuberance of the withers and the dip in the line of the back, as well as being generous in the cut of the neck hole. Unfortunately no trade is more bedevilled with cheap-jacks selling inferior articles at what appear to be attractive prices, and many of the products of these people are so skimped and badly cut as to be useless.

To fit properly a rug must be long enough, almost up to the dock, deep enough, well down the flanks, and must not be tight round the neck and shoulders when fastened at the breast. In fact, for a proper fitting there should be a dart or pleat at the shoulder.

As a rough guide the following sizes are appropriate:

Over 16 hh	6 ft–6 ft 3 in (Heavyweights possibly 6 ft 6 in)
15.2 hh–16 hh	5 ft 9 in–6 ft
15 hh–15.2 hh	5 ft 6 in–5 ft 9 in
14.2 hh–15 hh	5 ft 3 in–5 ft 6 in
13.2 hh–14.2 hh	5 ft–5 ft 3 in and proportionately thereafter.

For high days and holidays, including taking your friends round the stables on Sunday mornings, one may indulge oneself and one's horse in a day rug. This is a wool rug, of almost any colour you like, which can be further embellished by the addition of the owner's initials and replaces the canvas top rug on these occasions.

The use of wool bandages, used primarily to keep the extremities warm after exertion, is dealt with elsewhere in this section.

(No area of the horse equipment market has expanded like that of the horse-clothing manufacturer and some very significant advances have been made in insulating materials and so on. I welcome, particularly, the use of cross-over surcingles as being the best way to keep a rug in place without the risk of chafing. The fit of rugs is also much improved, many of them having accommodating darts and pleats at the point of the shoulder and being shaped well down at the dock. The choice, indeed, is almost confusingly wide. The only limiting factor for most of us, I suppose, is the price. *Author's note.*)

Care of the Stabled Horse After Exercise

A horse tired after strenuous work, such as a day's hunting, an endurance ride or the speed and endurance phase of a three-day-event, requires special, immediate and swift attention. It is in this state that the horse can most easily suffer from slap-happy management. The rule is always to see to your horse's needs first and your own afterwards.

If the horse is brought in dry and cool, remove his bridle and saddle and offer him a warm drink, if he likes a bottle of stout in it, so much the better. If at this stage he wants to roll allow him to do so. Sponge the sweat marks from the saddle patch and round the girth and dry thoroughly. Put his rug on and make him comfortable by sponging his head and throat and again drying them. Strip his ears, that is hand rub them, to get the circulation going. Sponge between the hindlegs, under the tail and round the sheath and do the same round the elbows, taking good care to dry the horse thoroughly.

Now inspect the legs for injuries and attend to them at once, including even the smallest scratch. If the mud is dry brush it off smartly, have a look at the feet and then give a quick all-round, upward (toward the heart) hand rubbing with Radiol spirit lotion. Check the heels are dry and bandage the legs. If the circulation is stimulated and the extremities then kept warm the temperature will not drop.

Lastly, groom the horse briskly with the body brush and, if necessary, hand rub the mud off the belly, and put his clothing on. He can then be given his feed, a soft bran or linseed mash, which will not strain his tired digestive system, and left alone for an hour or so.

When you have done this go back to the horse and check that he has (a) eaten up and (b) has not started to sweat again – if he has you must set about drying him. Feel his ears to see if they are warm and if they are not hand rub them until they are. He can now have a haynet strung up and you can have your dinner, after which you must inspect him again.

If the horse is brought in hot, as he may be after a competitive event, he can be sponged down to remove the sweat and must then be dried off by hand and by walking about. He should have a light sheet put over him to prevent his catching a chill. Very often, particularly after racing, a mesh rug is thrown over the horse, which in itself has little value. The mesh sheet is only effective when it has an outer covering, and only under these conditions can its insulating properties be brought into play.

Whether horses, or parts of them, should be washed is a point upon which the experts differ, often violently. I have no objection, *provided the horse is properly dried.*

If mud is washed off the legs after hunting (usually it can be brushed off if it is dry) it is, of course, very important to dry the legs, and particularly the heels, very thoroughly. To this end a little bran packed into the heel, after it has been dried, and covered by leg bandages is an effective drying agent and will prevent cracked heels.

It must be realised that when the body is in a weakened physical condition its functions are weakened correspondingly. It is of paramount importance, therefore, that the rate of circulation and the body temperature are maintained and that the digestive apparatus is not overburdened by unwise feeding.

Handling the Horse in the Stable

I am increasingly convinced that the foundation of a satisfactory partnership between horse and rider can more easily be laid by having a proper relationship in the stable than in any other way. I am not saying that it is impossible to build up a partnership in the field without the rider also acting as a groom to his horse, but I do say that a real understanding between the two is attained more quickly if a basis of trust has already been established by a contact, apart from that experienced during work.

The horse is by nature gregarious and in the herd all, with the exception of the herd stallion or the group leaders, are prepared to follow and be led without the exercise of personal initiative. When the horse is removed from his herd he does not leave his herd instinct behind, and if we are wise we recognise this and use these instincts to our advantage. In the herd the horse looked to the dominant stallion for leadership and submitted to his authority. Taken from this environment the horse seeks, if we allow him, to transfer this allegiance to his human master, who cares for him, corrects him when necessary and supplies him with food – always a preoccupation uppermost in the horse's mind.

Man is, therefore, always the dominant personality in the relationship, always the leader.

Leadership of any kind is, however, dependent upon mutual respect and trust. Discipline comes into it, certainly, but discipline is not a matter of unquestioned obedience to authority. There is a sort of discipline based on fear, but it is never a truly satisfactory or successful one. When the real question is asked, or to use a modern parlance, when the "crunch comes", it disintegrates.

Discipline is a two-way bond and a man cannot exercise it over men or animals until he first disciplines himself.

In the case of the horse there is another characteristic to be considered. He is by nature quick to panic, and he is highly nervous of unexpected sounds or swift movement; if man, therefore, is to be his leader, man must recognise not only this characteristic, but must also realise that at no time must he undermine the horse's confidence in him by being the source of fear.

All living things require a basis of security. A child needs the security of a home and parents, a fox finds security in his earth, a timid hare finds hers, without appreciating its insecurity, in her form and the domesticated horse finds his in his own familiar paddock and, even more strongly, in his stable. This is why a horse in new and strange surroundings, or even a horse in familiar ones, may display reluctance to leave his box, the centre of his security, and will always evince the greatest eagerness to get back to it when turned towards home.

In addition he is made even more secure, or he can be, by his proximity to his human leader, if, that is, he has learnt to trust him.

Where this trust exists it is possible for a horse to overcome fear, or at least to have it allayed, by relying upon his two-legged leader. Properly handled horses will respond to human leadership in almost the same way as a child. Instinctively, if frightened or hurt, a child calls for, or goes to, its mother, and much the same relationship can exist between horse and man.

As an example, my horses' paddock at our old home was adjacent to an open space fronting the church, and it was the custom of the local Salvation Army band to play in this space on certain Sunday afternoons. The horses had only recently been running out in this paddock when the band appeared one Sunday. The drum banged, the trumpets blared enthusiastically and both animals were prepared to jump the church to escape what for them could hardly be the consolation of religion. I happened to be in the paddock, inspecting the trees, which they were both partial to chewing, and called to them. Almost at once they galloped over and stood by me. I patted them and spoke to them until they lost the wild eye that betokens extreme alarm, and finally they walked back to the fence with me. They were then separated from the band by a matter of only a few yards and spent the rest of the afternoon happily listening to the proceedings. They became the band's most regular and attentive admirers. By coming to me when they were frightened they were showing the trust they had formed for their "leader".

If we recognise this need for leadership and for security in the horse it will influence our handling of him in the stable. Nothing we do will disturb his sense of security, so blows, raised voices, sudden movements have no place within the four walls of his box. This is not sentimentality, but just sound common sense. Break the security of his box and we remove an elementary prop in his existence and at the same time we lose his trust. To a point we may continue to dominate him, but for the wrong reasons.

We should be prepared, with a nervous horse, to spend hours doing nothing more than sitting in his box with him, talking to him or just reading a book until he comes to accept us as a necessary adjunct to his surroundings. We should handle him frequently, and when we feel we have reached a certain point, we can begin to ask him to move over in response to the voice, to lift his legs in the same way and with the aid of a carrot or two one can teach him to take two or three steps backwards. This is easily done by standing in front of him holding the carrot behind his nose. As he drops his head for the titbit a slight backward push on his nose coupled with the word "back" will induce the required reaction.

Later he will learn that a touch behind the girth is a request to move his quarters away and it is not too difficult to teach him to make one or two side steps. All these little exercises, carried out in a relaxed atmosphere, are teaching him to co-operate willingly, preparing him for future work, and accustoming him to the acceptance of discipline. When he co-operates willingly in small things he will co-operate as a matter of habit when more is asked of him.

When approaching the box always speak first to warn the horse of your arrival, when in the box move quietly, but purposefully, and always make sure the horse knows where you are before walking round his quarters. Few horses will kick viciously in stables and when they do it is always the fault of some groom who has mistreated them. A horse that has had his legs banged with a brush may kick when he sees his groom with one in his hand preparing to brush the particular leg. An animal that has had its tail pulled out in handfuls may react in the same way when you handle that part of him. If you scuttle round the back of him he may be frightened into making a defensive kick, although in nine cases out of ten it is likely that he will run forward, *away* from the suspected danger rather than attacking it.

The horse's defence, unlike the dog's, never lies in attack, but always in flight. Always, whether ridden or in the stable, he will try to get away from pain, or the fear of it; very, very rarely, if ever, does he turn and retaliate.

Nevertheless, when moving round the quarters precede the movement by placing a hand on him and walk round as close to the horse as possible. If by chance he should kick you will be too close to receive much more than a bump and you will avoid the full strength of the movement. Some horses will lay back their ears when food is brought round. Disregard it and walk quietly to the manger, speaking firmly to him. The reason for his apparent bad temper is a temporary reversion to the wild state. When feeding, horses do not share their particular patch with others, but rather drive intruders off. Temporarily, you, carrying the food, become in the mind a source which may deny him his rightful share, and so he makes faces. A firm word and a resolute step may not remove the scowl from his face, but it will prevent it becoming anything more unpleasant.

The horse is probably more responsive to the human voice than to anything else. He has an acute sense of hearing and although he doesn't understand what you say he will recognise the tone in which you speak to him. This is a great weapon in the horseman's armoury and should be developed and used accordingly. Normally, the quiet, soft voice can be used; if we want a reaction, however, the tone must be firmer, not louder, and can have an executive snap to it.

The contact of the hands on the horse's body is also important, a horse relaxes under the firm, confident hand, whilst he becomes nervous and jumpy with one that is not so confident, or is rough.

Biting is not to be encouraged and should be checked. I, as I have already mentioned, administer an immediate retaliatory nip on the muzzle which works wonders. The feeding of too many titbits is a frequent cause of biting and bad temper. Horses, particularly ponies, tend to bully if the expected titbit is not forthcoming and then to bite in temper. Reserve the titbits, therefore, as rewards for work well done and as a bed-time treat.

Horses may also nip when being groomed, particularly if they are ticklish. This can be avoided, not by shouting at the animal, but by being a little more gentle in your work and keeping a hand on the neck.

As our object is to win the animal's confidence it is hardly an expression of trust or good will to tie him up when you are grooming him. Leave the horse's head free and you will find he submits to your handling it with far better grace than when under restraint. (If he persists in biting then tie him by all means, it is better to tie than to be bitten.)

Never hit a horse in his box, your voice is sufficient punishment for most misdemeanours. The man who takes a horse into the box and punishes him for a resistance committed outside (such people talk about "squaring him up") is not only a fool (the horse cannot understand why he is being beaten), but is also a coward.

When turning a horse in a box remember that you must give him as much room as you can, and when you lead him in and out, take him through the door straight, so that he cannot bang his hips.

I have said that by nature most horses are followers and are willing and even glad to co-operate, occasionally, however, one comes up against a "leader-horse", the "dominant" subject, who may not submit so easily.

Such a horse needs a skilled, extra sensitive, horseman to manage him. If he gets less than this he may be turned into a rogue and become virtually unmanageable, on the other hand with the right master he can be the horse of a lifetime.

(If there is one thing that I have learnt about horses it is that they are able to communicate with us better than we with them – if, of course, we allow them and if we are prepared to learn the art of observation. *Author's note.*)

CHAPTER 6

Managing Grassland

While for reasons of economy and feed value it is most desirable to practise good management of pasture-land, a little study of the subject will bring one to an inevitable conclusion. The more grass one has the easier it is to manage it properly, whilst the person possessed of a very small area will find management correspondingly difficult, even though the need for proper control is of more importance.

Drainage

Nevertheless, any effort at improving the quality of the feed is well worthwhile, since good pasture will feed twice as many animals, twice as well, than the same acreage of neglected land. The first consideration is drainage, which is no problem on most chalky, sandy or gravel based soils, but a very large one on clay soils. Clay sub-soils absorb only a little moisture and the topsoil quickly becomes waterlogged in wet weather; there is also practically no aeration possible in the sub-soil. Under such conditions it is impossible for plant life to thrive and no satisfactory crop will be obtained until the land is drained.

At the least this entails the existence of good, clean ditches, but in many cases pipe drainage is the only real solution, and an expensive one at that, although it pays in the long run through the results achieved.

Soil Analysis

The majority of pastures, particularly old ones, suffer from deficiencies of the essential components for abundant plant life, namely, lime, phosphates and potash. It is, however, no good embarking upon a scheme of improvement until the extent and type of deficiencies have been determined by a scientific soil analysis.

If the owner of the field has a Registered Holding number with the Ministry of Agriculture it is easy enough to arrange for an advisory officer to take a sample. Otherwise the Ministry local office will be able to advise on how an analysis can be taken. It will involve sending a sample of soil away and paying a small fee but in return you get not only the analysis but advice on the best method and type of fertiliser to be used. Apart from the important factor of soil analysis as a basis for improvement a visual examination of the pasture will provide a guide as to the line which should be followed.

Quality of Pasture

A good pasture will carry leafy grasses in great variety, as well as clovers, and there will be a noticeable absence of weeds. Moderate and poor pasture will display these attributes in correspondingly less abundant a fashion. Matted grass, thick fog, mare's tail and sorrel indicate an acid soil in need of lime. This is, also, the case where there is a preponderance of buttercups and surface moss. A phosphate deficiency is shown by the absence of clovers.

Re-seeding

Nothing much can be done with really poor pasture and it is better and cheaper by far to plough it up and re-seed it. If this method is decided upon preparation of the seed bed is a vital factor. After deep ploughing, to bury the old turf, heavy rolling should be alternated with harrowing, until a fine top tilth is acquired. After seeding the seed should be covered by a light harrow and the surface then rolled again. Manuring will be according to the soil analysis, but during harrowing 6–7 cwt per acre of basic slag and 2–3 cwt of potato or beet manure can be worked in profitably.

The seed mixture will vary according to the soil, but should, in any case, include such deep-rooting, palatable herbs as yarrow, burnet, chicory and ribwort plantain and have a clover/grasses ratio of about 30 to 70. By ploughing and re-seeding a poor pasture can be converted to a first-class sward in *one* year.

It is possible to alter the constituent growth of poor land by a process of grazing with sheep, so as to remove the matted grasses and allow soil aeration, and by constant deep harrowing and applications of lime, phosphates and potash, together with supplies of nitrogen, but the process of conversion may take anything between five to eight years and the cost of sheep fencing is very high.

Moderate grassland will be improved by resting, harrowing and manurial treatment, whilst good grass will only remain so if subjected to the same treatment.

Rotational Systems

In order to carry out cultivation and fertilising and to give pasture adequate rest periods for the making of new growth it is obvious that the available area must be divided either by permanent or electric fencing, so that animals graze one part whilst the others are being rested or treated.

How this rotational system of preparation, rest, growth and grazing periods is arranged depends on the number of animals, the quality of the grass, the acreage available and the individual circumstances.

It is, however, essential that such a rotational system is carried out if the best results, and the most economical ones, are to be obtained from the land available. An arrangement should, therefore, be made to ensure a maximum amount of grass being available throughout the growing season from spring to autumn. Ideally horses should have large acreages to graze over, but unless we are possessed of a 200-acre park this will not be possible, and the land at our disposal will have to be divided into small units, varying from say six acres at the outside to a minimum of one-, or even half-, acre strips, depending upon the acreage and the number of horses involved. Land required for spring grazing or for haymaking must be left free from the previous autumn.

Fertilising

Liming, best done in November, can then be carried out at a rate of ½ to 2 tons per acre at an interval of five years on lime deficient land. The rains will then have ample time to wash in the dressing.

Periodic dressings of a phosphate fertiliser are necessary for maximum grass production. These are applied in the autumn, at intervals of between three and five years, at a rate of 8 cwt per acre. Phosphates stimulate clover growth and being slow remain active for a long period.

Clovers, apart from being highly nutritious, attract oxygen from the air and so assist the root development and growth of the surrounding grasses.

Land which is notably deficient in potash (sandy soils are particularly affected in this respect) require occasional dressings of potash salts, which are applied at a rate of between ½ to 1 cwt per acre.

Just as important as these fertilisers, however, is the provision of humus, containing nitrogen, in the form of honest farmyard muck if it is obtainable. Autumn is again the best time for manuring the land, but land so treated must be kept for haymaking, as it will not be fit for grazing until after haymaking time in June. Horse manure is not suitable because of the likelihood of reintroducing parasitic worms. Never, on any account, use liquid manure from pigs or poultry. Neither are horse friendly and both create a variety of serious and complicated side effects in youngstock and in mature horses.

Nitrogen, in the form of nitro-chalk or sulphate of ammonia, if spread on pasture land in February (2 cwt per acre) greatly assists growth and will produce a pasture suitable for grazing considerably earlier in the spring.

Because certain grasses come into growth earlier than others it is unwise to carry out a rigid rotational plan always using the same paddock or strip for early grazing, or hay, as the case may be. Unless the plan is varied from year to year the result will be for certain grasses to disappear entirely, thus altering the balanced composition.

Harrowing

The remaining partner in grassland management is cultivation achieved by harrowing, which should be carried out when the field has been grazed thoroughly.

The object of harrowing is firstly soil aeration, achieved by opening the soil up and removing the old growths, mosses, etc., which choke it and prevent the access of air and nitrogen to the root systems. Harrowing also spreads the droppings which, if allowed to remain in heaps, soon sour the ground and encourage tufty growth which horses will not eat. Moreover, heaps of dung breed parasites and are the principal vehicle, apart from the animal itself, in the red-worm cycle. It is particularly important on small acreages to remove droppings regularly for all these reasons.

Harrowing operations should be carried out when the land is just damp, and never during or after a frost when great damage could be done. Harrowing should be drastic and carried out in both directions, the more the sward resembles a ploughed field at the finish the more effective is the operation.

Rolling

The other form of cultivation, of almost equal importance, is rolling. The winter frosts and heavy rains loosen the topsoil, creating a condition not conducive to vigorous plant growth, which needs firm ground if it is to thrive. Rolling makes the topsoil firm and supplies the necessary growth conditions.

Inter-Grazing

Whilst the treatment of pastures advocated will undoubtedly produce excellent grazing it is, unfortunately, true that the horse's eating habits are not helpful in achieving ideal swards without the assistance of other animals.

Horses are selective grazers, leaving whole patches completely untouched and grazing others entirely bare. The left-over patches soon become coarse and tufty and the only satisfactory way of achieving level grazing and preventing horse-sick pastures is by alternating bullocks with horses.

Unfortunately, the vast majority of horse-keepers do not have bullocks, and most of them will find it difficult to make an arrangement with someone who does. Be that as it may, if it is at all possible every effort should be made to inter-graze cattle with horses.

Cattle and horses appear to be complementary in their grazing habits, the one eating what the other leaves and vice versa. Each will graze over the droppings of the other, whilst refusing to do so over its own. Cattle, too, combat red-worm infestation, the worm being eliminated when taken into the body of any host other than its natural one.

Horses graze on shorter grasses (four to five inches is ideal) by biting, whereas cattle prefer longer growths, which they pull off with their tongues.

As a result a field in which horses have little grazing, will, if it has tufty high grasses in it untouched by them, provide a feeding ground for bullocks. Conversely, a field grazed by bullocks, who are unable to cope with the shorter growths so effectively, will offer adequate feed for horses, and when grazed by both, alternately, will be level.

No field should be grazed bare, whether bullocks are employed or not, otherwise there will be no covering left to retain moisture and the recovery period will be protracted. Once the field or strip has been used, the harrows should be put on to aerate the soil and spread the droppings, if these have not already been removed by hand.

For many people the problem of harrowing may appear, at first sight, insuperable. How, in fact, to obtain harrows and then, how to drag them across the fields?

A small chain harrow is not, however, very expensive and with a little searching around a second-hand one may be found for very little money.

A tractor is not, perhaps, so easily obtained or borrowed, unless one is engaged in farming, but a Land Rover, or even a Mini will pull a harrow, and if the fields are not too rough the Mini will not suffer.

A friend of mine, determined to practise good grass management, but too car-proud to risk his immaculate vehicle, has solved the problem by improvising some harness and pressing his hunter into service. Despite one or two occasions when the field was harrowed rather more swiftly than would be considered necessary, neither he nor the hunter seem to have suffered any ill-effects.

Fields that are constantly grazed short will usually produce a crop of weeds including docks, nettles, thistles, ragwort, brambles and brushwood.

The only sure method of control is by chemical spraying which responsible green-minded horse-keepers may not find acceptable, otherwise, of course, the answer is in good management on the lines suggested.

Should one resort to spraying watch out for that most pernicious and persistent of weeds, the yellow ragwort, which is a killer. Spraying when the buds are forming on the plant will kill the weed but it is advisable to pull up the shrinking stems and burn them before putting horses back into the paddock.

Othwerwise organise ragwort pulling parties, pull up the weeds and burn every single one. To allow ragwort to grow unchecked on land is an offence and should you have a neighbour who grows a goodish crop of the weed you are within your rights to insist on its immediate removal.

CHAPTER 7

The Foot and Shoeing

Inevitably no chapter devoted to the horse's foot can omit the old saying, "No foot – no 'oss". There are many horsy sayings that amount to nothing more than uninformed nonsense, but this one is clear, shining, gospel truth.

The necessity to shoe the horse with rims of iron is a direct result of domestication, the horse in its feral state having a hoof which is sufficiently hard to withstand the wear caused by the distances and the country over which he has to travel.

Working, however, under weight, at speed, and nowadays for a considerable part of the time on roads, the horn would wear too quickly, would break away and the animal would become footsore unless the foot was protected.

As a result of our interference and the shortage of qualified farriers we can land ourselves, or rather our horses, in considerable trouble. It, therefore, behoves us to know something of the construction of the foot and of the simpler principles of shoeing.

Structure of the Foot

The foot is a sensitive, vascular structure containing three bones, the "coffin" or pedal bone, the navicular bone and the lower parts of the coronet bone; together they form the foot, or pedal, joint. These bones are covered by the soft structures which produce the horn of the hoof, are separated by gristle on their bearing surfaces and the whole joint is surrounded in "joint oil" to assist its working. To these bones are also attached cartilages, ligaments, and the tendons from the muscles of the forearm.

The whole is contained in an outer protective case, consisting of the wall, a horny substance which grows down from the coronet and can be likened to our toe or finger-nails (the forefoot of the horse would seem in fact to correspond to the human finger, whilst the hock corresponds to our ankle, so that he proceeds, as it were, on finger tips in front and

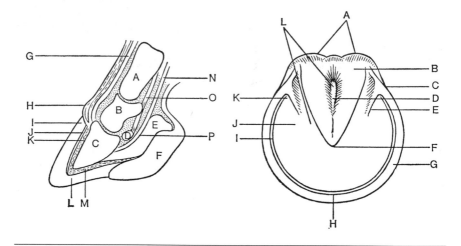

Section of the foot.

A Long or great pastern bone (os
    suffraginis)
B Short pastern bone (os coronae)
C Coffin bone (os pedis)
D Navicular bone
E Sensitive frog
F Insensitive frog
G Extensor pedis tendon
H Coronary band
I Crust or wall
J Insensitive laminae
K Sensitive laminae
L Insensitive sole
M Sensitive sole
N Flexor perforans tendon
O Long inferior sesamoid ligament
P Seat of soreness where tendon passes
    over navicular bone

Parts of the foot.

A Cushion of heel
B Frog
C Angle of heel
D Cleft of frog
E The bars
F Point of frog
G Wall of foot
H Seat of seedy toe
I White line
J Sole
K Seat of corn
L Seat of thrush

on toes behind). The wall continues round to the heels and there turns inwards to form the bars, which rigidly secure it in position.

The underside of the foot embraces the sole and the frog, the triangular, rubbery substance lying between the angles of the heels.

The outside of this protective case is insensitive, but the inside of the case, surrounding the pedal bone and running back to the heels, is fleshy and, therefore, sensitive.

If we look at the sole of a scrubbed, unshod foot we shall see what is termed the "white line" running round the inside of the hard wall. This line divides the outer, insensitive area from the commencement of the inner, sensitive one. As the shoe is fitted to the horny, insensitive wall there is, therefore, very little room for mistake on the part of the farrier when driving home his securing nails.

The horn of the wall is thickest at the toe and the heels, but in the "quarters", the sides, it becomes considerably thinner.

The white line marks the merging point of the hard outside wall with the horny, but less insensitive "leaves", which in turn merge into "fleshy leaves" of great sensitivity which connect the wall to the inside structures of the foot.

The sole of the foot is similarly constructed, having a hard, insensitive outer covering protecting an inner sensitive casing. The latter is known as the fleshy sole and is the source of the life and growth of the horny sole.

A healthy sole is slightly concave in shape to afford a better foothold and to be less prone to bruising. The horny sole, apart from helping the narrow wall of the foot to carry the weight of the horse, fulfills the purpose of protecting the fleshy sole. In order to do this effectively it needs to be as thick as possible. Nature arranges for it to be continually growing and when it is almost three-quarters of an inch thick the old growth shells off from the foot to make way for new horn. This process causes the sole to look ragged and tempts the unknowledgeable horse-shoer to pare it off. This should not be done, otherwise the sole will be weakened irreparably.

The frog is a wedge-shaped piece of rubbery horn, growing from and protecting the fleshy, sensitive frog above it. Its purpose is to assist in bearing the animal's weight and to form a "pluperfect *prestissimo*" shock absorber and anti-slip device.

The construction of the foot, therefore, is one that places the burden of the horse's weight upon the outer edge of the wall and the bearing surface to which the shoe is fitted. These are assisted in their task by the sole and the frog.

The sole supports the weight through its naturally flat outer edge and, also, from above by means of its central arch, whether or not, according to whether the going be hard or soft, it actually bears on the ground.

The weight-bearing quality of the frog will be qualified to a degree on the shod foot, because the thickness of the shoe will prevent the frog, on hard surfaces, from coming into full use. On soft going, however, the frog fulfils its complete function of weight carrier and shock absorber. From this point alone it is easy to see how inadvisable is the practice of using fast paces on hard surfaces.

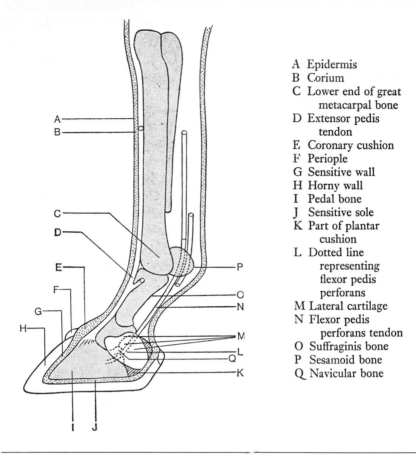

A Epidermis
B Corium
C Lower end of great
    metacarpal bone
D Extensor pedis
    tendon
E Coronary cushion
F Periople
G Sensitive wall
H Horny wall
I Pedal bone
J Sensitive sole
K Part of plantar
    cushion
L Dotted line
    representing
    flexor pedis
    perforans
M Lateral cartilage
N Flexor pedis
    perforans tendon
O Suffraginis bone
P Sesamoid bone
Q Navicular bone

Lower part of the leg.

The Function of the Frog

The importance of the frog in the anti-concussion apparatus of the horse is worth considerable consideration.

In movement the toe of the foot is slightly raised to allow the heel to meet the ground first. Some of the shock is absorbed by the interplay of the pastern and the variation in the angles made by the shoulder bones, but the greater part is sustained by the two springy cartilages, at the back of the foot, and the india-rubber frog, separated from them by a thick, elastic cushion. The frog, as it touches the ground, is pressed forwards and downwards, taking the initial shock and providing a firm non-slip hold. It and its supporting cushion spread under the weight and then, with the aid of the supporting cartilages, regain their shape as the pressure is removed.

Having appreciated something of the construction and functions of the foot it should be clear that the paramount consideration in its care is the preservation of the protective outer casing, and the ensurance of its complete freedom and natural action when given the additional protection of a shoe.

Preparation of the Foot

To achieve these objectives certain common-sense rules should be observed in the preparation of the foot.

In the regularly shod foot the horn which has grown on the wall (the rate of growth varies between ¼ to ⅜ inch per month and, therefore, necessitates attention every four weeks if it is not to alter the action of the foot) must be removed by rasping after the old shoes are removed. This operation should not in any way alter the absolutely level bearing surface of the foot, nor should the length of toe and heel be affected.

Ragged pieces of frog may be cut off and any obviously removable flakes on the sole pulled away. For the reasons explained *no further paring or cutting* should be allowed on these two parts.

Some smiths attempt to bring the frog closer to the ground, when preparing the foot, by rasping the wall at the heels. This is in any case impossible due to the thickness of the new shoe and only serves to weaken the wall at a very vulnerable point, as well as to throw more strain on the tendons and ligaments by lowering the heel.

A common fault in preparation is the "dumping" of the foot. This is when the toe is rasped either to shorten it or to make the foot fit the shoe. If the toe is in need of shortening it must be effected by rasping from the ground surface. Rasping the front of the wall removes a part of the already thin layer of insensitive horn and affords a smaller area into which a nail can be safely driven.

The bars of the foot should not be cut away in an effort to make the heels look wider. This practice weakens the heels, causing them to contract and to be unable to fulfil their purpose.

Feet which *turn in or turn out* can often be corrected by rasping the overgrowth which is usually the cause of these failings.

When toes turn in the overgrowth occurs on the inside wall and the action is corrected by rasping it level. Conversely, toes turning out do so because of an overgrowth on the outside wall.

Foot Pastern Axis (FPA)

The ideal FPA corresponds very closely to the slope of the shoulder. Specific angles are produced at fetlock, toe and heel to ensure the most economical and least concussive flight path for the foot. The ideal inclination of a good riding shoulder from the highest part of the wither to the point of the shoulder is between 43–45 degrees and the FPA should relate to that slope.

Abnormal FPAs resulting in a faulty flight path are caused by the toe being too long or, conversely, when the foot is too high at the heel. In both cases the proper FPA can be restored by correcting the growth at toe or heel.

Hot and Cold Shoeing

Following the preparation of the foot the shoe can be fixed by either hot-shoeing or cold-shoeing.

Hot-shoeing involves heating the shoe and placing it for a few seconds on the foot, burning a brown rim where it touches. The object is not to provide a more accurate seating for the shoe, but to check the fitting and to ensure the whole is in perfect contact, as will be shown by a complete brown rim. An incomplete rim entails further rasping until the surface is level.

Most blacksmiths prefer to shoe hot as it is the surest way of getting a perfect fit but, today, cold-shoeing, where the completed shoe is nailed to the foot without being heated, is becoming increasingly necessary and prevalent. The only disadvantage of hot-shoeing is when a smith makes the shoe too hot and holds it against the hoof too long, thinking he is making a good "bed" for it. What happens, of course, is that the burnt horn breaks away and the result is just the opposite.

I have, in fact, read an American authority who condemned hot-shoeing entirely for this reason, advocating cold-shoeing under all circumstances. I cannot agree with him and I have the feeling that his conclusions were probably made out of necessity.

The Well-Made Shoe

The shoe itself must follow the rim of the wall. It must be neither too wide, too long nor too short.

Too wide a shoe encourages brushing, the striking of the opposite leg; too long a shoe, projecting beyond the heels, is liable to be torn off

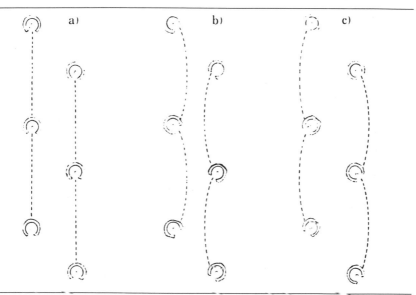

Flight of forefeet: a) normal; b) toes turned out; c) toes turned in.

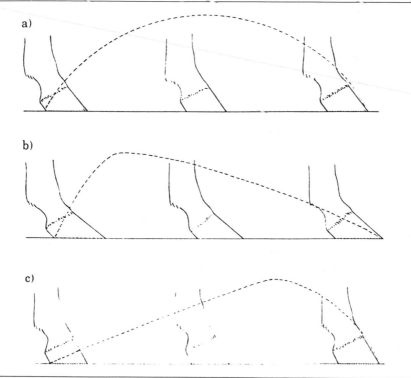

Flight of foot with FPA: a) normal; b) sloping; c) upright.

by the hind shoe, whilst a shoe that is too short allows bruising of the heels and the formation of corns.

"Dumping" can also occur in the fitting of the shoe when the latter is too small. It is a most reprehensible practice.

The number of nails required to secure the shoe should be as few as possible. Each nail weakens the wall and the horn surrounding it becomes brittle, making it more difficult to place the nails at subsequent shoeings. For a hunter four nails on the outside and three on the inside are usually deemed sufficient.

The actual driving home of the nails in the narrow space of the insensitive horn available is a matter calling for experience. A nail too close to the fleshy leaves is said to "press" and causes bruising of the sensitive laminae of the inner wall. One that enters the sensitive wall is said to "prick" and causes immediate lameness.

Nails leaving the wall too high ("high" nailing) or too low ("shallow" nailing) are usually indicative of faulty workmanship, although in the case of brittle or broken feet both may be necessary.

When the nails are driven home the protruding points are wrung off and the shanks turned up to form the securing "clenches", which are then hammered down.

Rasping the wall of the hoof after the shoe is secured to finish the job off is another foolish practice which removes the natural oils in the wall as well as weakening the structure. The clenches may be rasped briefly, but nothing more is required.

The weight of the shoe has a particular effect upon the action. Heavy shoes encourage the foot to be raised higher and contribute to a greater knee action as a result.

Too heavy a shoe adds to the effort which has to be made with every stride. It puts extra stress on the limbs and causes unnecessary fatigue.

Light shoes, on the other hand, produce the sort of long, low movement we look for in a riding horse. But, of course, it won't stand up to as much wear as a heavier shoe and if it is too light it will need replacing very frequently and the wall will begin to resemble a pepper-pot because of the constant nailing.

Points of a Well-Shod Foot

The points noticeable in a well-shod foot are:
    (1) No rasping of the wall.
    (2) No "dumping" of the wall.
    (3) Shoe fits the foot.

(4) Clenches are even, no "high" or "shallow" nails and none driven into old nail holes.

(5) No nail heads protruding below the ground surface of the shoe.

(6) No paring of the sole or frog.

(7) No cutting of the bars, heels level.

(8) No interference by the shoe of the frog.

(9) No uneven bearing between foot and shoe.

Types of Shoes

The types of shoes available are very numerous and the skilled smith can assist weak feet or faulty action by employing one which is appropriate.

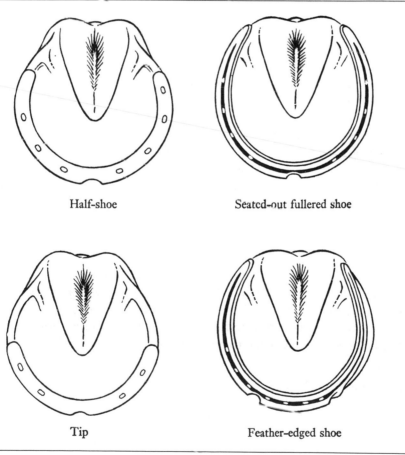

Half-shoe   Seated-out fullered shoe

Tip   Feather-edged shoe

Types of shoe.

The commonest one, however, is the *fullered* shoe with the centre hollowed out, which, it is claimed, is lighter, gives a better hold and helps the fitting of the nail.

It does not, however, wear so well and the nails are not so secure as in a *plain* shoe with a "stamped" hole embracing the nail on all four sides. The plain shoe is one in which the ground surface is flat.

A fullered shoe is frequently a *concave* one also. A concave shoe being narrower on its ground surface than on its bearing surface. It is lighter and not so likely to be pulled off.

A *feather-edge* shoe is used on horses that go so close as to "brush". The inside edge being made very thin and sloped inwards from the top, necessitating the show being nailed on at the toe and the opposite quarter.

A *seated* shoe is one hollowed so that the bearing surface is on the wall alone. Its object is to remove pressure from the sole, which will be necessary in horses having flat, instead of concave, soles. Its disadvantage is that it is very prone to getting pulled off in anything but perfect going.

For jumping, to give greater grip and as anti-slip devices, studs can be inserted into shoes. To insert studs a threaded hole must be made in the heel of the shoe, which needs plugging when the stud is not in actual use, and one is supplied with a "tap" to clear the thread. Jumping studs are usually used on the outside of the rear heels.

Road studs which give a much improved grip on slippery surfaces can be set permanently in the heels of the shoes, one on either side. Because they are low and broad they do not interfere with the balance of the feet.

Care at Grass

Unshod feet of horses at grass require just as much attention as those of the horse at work. Feet should be inspected once every six weeks and the horn growth rasped off and rounded to prevent splitting of the horn.

Toes or heels may have to be lowered to keep the foot in proportion and the animals should be trotted out frequently to check for any signs of lameness or foot-soreness. If an animal is footsore it is better to put shoes on again to allow the feet to grow. Feet which break easily may be protected by shoeing with "tips", half shoes fitting round the toe only.

Oiling the Feet

Hoof oil or ointment is usually brushed on for its cosmetic effect without folk appreciating that the preparations have an important role to play as a means of controlling moisture content and evaporation.

When horses are stabled for long periods, possibly without having the opportunity to run out for a part of the day, the foot is unable to keep up with the loss of moisture caused by evaporation. As a result it dries out, becomes brittle and may crack badly.

The moisture can be replaced by daily washing of the feet, using a *soft* brush which will not damage the essential periople.

By applying oil or ointment that moisture can be retained.

In the normal way oil should be applied *after* exercise or turning out. If it is done before, whilst it may look very smart, the waterproof coating which has been so lovingly brushed on the hoof will actually prevent moisture being absorbed.

These are the rules about oiling:

Normal conditions. Use oil if you must but remember that continuous applications of impervious dressings will prevent evaporation and cause the horn of the foot to become soft.

Wet conditions. Dressing the foot in these circumstances prevents *excessive* absorption of moisture and so prevents the horn softening.

Dry conditions. Oiling prevents loss of moisture content. If brittle feet are soaked in water then dressed, the oil or ointment helps to retain the moisture.

(Brittle feet respond very well to biotin preparations being given in the feed.)

Farriery Qualifications

Under the Farriers Acts of 1975 and 1977 it is unlawful for persons to shoe horses unless he/she is listed in the Register of Farriers maintained by the Worshipful Company of Farriers.

Before employing a farrier check that he is qualified.

CHAPTER 8

Common Ailments and Their Treatment

It should be understood quite clearly that while it is important for the horse-owner to be able to diagnose and treat the more common ailments and injuries, it is even more important that he or she should know when to call in the veterinary surgeon. Nothing is more dangerous than amateur, unskilled treatment, and the motto of the horse-owner should be "When in the slightest doubt – call in the vet."

There are all sorts of horsy remedies, they are as numerous as horsy sayings and often as far removed from the truth. As a well-known vet. wrote recently: "There are no magic cures any more – they have all been put into bottles, tins and syringes." There are, however, certain straightforward, common-sense methods of dealing with the simpler ailments which are within the province of the horse-keeper and with which he should be conversant.

The General Signs of Health and Disease

The horse quickly reveals the state of his health through the appearance of various parts of his body, his excreta, and by means of his temperature, pulse and respiration.

In health the eye is bright and big and the membranes under the lids and those of the nostrils are an even pink in colour. Redness denotes inflammation, white shows debility, a yellow colour is symptomatic of liver disorders and bright purple is indicative of improper blood aeration, as in pneumonia, etc.

The coat lies flat and has a sheen on it, although this will not be apparent in horses wintering out. A staring coat can mean general malnutrition. When the coat is easily pulled from the mane it is as well to look for other general symptoms of ill-health.

The skin is loose and clean. If it is tight it may be due to malnutrition or the onset of some disease.

Lice infestation also makes the skin tight, but is more easily discernible than most troubles.

Limbs should feel cool and free from swelling. Puffiness indicates sprains, poor circulation, irritation or possibly a heart condition.

Droppings will vary in colour and consistency, but should be generally well formed, slightly moist and not be strong smelling. The accompaniment of mucus is the result of a deranged digestion. Yellow, strongly smelling droppings may denote disorders of the liver and the presence of red worm.

The urine should be almost without colour; thick, highly-coloured urine indicates kidney trouble and bloody water an inflammation of that organ. An excessive urine flow means diabetes, whilst a constant and obvious dribble accompanies bladder inflammation.

The normal temperature of the horse is 100°–101·5°F. Above this level gives reason to suspect a general infection.

As horses vary in their normal temperature, it is wise to take and note the normal temperature when in health for future comparison. Using a clinical thermometer, shaken before use, which has been dipped in glycerine, insert the instrument for some three minutes into the rectum. As the temperature is inclined to rise slightly in the day time it is as well to take two or three readings at different times. After use wash the thermometer in cold water. Clinical thermometers register up to 110°F and will burst in water hotter than this.

The normal rate of the pulse is 35–40 beats per minute. An increase in the pulse rate when at rest usually signifies a fever. Up to 50 beats per minute can indicate that the horse is in pain. The pulse is conveniently taken on the inner surface of the lower jaw, just behind the elbow or just above and behind the eye. Count the number of beats in 20 seconds with a stop-watch, then multiply by three to obtain the pulse rate.

Respiration at rest is between eight and twelve breaths per minute. Faster than this indicates pain and an almost certain rise in temperature. Stand behind the horse and count the number of times the flanks rise and fall in 60 seconds. Each rise and fall equals one breath.

The teeth are in need of attention if food, left in the manger, is wet or balled.

Tetanus – Equine 'Flu

It is advisable for all equines to be injected against tetanus and be vaccinated against equine 'flu. Obviously, it is just as important for the humans looking after them to be similarly protected against tetanus.

The incidence of equine influenza has increased rapidly over the past 20 years, more particularly perhaps in the last decade, and serious outbreaks are not infrequent. If there is a 'flu epidemic in your area keep your horses at home, even if they have been vaccinated. To stage shows, events, etc. during an epidemic is as irresponsible and reprehensible as taking a horse which has been in contact with the virus to such gatherings. Even vaccinated horses can suffer a mild attack of influenza should they come in contact with affected animals.

Only recently my own mare suffered just such an attack. She had been vaccinated but she had a runny nose and a cough for some days. She had no temperature but she was off work for two weeks and on walking exercise for nearly three weeks after that, and just before the hunting season, too. Our young pony, not then vaccinated, suffered far worse. He survived only because of devoted round-the-clock nursing over a full three weeks. The veterinary bill on account of broncho-dilators and daily antibiotic injections amounted to more than the value of the pony. The expense was not grudged but I urge you to take heed.

Without doubt the much greater movement of horses about the country, and the comparative ease with which horses can now be transported internationally, has contributed to the spread of viruses in much the same way as human viruses have increased as a result of improved world travel facilities.

Because of the serious nature of equine 'flu and because it is so highly contagious, the Jockey Club has made vaccination compulsory for all horses entering racecourse premises. This was in 1981 and since then the same ruling has been applied at shows and major competitive events which attract large numbers of horses.

The requirement is for a primary vaccination, which must be followed by a secondary one in not less than 21 days or more than 92 days. Thereafter booster vaccinations are given at intervals of not more than 12 months. All vaccinations need to be entered on the horse's identification/vaccination card.

There are two main strains of the equine influenza virus, far less than the numerous human strains, but new strains have been discovered in recent years.

Type 1 is the Prague virus, discovered in the city of that name in 1956. The second is the Miami strain found in Miami, Florida in 1963. Both are covered by the modern 'flu vaccine.

The virus is very contagious and spreads rapidly either in a stable-yard or on a showground. Horses do not have to rub noses to become infected, and a coughing horse obviously increases the likelihood of infection by spreading the viruses.

The incubation period is between three to ten days. Horses are off-colour and usually lose interest in food – swallowing may, indeed, be painful as the attack progresses. There is a nasal discharge accompanied by a high temperature of around 104°F (normal temperature at rest is 100°–101·5°F) and a notable increase in the pulse rate.

The cough may persist for as long as three or even four weeks and because the virus can cause damage to the lungs and also the heart, *complete* rest is essential for at least six weeks before the horse can begin light exercise. In essence, therefore, the infected horse may be off work for almost three months and will then spend some six weeks getting back to the original condition of fitness. All that apart, there is the heavy expense of veterinary fees, medication, etc. to be met as well as the inconvenience which is part and parcel of infectious diseases. The virus can, for instance, be transmitted on clothing, so one does not invite friends with horses to visit. Similarly the owner of an infected horse is not entirely welcome at other yards.

Young horses and particularly foals, of course, are particularly at risk and a 'flu infection may well cause death.

Then there are the after effects of infection, which may be more serious than is generally understood.

It is accepted that the possibility of SAD (Small Airway Disease) is increased following a bout of 'flu and it is possible for animals to become increasingly allergic to moulds, etc.

There may also be a long-term effect decreasing the level of subsequent performance over an extended period of time because of the effect of the virus on the air ways. It is not yet clear whether the damage sustained is more or less permanent. However, there seems little doubt that horses that are not allowed a sufficient period of convalescence following an infection will be permanently affected.

(For buyers of horses this is yet another reason to beware and exercise caution. It would, perhaps, be prudent to ask of the vendor, "Has this horse ever had a 'flu infection?" Under the law he is required to answer that and any other pertinent question truthfully.)

There is a school of thought which holds that vaccination has an adverse effect upon performance. There is another claiming that the cost is too high.

So far as we know there is no conclusive evidence to support the first assertion and, of course, the cost, financially as well as otherwise, of an unvaccinated horse suffering an infection of the 'flu virus is far and away higher than that of the vaccination itself.

What is certain is that vaccination immunises the horse almost completely, saves pain and discomfort and obviates the possibility of serious damage being done to essential organs.

Injuries and Wounds

Wounds fall into one of the following categories: Punctures, Cuts and Tears, Deep Wounds, Bruise Wounds.

The most common form of puncture is that caused by a thorn and, therefore, a painstaking inspection of the legs is necessary after hunting. On locating a thorn, remove it at once. If it cannot be withdrawn expert help is needed to cut it out. Poulticing is rarely effective and can result in a big leg for some time. Once the thorn is removed, however, a poultice of Epsom salts and glycerine will draw out any residual infection.

Puncture wounds from stakes, nails, etc., as well as from thorns, are dangerous if they are near, or likely to affect, a joint and need expert attention; otherwise treat as for thorns.

Punctures of the sole of the foot are also dangerous, as there is a likelihood of the horse coming into contact with material carrying tetanus germs. Regular tetanus injections should be the rule, but if these have not been given an immediate injection is necessary. The puncture has to be opened, to allow drainage, a job best left to the vet., and then poulticed. A good old-fashioned way is to put the foot in a bucket of salt water for half-an-hour and pack the sole with a poultice of wet, unheated, brewer's yeast. To draw the wound the foot can be wrapped in plastic, or something similar. In days gone by the whole thing was secured in a stout sack, but sacks of that sort are now in short supply

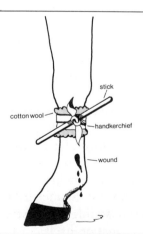

A simple tourniquet applied above an arterial wound.

and it is easier and more convenient to use one of the purpose-made rubber poultice boots.

Yeast has the property of killing infection and should not be used with other antiseptics which will destroy this characteristic. The poultice will need to be changed twice daily for three days, after which a dry dressing of sulphanilamide may be used to prevent excessive formation of healing tissue (proud flesh). Wounds of this nature usually require veterinary supervision.

Small cuts should be washed well with hot water to which a handful of salt or Epsom salts has been added and dusted twice daily with sulphanilamide powder or something similar.

More serious cuts or tears should be cleansed with a mixture of four parts salt to one part citrate of soda in a solution of one teaspoonful to one pint of boiled water. A lint dressing soaked in the solution and bandaged lightly can then be fixed and left for 24 hours.

Salt induces a flow of lymph and on removing the bandage this will be present as a yellow, sticky substance. This should be swabbed off with the same solution and the wound recovered.

Once tissue (proud flesh) begins to form, a dry, coagulating, dressing (boracic powder) can be applied. A scab will then be made, under which the process of healing will continue.

Deep, large wounds require different treatment. If bleeding is of a venous nature it is easily stopped by copious applications from the hosepipe. The blood in this case is dull red. Arterial blood is bright scarlet and issues in fairly violent spurts from the wound. To control arterial bleeding place a tight bandage or a tourniquet above the wound, nearest to the heart, and bathe continuously with cold water. Arterial bleeding requires veterinary assistance.

Once bleeding has stopped all dirt must be removed from the wound and penicillin applied very freely or, in these modern times, the horse can be given an expensive antibiotic injection. A dressing of powdered Epsom salts mixed into a paste with glycerine is then applied on lint, the whole wound covered with oilskin or plastic to promote drawing, and finally bandaged.

Over-reaches are a common form of wound, caused by a blow from the hind shoe lacerating either the bulbs of the heel or the back of a fetlock joint.

Healing in the first case is slow. Any flap of skin and tissue should be removed and the wound cleansed with salt and water. A brewer's yeast poultice, followed by dressings of sulphanilamide powder, should be applied as for a sole puncture.

Should there be excessive proud flesh it can be controlled on a DIY basis by dusting with powdered blue-stone. A blow on the joint is far worse as the tendon, or rather its sheath, will almost certainly be damaged, in which case there will be a yellow synovial discharge. Treat as for an over-reach on the heel, but call the vet.

Bruise wounds may be caused by blows or kicks and are not always very conspicuous. They should be treated with cold water to relieve the pain and then gently massaged with a cooling lotion, such as vinegar and water, or a mixture of one part petrol or methylated spirit to ten parts water. The horse should then be rested and given only gentle exercise.

Kicks in the area inside the second thigh, where the bone is near the surface, are dangerous as they may involve bone damage. A horse suffering a kick of this nature should not be ridden for about a month, but should be rested to give the bone time to heal.

Broken knees, the result of a fall, may vary from a light graze to a deep wound. In the first case continual bathing with salt and cold water will effect a cure. If, however, the wound is deep and discharging, a poultice of glycerine and Epsom salts smeared on lint and kept in place by a light bandage must be applied twice a day for three or four days. This can be followed by an antiseptic ointment and the wound allowed to make a scab. Hot applications should *not* be made and the bandages never kept on longer than necessary or the specified time.

To encourage the growth of hair on the knees after they have healed there are a number of recipes – most of which have not yet been bottled or tinned. I am assured that melted butter (or even, perhaps, a low-cholesterol margarine) mixed with the scrapings of burnt cork until the mixture is brown is most efficacious. It should be rubbed in for 20 minutes twice a day, massaging downwards. I have also found a mixture of black sulphur and vaseline to be effective. This mixture must be melted in order for the constituents to merge. Plain lard, or even goose grease, is probably just as good.

Girth, Saddle and Bit Galls

These are the result of bad horse management and prevention is better than cure. Rest is the solution and the removal or repair of the offending article of saddlery.

Bit galls can be treated with salt water to harden the skin. In other cases the wounds can be washed with salt water and dusted with sulphanilamide powder.

A more severe injury of the back caused by a badly fitting saddle is when a portion of skin dies due to pressure restricting the blood circulation. This dead portion separates from the living tissue and pus is formed.

A kaolin poultice will help the removal of the core, but it may take time and be so obstinate as to need cutting out by the veterinary surgeon. Once the core is removed the wound must be bathed twice daily with salt water and treated with penicillin ointment.

The only way to prevent galls of this sort is to keep saddlery in good repair and properly cleaned, and to ensure that it fits the horses. Felt numnahs with holes cut in them to avoid sore places are not the answer nor, indeed, is any sort of therapeutic numnah used in this context, but rather it is an admission of incompetence in horse management.

Simple Remedies

A lot of remedies recommended in this chapter may be unfamiliar to the modern horse-keeper who may be more accustomed to the injection as the panacea for most equine ills. Nonetheless, they have stood the test of time, in conditions far more demanding than most of us experience and should not be discounted. They are, also, of course, far less expensive.

In the forefront of these basic items which, in my view, should form a substantial part of the contents of every veterinary chest is that cheap and very under-rated commodity, Epsom Salts.

It is probably the most versatile substance at our disposal and with cold water and common sense forms an essential and inexpensive trinity in the treatment of all sorts of minor ailments. (If the trinity were to be upgraded to a quartet, the final member would be *rest*. Rest and allowing nature to bring about the cure is an all too neglected remedy. There is a place for the needle and the wonderful modern drugs, but they (and the horse) can be abused on account of an entirely selfish human interest, which demands that come what may the horse must be fit to compete on Saturday.)

When my favourite mare went off her food for a few days, two or three doses of Epsom salts (a single handful – a teaspoon will do no good – in a bucket of water) had the effect of clearing her system and bringing back her appetite. Some horses will not drink water doctored in this way but the addition of a bottle of beer will usually overcome their inhibitions.

The salts are a useful addition to bran mashes, where their presence is more easily disguised, as well as being effective in all types of digestive derangements.

Were I to have a horse with *lampas*, discussed later in this chapter, a condition usually caused as a result of digestive troubles; or one suffering from that pimply condition of the spring we call *humour*, or worse still from nettlerash (*urticaria*) which has nothing to do with nettles and a lot to do with a dietary "lurgy", I should resort to Epsom salts, either straight or, in the case of lampas, as part of a prepared mixture. Indeed, there is a simple remedy based on Epsom salts (the other ingredients being bicarbonate of soda and potassium nitrate) for the treatment of what used to be called a "stomach cough" (the harsh, dry one which is not accompanied by a rise in temperature).

Although Epsom salts cannot be considered as the all-embracing panacea, it is one of the few items which is just as useful when applied to the outside of the horse as when taken internally. Used as a poultice it has drawing properties and is most useful when alleviating the initial symptoms in *azoturia*, the tying-up syndrome. Towels soaked in hot water, to which a double handful of salts has been added, and then placed over the loins will form a comforting compress to draw the fluid and ease the muscles.

Cold water and exercise can reduce swollen legs to respectable proportions but Epsom salts can also be employed most profitably. Mixed with glycerine to form a paste and then covered with bandages after it has been plastered on the legs it is, in my view, the sovereign remedy for the condition and far cheaper than an expensive proprietary mix which I tried recently and which had no beneficial effect at all.

Lameness

In cases of all but obvious lameness the horse must be trotted out to ascertain the source. Lameness in the forelegs can be ascertained by watching the head of a horse trotted towards you. If the head appears to rise and fall the lame leg is the one on which the head is raised.

Lameness behind can be seen by watching the highest part of the quarters as the horse trots away. If the horse is lame in either hindleg there will be a definite rise and fall of this point, the affected leg being the one upon which the corresponding hip is raised.

There will possibly be heat in the affected leg or hoof and in extreme cases the horse will stand with a foreleg pointed out in front. In slight lameness the pastern of the same leg is slightly straighter than that of the sound one.

Shoulder lameness is more difficult to detect, but in general the toe of the painful leg is dragged and the whole leg does not reach as far forward as the sound one. At rest the affected limb is held, with the toe on the ground, behind the sound one.

Common Causes of Lameness

Bruised Sole – caused by treading on a sharp stone or something similar. It will occur more frequently with those horses having a tendency towards a flat, dropped sole which may also be thinner than desirable.

Horses with notably flat feet can be fitted with a *seated-out* shoe to ease pressure on the sole. (A seated-out shoe has the inner edge sloped so as to relieve pressure on the sole's border. It has the disadvantage of being more easily pulled off in heavy going.)

A slight bruise will clear up if the horse is rested for a day or two but in more severe instances, when there will be heat in the foot, the shoe has to be removed and the foot poulticed.

Corns – When bruising occurs between the wall and the bars of the foot (the "seat of corn") it is termed a corn. The condition is recognisable by a red discoloration of the horn and the corn will fall into one of three categories: *dry, moist* or *suppurating*. In the case of the former, removal of the shoe and a few days' rest will usually be sufficient to effect a cure, although the horse must then be shod with special care.

In more severe cases, when infection may be present, veterinary assistance will be needed to cut away the affected part. Poulticing will probably be necessary and the subsequent cavity will need to be packed with tow and Stockholm tar. Serious types of corn can lead to permanent lameness.

Some horses seem to be more prone to corn problems than others but the cause is almost always concerned with bad shoeing, when the shoe is made too short or fitted too close, or (which is more common) by the shoes being left on for too long a time.

Corns occur in the forefeet.

Seedy Toe – an affection where the wall of the foot separates from the sole at the toe. A cavity is formed which becomes filled with crumbling horn. This latter has to be removed and the cavity packed with tow and Stockholm tar. It is advisable to fit a plain stamped shoe. Horn growth can be stimulated by external treatment, ointments, etc., and by a diet including biotin. No lameness occurs in the early stages and the condition may pass unnoticed until the shoes are removed.

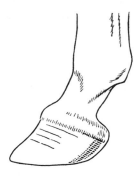

Appearance of the foot affected by laminitis.

Sand Crack – a crack in the hoof wall extending downwards from the coronet. A V burnt by the smith at the base of the crack, or the fixing of a clip, will facilitate healing. A horn stimulant should be applied.

Laminitis – a condition sometimes known as foot-fever. It is an acute form of inflammation within the outer protective casing of the foot, affecting the sensitive laminae. The outer wall cannot expand so the condition is very painful. The temperature rises, there may be sweating and the animal is unwilling to move or to rise if down.

It is caused by hard work when in unfit condition, too heating a diet with an insufficiency of exercise, galloping on hard ground and, in the case of ponies, who are particularly susceptible, grazing on lush pasture and being overweight.

Cure lies in restricting the diet, feeding laxative foods and cutting back the feet under veterinary supervision. Injections can be given and the animal will have to be forced to walk on hard ground until the circulatory troubles are resolved.

Navicular Disease – Until recently, the manuals, both veterinary and otherwise, talked of concussion as a principal cause and pronounced the disease as being incurable.

Today, much more is known about the contributory causes and although it seems that a complete cure is unlikely the condition can be alleviated.

Essentially, the disease is caused by a blockage of the blood supply to the navicular bone, which causes the latter to degenerate. The result is lameness, always in the forefeet. Initially, the lameness may be intermittent but without treatment it will become chronic. The horse will "point" a limb to relieve pressure on the foot and begin to move on his heels. The disease can be diagnosed specifically by X-ray.

Undue concussion can be a contributory factor but the principal cause (which may, indeed, result in uneven concussion) is concerned with the care of the foot and the shoeing of it. If toes have been allowed to grow too long, so that the heels become low and weak the blood flow will be affected. Shoes made too short or left on for too long a time cause this sort of condition and emphasise the need for the foot to be balanced correctly and the FPA maintained carefully.

Treatment involves the correction of the shoeing and possibly the fitting of a surgical shoe like an *egg bar* or a *wide web* shoe fitted long and wide to support the rear of the foot.

Secondly, it is necessary to improve the blood supply by the means of drugs which dilate the blood vessels in the area.

With proper care of the feet this disabling condition may be prevented.

Ringbone – a condition affecting the pastern bones resulting in a bony enlargement round the top of the hoof (low ringbone) or round the pastern bones (high ringbone). If caused by a blow or undue concussion, rest may effect a cure. If the condition is hereditary, involving the joint itself, recovery is unlikely.

Sidebone – an interference with the ligaments of the foot caused by the sesamoid bones becoming injured or inflamed due to concussion. There is much pain and a *hard* swelling is apparent on the joint. Rest and veterinary attention may affect a cure, but the action is usually "pottery" after the disease.

Pedal Ostitis – inflammation of the pedal bone usually due to concussion. Acute lameness is caused and the foot is sensitive to a tap with a hammer on the sole. Surgical shoeing involving the use of pads can sometimes be helpful.

Sore Shins – an inflammation of the cannon bone membrane accompanied by noticeable swelling of the forelimb and considerable tenderness. It is commonly supposed to be caused by the effect of concussion on immature bone and is found in very young animals. The animal should be rested, given laxative food and a kaolin poultice applied.

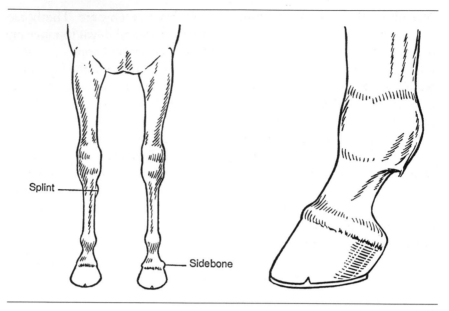

Splint and sidebone.   *Sesamoiditis.*

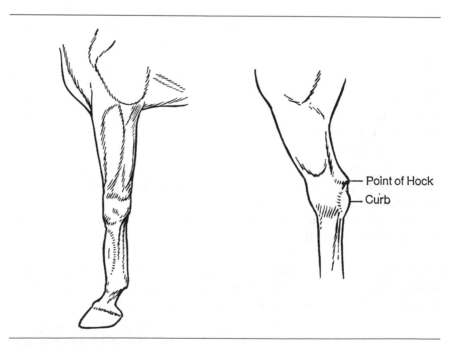

Sore shins.   *Curb.*

Spavin – inflammation of bones in the hock, giving rise to a bony enlargement on the inside of the joint. Flexion causes pain and movement is restricted, there is a dragging of the toe and the limb is thrown outwards. Lameness tends to decrease with exercise. Complete rest and the use of anti-inflammatory drugs may bring the horse back into use or surgical treatment to fix together the bones of the hock is sometimes successful.

A "bog spavin" gives far less cause for concern. It occurs on the front of the hock and is to all intents a bursal enlargement in the nature of a windgall. It does not cause lameness and can be treated with cold compresses.

Swollen Legs – old horses are particularly susceptible to swellings in the fetlock joints due to wear and tear and a consequent blood congestion in the limbs. Upward hand-rubbing of the legs is helpful, and the hosepipe and pressure bandages also relieve the condition.

Sprains – tendon sprains in the flexors of the foreleg are fairly common and a horse experiencing such a sprain is often described as "broken down". The causes of such sprains are either associated with fast work, jumping or sometimes they may be the result of a conformation not best equipped to meet excessive demands in the way of speed. The extent of the strain varies between very slight, when heat is present with a little swelling but possibly no lameness, to severe, when the fibres are ruptured and there will be extensive swelling and lameness. Finally there is the complete breakdown when both the superficial and deep tendons are ruptured. Swelling is now even more evident, lameness is acute and much pain is present.

Treatment involves REST, application of *cold* dressings (there are now some very effective ones which are prepared by refrigeration) and *support* of both the good and the bad leg by bandaging. All to be carried out under veterinary supervision.

The suspensory ligament which runs from behind the knee to hold the fetlock joint can be damaged when a rupture of the tendon occurs, but it is usually caused by jarring on hard surfaces. Lameness does not occur, but the stride is shortened. Providing it is not connected with tendon ruptures it can be treated with hot water fomentations and kaolin poultices followed by a few weeks' rest.

A Curb – is a strain of the ligament joining the hock to the cannon bone and is seen as a thickening immediately under the point of the hock. Slight lameness may result initially. The condition is confined usually to young horses and does not appear to affect performance.

Misdirected Nails – as discussed in the chapter on shoeing – are obvious causes of lameness.

Bursal Enlargements

Exemplified in *thorough-pin*, a soft swelling above the hock on either side; *bog spavin*, in front of the hock; *windgalls*, above the fetlock joint; *capped hock*, on the point of the hock and *capped elbow*, occurring on the elbow itself and caused by the shoe of the forefoot exerting pressure when the horse is lying down.

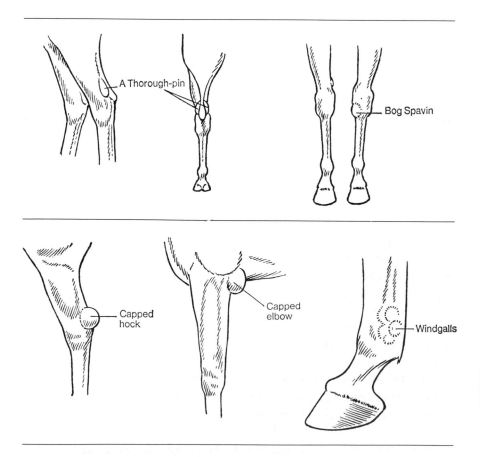

Bursal enlargements.

A bursa is a sac of fluid acting as a buffer between a ligament, tendon or muscle passing over a bone. If through pressure the sac is stretched it becomes filled with fluid.

Hand-rubbing with an astringent can be helpful as well as the application of cold compresses.

A capped elbow – is best cured by putting a "sausage" boot round the fetlock to prevent the foot coming into contact with the elbow.

Digestive Complaints

Colic – a severe stomach-ache to which the horse, by reason of his stomach structure, is particularly susceptible. It can be caused by almost anything to do with his food, from eating too much at one session to sudden changes in his diet or eating bad food. Worm infestation in youngstock is a notable cause of susceptibility to colic in later years.

Usually the horse displays his uneasiness by looking at his flanks, kicking at them, pawing the ground, getting down and up again, and attempting to pass water. The temperature is not affected, but the pulse rate may increase and the breathing be laboured. In more acute cases the membranes of the eye may become inflamed and the horse will break out in a sweat.

For more years than I care to remember horse-owners dealt with colic attacks quite effectively by the administration of a "colic drink". There are still a number of proprietary "drinks" on the market and if they do not have a chlorodyne base, which deadens pain and consequently the nerves, therefore militating against nerve impulses which would promote bowel action, I imagine they work as well as they ever did.

Twenty years ago, when this book was first published, I relied upon two home-made remedies and always had the ingredients to hand. The first comprised a pint of kaolin emulsion, half a pint of water and two tablespoons of sal volatile. The second was made up from one and a half pints of linseed oil, two tablespoons of precious whisky or brandy and a similar quantity of turpentine.

To administer the "drench", as it was called, you needed an assistant, a drenching bottle, a two-tine pitchfork, the ends of the prongs being protected with corks, and the know-how acquired at one's mother's knee.

However, all that is now strictly taboo and veterinary surgeons, for the most part, will advise owners that "treatment . . . is not a matter for the horse-owner". Furthermore, they hold that colic drinks "are not only of no therapeutic value" but that "the giving of liquids to a horse by mouth is dangerous" because of the likelihood of the liquid going down the wind-pipe into the lungs.

In the present climate of horse-management their opinions have to be respected – after all the administration of the drench does not form any part of our modern training qualifications.

Opinions of the merit or otherwise of walking the horse about during colic are divided, when, indeed, they are expressed at all. My belief, based on experience, is that in mild cases walking can be done while a spasm is taking place to prevent the animal from hurting himself by rolling violently in the box. The horse should however be allowed to rest between spasms.

In mild cases, cover the horse with rugs and watch for an hour or so. If he has eaten unripe apples or damsons (a particular perversion with my own horses despite all attempts to remove the fruit) the attack will pass. However, if the pain continues beyond that time or if it is severe *call the vet. at once* and do everything possible to keep the horse moving and to prevent his throwing himself down until the vet. arrives.

A twisted gut – regarded as a form of colic can arise from a violent attack when the horse might throw himself to the ground. It can also be caused by a fall when the bowel is overladen with food or by a very strong purgative causing excessive bowel action. The gut lies in coils along the length of the back, supported by a membrane called the mesentery. Should the mesentery be torn from the gut it resolves on itself causing acute pain. If the veterinary surgeon can operate quickly there is a chance of survival, otherwise the condition is fatal.

Constipation – usually the fault of the diet and the best cure is to feed grass and bran mashes. Otherwise an enema of warm soapy water works wonders.

Diarrhoea – the treatment for diarrhoea caused by diet, such as a sudden change to green food, is obvious, but if the condition persists then it is probable that the bowel may be inflamed, either due to heavy worm infestation or to some irritant food. The temperature will be normal in this case; if, however, it is not, then there may be an enteritic infection. It is then as well to call in expert advice rather than to indulge in home doctoring in the form of purges.

Lampas – a condition in which the upper jaw, behind the incisors,

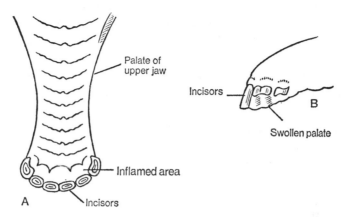

A Palate showing inflamed area   B Side view (cut away) to show swollen area

Lampas.

becomes swollen. It is due to a digestional derangement and its cure lies in improving the animal's general condition. A ten-day course of one tablespoon, given night and morning either in the feed or in water, of a mixture of 8 oz Epsom salts, 4 oz glucose, 2 oz bicarbonate of soda, ½ oz Nitrate of potash will act as a corrective, but the cure is in the conditioning of the animal.

Skin Diseases

These can be divided into those which are contagious and those which are not. Principal among the contagious skin affections is *Mange,* of which there are three types, all caused by parasites.

Sarcoptic Mange – affects the head, neck, withers, shoulders and some parts of the sides. It is characterised by small lumps from which issues a yellow discharge. At the discharge dries the hair falls out and a scaly patch remains. The animal is constantly rubbing and there is intense irritation.

Psoroptic Mange – is similar, but affects the base of the mane and tail. Both diseases must be notified under law and outbreaks are controlled by an appointed veterinary surgeon of the Ministry of Agriculture.

Symbiotic Mange – is unpleasant, but does not come in the same category. The lower legs, knees and hocks are affected, hair falls out and there is again intense irritation. The hair must be clipped off and the legs washed twice a week with Dermoline, or something similar, followed by an anti-parasite dressing. The horse should be isolated, his box disinfected and all his clothing, etc., fumigated, disinfected or burnt. Clothing worn by the attendant should not come in contact with other animals.

Itchy Mane or Tail – This sort of irritation can be caused by a parasite or by a high blood condition. In the former instance treatment is as for mange. In the latter the parts should be washed in a medicated shampoo and the horse put on laxative foods. Coconut oil, rubbed in gently, is often an additional help. Irritation around the dock and rectum can be caused by whip or seat worms. They can be dealt with by giving an enema of salt and water (see chapter on Worm Control).

Ringworm – is very contagious and is caused by a fungus. Symptoms are raised circles of hair, on the neck and shoulders initially, from which the hair falls out, leaving grey-white crusts. As the fungus is under the crusts they must first be removed by scrubbing before applying Gentian Violet or Iodine ointment. Isolation and disinfection routine must be carried out to prevent the disease spreading to other horses.

Lice – are found on horses in poor condition, but can also be picked up when animals are out at grass. A heavy infestation causes loss of condition due to the blood sucking propensities of the parasite. The coat appears blotched (hence the dealer's euphemistic description "touch of the frost") and the horse rubs continually. The lice will be visible to the naked eye. There are numerous anti-parasitic preparations, the majority of which are highly effective.

As with ringworm, clippings of hair, etc. should be burnt and, as a precaution, the stable disinfected.

The non-contagious diseases are:

Mud Fever – this is a skin irritation, derived from mud, which affects the legs and sometimes the belly. Certain soils are more prone to cause the disease than others. The legs are hot and swollen, a thin discharge is noticeable on the hair and cracks form on the skin. The horse moves very stiffly. The horse should be fed a laxative diet with no heating foods. Mild attacks can be treated with one of the proprietary ointments or with udder-salve, but severe attacks displaying the symptoms mentioned may require the application of heat by means of boracic lint soaked in boiling water and squeezed out in a towel. The lint is then *quickly* applied to the leg, cotton wool put over it and the whole secured with a stable bandage. The effect is to reduce congestion in the blood vessels. The treatment is carried out twice daily until the inflammation is lessened and this is then followed by the application of an antiseptic ointment.

Cracked Heels – are similar and caused by mud or neglecting to dry wet heels. The heel becomes chapped and the horse moves with difficulty. The same treatment as for mud fever is effective. The condition can be avoided by greasing the heels with either an ointment or grease saved from the Christmas goose before turning horses out.

Humour – is a pimply skin condition caused by "overheated blood" and is best treated by a laxative diet and a dose of 4 oz Epsom salts in one pint water.

Nettlerash or Urticaria – is caused by an allergy to something in the diet. Areas of varying size become raised with the hair standing erect. They can be treated with a solution of bicarbonate of soda – two tablespoons to one pint water, and the horse should be given a laxative diet with a dose of Epsom salts. (The homoeopathic remedy *Urticaria urens* is very effective as are raw nettles.)

Warts – of the small pointed type occur usually on the nose, lips and ears. They often disappear of their own accord, but may be treated with treacle, castor oil or sump oil. Caustic potash may also be used, but with care.

A cylindrical wart appears on the under surface of the belly and round the sheath. Single warts may be removed by tieing a piece of thread round their necks to cut off the blood supply, when they will eventually drop off. Where these warts appear in large numbers they may need expert surgical attention.

Warbles – lay their eggs in the late summer on the horse's skin and the resultant larvae work their way into the back and sides. The following spring a hard lump appears under the skin, which becomes larger until a small hole can be seen at the top. If the lump is squeezed before the larva is ready to be pushed out, or if the lump is ignored and receives pressure from the saddle, the larva will burst and the ensuing infection will cause a large swelling lasting for some weeks.

If it is possible it is best to wait for the maggot to mature and leave the horse naturally rather than mess about with fomentations which will certainly remove any pus which might have formed but may kill the maggot and aggravate the condition. Otherwise, seek veterinary assistance.

Sweet Itch – occurs in spring and summer and veterinary opinion inclines now to blame this distressing condition on a midge called *Culicoides pulicaris*. Areas of the neck, mane, tail and withers suffer intense irritation and inflammation. The animal rubs continually, a yellowish discharge is present and the hair falls out. Corticosteroid and antihistamine preparations are widely used in the treatment of sweet itch and so is the old favourite Benzyl Benzoate.

A partial solution is to stable the animal in the early morning and from late afternoon to late evening when the midges are most active. The use of synthetic pyrethrum spray is also recommended, the whole body being sprayed every fortnight and every week in wet weather.

Hidebound – is not a disease, but a sure sign of worms and should be treated accordingly. The skin is dry and dull and the animal is generally in poor condition.

Respiratory Diseases

A great deal more is known about respiratory diseases, their cause and treatment than was appreciated even ten years ago.

We now talk about COPD, Chronic Obstructive Pulmonary Disease or SAD, Small Airway Disease.

In the past this was known as "broken wind" and was thought to be caused by over-distension of the lung vesicles. The breathing after exertion becomes noticeably laboured, a cough is present and a nasal discharge. A line appears between the abdomen and the chest wall, the "heave" line, hence "the heaves", and there is a double expiratory effort. Obviously, horses affected are not capable of even the lightest work.

The cause is now traced to a dust allergy and if the dust is removed the condition, so long as it is not advanced, is eliminated. That means bedding on shavings or shredded paper, soaking hay to remove the dust spores or feeding the dust-free bagged hay and being very careful to ensure that the horse has no contact with dust from straw or hay being used elsewhere in the yard.

Fortunately, there are modern drugs like the broncho-dilators which can bring significant relief.

Horses will still, of course, contract coughs and colds from changes in temperature when stabled and very particularly from lack of proper ventilation.

A simple cough and runny nose are best treated by plenty of fresh air, rest, a laxative diet and a cough electuary smeared on the tongue and possibly by the administration of antibiotics.

Like humans, horses get colds in the head. Antibiotics will once more be helpful but the horse must be rested, and given a soft, laxative diet and whilst being well rugged get plenty of good, fresh air.

The condition can be relieved by eucalyptus inhalations. To administer the inhalation two sacks are needed, one inside the other. Put some hay in the sack, sprinkle it with a tablespoon of eucalyptus and then add a kettle of boiling water. Hold the sack over the animal's nostrils.

Whistling and Roaring – are affections of the wind, but are concerned with the larynx and are the result of a paralysis of one of the main nerves on the left side. Roaring is an exaggerated form of whistling.

Whistling may be due to fast work when the horse is out of condition, or even galloping when at grass, or it is possibly an after effect of some septic infection, such as strangles. Treatment is surgical and if performed early has every hope of success.

Big, heavyweight horses are more prone to these affections than others. Ponies, for instance, very seldom, if ever, suffer from whistling. Thick, bull-necked animals would seem to be more easily affected, particularly when they carry their heads somewhat "over-bent".

Other Diseases

Azoturia – is commonly known as "Monday morning disease" because it sometimes occurs following a Sunday rest day. The incidence of azoturia is certainly more noticeable in highly-fed horses whose exercise has been insufficient to cope with the intake of heating foods. When that is the case the fault lies with bad horse-management, but it is not always so. The cause is a build-up of lactic acid in the muscles of the loins and quarters because the circulatory system is unable to remove the products of metabolism and this is more pronounced in some horses than in others.

It occurs after a short period at exercise. There is a marked stiffening in the loins, followed by sweating and general signs of distress. The muscles are hard and painful to the touch. The temperature rises and if urine is passed it is coffee coloured and smells, of all things, of violets.

The loins should be kept as warm as possible and the horse got back to the stable with all speed, which may well involve the use of a horse box.

The vet. should be summoned and until his arrival the back is best covered with hot blankets.

Vit.E/solenium additives have proved successful in the treatment of this complaint.

Strangles – This is a contagious disease caused by an organism called the streptococcus of strangles. Young horses are more susceptible and the disease can be caught from mangers, stables, paddocks, etc., carrying the infection.

The most recognisable symptom is the formation of abscesses in the glands behind and under the lower jaw. These are hot and painful. There is a rise in temperature, the horse is dull and off his feed and a thick, yellow, nasal discharge occurs, together with a cough.

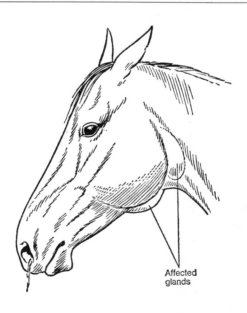

Affected
glands

Strangles.

Isolation and disinfection routine must be carried out and the horse kept warm with rugs and bandages. The first objective is the bursting of the abscesses. To this end hot fomentations should be applied. If this is not done the infection spreads to the rest of the body.

Cough electuaries can be given to soothe the throat. Complete cure lies in rest and good food after the attack to restore condition.

The main constituents of the veterinary chest are:
 thermometer – a digital one is easier to read
 round-ended scissors
 safety-pins
 surgical tape
 cotton wool and Gamgee
 veterinary bandages
 vaseline
 zinc and castor-oil cream
 antibiotic (wound) powder
 sulphanilimide powder
 gauze
 kaolin poultice
 Animalintex poultice
 antiseptic cream
 Epsom salts
 witch-hazel
 Stockholm tar
 vapour rub
 disinfectant
 fly repellent
 antiseptic terramycin (purple) spray
 louse powder
 cooling lotion
 ice packs
 cough electuaries
 boracic powder

CHAPTER 9

Riding and Training the Horse

To attain the highest peak of perfection in the art of riding is beyond the aspirations and the capabilities of most people. Perfection is, indeed, a state beyond us all and to reach a stage where it can be even dimly discerned demands of the horseman much hard work, a high degree of dedication and far above average talent.

This is not to say, however, that the average, intelligent person of normal physique cannot obtain great satisfaction from riding, and with a little conscious effort become a competent horseman and horse-master.

To learn to sit on a horse and to be able to exercise a rudimentary control over his actions without falling off is not difficult. We shall, however, obtain greater enjoyment, ride with more consideration for our horses, and with greater safety to ourselves and to other people, if we devote a little time and thought to understanding the horse and increasing our ability in the saddle.

It is an unhappy fact that the number of horses who are mismanaged, badly ridden and generally abused rises in direct ratio to the increasing number of riders and horse owners.

This is not to say that the majority of horses are actively ill-treated, although there are such cases, but rather that there are too many who are abused, and consequently spoilt, through the ignorance and inefficiency of their riders.

Cruelty and Abuse

There is a difference between cruelty and abuse, although it is one which the horse may be unable to appreciate. It is cruelty when a man knowingly continues to ride an exhausted horse, possibly to its death, to satisfy his personal ego. It is abuse when a man does the same thing, but is too ignorant to know that his horse is exhausted. It is cruelty when a rider, in anger, spurs his horse violently and then with equal force tears at his mouth. It is abuse when an incompetent rider kicks his horse in the ribs and then, to preserve his balance, jags his mouth by hanging on to the reins.

Unfortunately the horse cannot differentiate between the two. To him the result is the same.

Security and Control

Although it may not be apparent in the standard of driving seen on the roads, it is a law that no person shall drive a motor-car, unaccompanied, until he or she has passed a test to prove their competence, which involves learning the technique of placing and controlling the vehicle. There is then a further legal requirement incumbent upon the car-owner, enforced for both his own and other people's safety, which is that his car must be in a roadworthy condition. Amongst other things this entails having a vehicle that has effective brakes and efficient steering.

It is a pity that similar laws are not practicable in respect of people wishing to ride and own horses, for the need is in some ways as great because a living animal is concerned.

It is of no great consequence if a driver tears the gearbox out of his motor-car as a result of his incompetence nor, I suppose, is it mine or anybody else's business if a rider wishes to break his neck on a horse he cannot control, although the cost and time expended in medical care is something to be considered. It is, however, a matter of concern if good horses are spoilt and abused because their owners have not bothered to learn the techniques of security and control.

There are two types of rider the horse could well do without. Those who regard themselves as God's gift to the horse (how salutary it would be to have the horse's opinion on the subject) and those who profess undying love for them in capital letters. In the former case they will not learn because they consider they know it all, and in the second they are too stupid to realise that their love is of the wrong kind and is no substitute for knowledge and ability.

A System of Communication

The foundation of equitation, a term which in its simplest form means sitting or riding a horse, is the establishment of communication between the rider and his partner.

The most primitive and basic communication is for the rider to thump his legs into the horse's ribs, reinforcing the action with a cut

Señor Nuno Oliveira on the Andalusian stallion, Ansioso.

Mr Gregory Lougher on one of his superbly trained Quarter Horses.

from the whip. This means "go forward", and most horses will get the idea in time. A yank on the sensitive mouth, into which has been inserted a piece of metal, which will vary in the intensity of its action according to its shape, means "stop".

Such basic signals, relying for their efficiency on the fear of intense pain, are not, however, anything to do with horsemanship and are unlikely to lead to a *rapport* between horse and rider. Surprisingly there are many riders (again, not horsemen) who do not advance much beyond this stage.

The result is usually a spoilt unhappy horse and a rider who never appreciates the enormous satisfaction and pleasure to be derived from riding in a civilised manner and in harmony with his horse. This is not to say the rider obtains no pleasure – I think he does, but it is a perverse enjoyment of the "show him who's boss" variety.

It is not in rough actions, but in the finer shades of meaning, transmitted through the quiet disposition of the body and the infinitely varied pressures of hand and leg, that the horseman establishes complete communication with the horse and obtains his full co-operation.

Before one achieves this happy state, however, it is obviously necessary for the rider to learn the system of signals and for his body to be able to transmit them. Secondly, and of equal importance, it is helpful, indeed essential, that the horse should understand the significance of the signals he receives from the rider. Unless, therefore, the rider knows his job it is unlikely that the horse will learn his.

The well-trained and intelligent rider will, therefore, improve his horse and the range of communication, and consequently the degree of co-operation between the two, will increase. Conversely, the ignorant rider on a horse that has received little education in the system is unlikely to advance very far, and if he obtains a horse that is capable, by virtue of his training, of a high degree of co-operation, his inability to transmit his wishes intelligibly will result in first confusing the horse, and later reducing him to the same level as his master.

Fortunately, the basis of communication is simple and the two signals "go forward" and "stop", in varying degrees of intensity, are pretty well universal. It is, of course, possible to build an individual system on these elementary actions which ultimately bear little relationship to the base. One could, for instance, teach a horse to canter by pulling his right ear and to halt when his shoulder was slapped. In time the horse would come to rely on these signals and would not obey the more conventional ones. In fact, it would be possible to devise a system which owed nothing to the accepted signals. To produce horses trained in such a way might be amusing, but few people are likely to appreciate so warped a sense of humour.

The Objective

It is only when a system or communication has been established, on both sides, that the rider can proceed to his objective. To my mind that is gained when one has a horse that is comfortable and safe to ride at all paces, jumps small and varied obstacles willingly and calmly and is obedient to the will of the rider. Many riders will decide that this is the ultimate objective as far as they are concerned. This stage of training will, indeed, be sufficient for the average rider, who has neither the time nor inclination to do more than hacking, hunting and to join in riding club events, and it is fairly easily accomplished.

Others, having completed this elementary training, will be more ambitious and will proceed to further, advanced objectives, which will enable them to enter the more demanding fields of dressage, showjumping or horse trials.

Which Method?

Exactly how this objective should be achieved will occupy the minds of horsemen for as long as men and horses occupy the same planet. What is certain is that complete agreement is never likely to be reached.

That this state exists need not, however, bother us in the elementary stages, for all theorists agree, or almost agree, upon at least one fundamental. The rider's legs and (depending on the school of thought subscribed to) his back and seat provide *forward movement* by activating the horse's source of propulsion, his quarters and hind legs, whilst the hands, acting as a sort of brake and steering wheel, contain the energy created by the legs and control the forehand, i.e. the part of the horse in front of the saddle. In fact, the horse is ridden from the back to the front, from the legs into the hands.

Collection Versus Extension

Almost from the beginning of man's association with the horse it is possible to discern the development of two distinct styles of riding both of which were governed by the circumstances of the peoples concerned and the manner in which they waged war. The growth of equitational

Supremacy of leg over hand.

theory and the development of equipment to facilitate its practice stem, indeed, from the use of the horse as an instrument of war.

Much of our history has its origins in Asia Minor, that cockpit of the early civilisations, where advanced societies existed thousands of years before any comparable development in Europe.

There seems little doubt that horses were first domesticated in the steppe-lands bordering the Caspian and Black Seas by nomadic Indo-Aryan tribes.

These peoples, the Scythians and Parthians of the pre-Christian era, who were, in turn, to be followed by related peoples like the Mongols and Huns, all belonged to societies in which the horse was central to the economy and way of life. Horses provided mobility; the means to make war; food and drink, for the mares were milked and the milk when fomented produced *kummis*, the fire-water of the Asian steppes. The hides were used to make shelters and clothes and the dung was dried for burning on the cooking fires.

These nomadic tribes, who considered it beneath them to walk, lived on the backs of their tough steppe ponies; they held their councils seated on that familiar vantage point, answered the calls of nature without quitting the saddle and had even, if the evidence of early Chinese artefacts is to be believed, mastered the seemingly complex business of amatory exercises on horseback.

They were the irregular horse-archers, using the short, double-curved horn bow to loose clouds of arrows at the enemy whilst riding at full gallop with the reins lying on the pony's neck. Their tactic was that of the guerilla's hit and run and the idea of charging home (which became the European concept) was quite alien to them.

Short-legged, squat men, they rode of necessity, for it takes two hands to draw a bow, with the horse extended from nose to tail, crouched and sitting forward.

On the other hand the people of the civilised world, the Greeks and Persians, adopted an upright seat on horses, which although ridden in snaffles, were "collected" in so far that the quarters were engaged under the body. They, of course, sought to operate as organised, cohesive bodies of horsemen.

The division between the light horsemen, influenced by the Middle-Eastern horse peoples, and the heavier cavalry which developed in Western Europe continues virtually to this day along with that older school (older than that of Europe) which became established on the Iberian Peninsula during the long Moorish occupation. The system employed in Iberia, where the horse is to all intents "mouthed" from his nose, went, along with the traditional saddlery, to the New World with the 16th century *conquistadores*. Adapted in principle but not in detail it survives today in the art of the infinitely skilful Californian reinsman – descendant of the cowboy of yesteryear.

"Classical" equitation has its roots in the 16th century Renaissance schools of Europe, reaching its apogee in the 18th century under the French riding master, "the father of classical riding", François Robichon de la Guérinière.

His principles are today exemplified in the work of the Spanish Riding School in Vienna, founded in 1572. The School uses Lipizzaner horses, descendants of the Spanish horses used to form the Imperial Stud at Lipizza, near Trieste, in 1580.

This Indian sowar *epitomises in his seat light horsemen the world over.*

The late Henry Wynmalen riding passage *on a pure-bred Arabian in the seat which would not have been unfamiliar in Classical Greece.*

The School Quadrille performed by the riders and Lipizzaner horses of Vienna's Spanish Riding School, where the classical art has been preserved for 400 years.

The school's classical pas de deux.

The "airs above the ground" remain the ultimate manifestation of collection.

Here are demonstrated the High School movements, the ultimate manifestation of true collection, such as *passage* (a lofty, cadenced trot of great energy) and *piaffe* (the same trot executed on the spot without the horse gaining ground). They require a very high degree of collection and complete submission on the part of the horse to the indications of the rider. Collection is a shortening of the outline, or the posture, of the horse obtained by the compression of the horse towards his centre. That is the hindlegs are engaged well beneath the body, and the head and neck are held high and withdrawn in accordance with the movement to the rear of the centre of balance. In extreme collection, as in *piaffe*, the forehand will be held high and the croup will be lowered as the hindlegs are increasingly engaged under the belly. Collection results in elevation of the paces and, therefore, a shorter stride. By the rider *influencing* the horse to assume this posture the balance of the horse, with the greater proportion of the body weight resting on the hindlegs, is correspondingly moved to the rear.

Such a system is ideally suited to obtaining the objectives required in High School or dressage riding, but slow, elevated and collected paces are of little use to the horse whose purpose is to jump and to gallop across country. In fact to impose so high a degree of collection on such a horse might well prove disastrous. In general, however, whilst not asking for advanced High School movements, the 19th century cavalry schools were influenced by the principle of collection to a considerable extent.

It was in opposition to these methods and principles that the Italian system, evolved by Captain Federico Caprilli (1868–1907) and known either as the Caprilli system, or the "forward seat", came into being at the turn of the century. The Caprilli system discarded collection as unnecessary and unnatural and was designed to meet the needs of mobile cavalry. The emphasis was upon cross-country riding and jumping and it encouraged extension (the lengthening of the posture) with the rider *not* imposing a balance upon the horse, but allowing him to adapt his balance to the conditions of the terrain without interference, the rider's body-weight being placed over, or in equilibrium with, the shifting centre of balance of the horse in motion. Contrary to the classical school the Italians did not *sit* in the saddle, but rather *perched* on it. In fact, the rider's body was to conform with the movement of the horse, instead of imposing an outline on the latter.

In extension, as in the gallop, the centre of balance of the horse moves forward as more of the weight is thrown on the forehand. The Italian rider, therefore, moved his body forward, seat out of the saddle, and let his hands follow the extended head and neck of the horse.

The rider in this position was the least possible encumbrance to the horse's movement. There was likewise no interference from the rider over fences. The horse was to position himself, without being "placed" at the fence by his rider, and the execution of the leap was his affair.

Today the system practised at Vienna is still the greatest influence in the production of the specialised dressage horse. Caprilli's system is, however, rarely practised *in its entirety*. Had not Caprilli died young, as the result of a riding accident in his early forties, it is probable that he would have developed his theories and even altered them. As it is, the pure Italian system, whilst remaining in its essentials the basis of riding over obstacles, has been adapted to suit the needs and temperaments of individuals and nations.

The Germans, for instance, adopt the forward seat over fences but do not embrace the theory of non-interference, nor do they discard collection. They ride their horses with great accuracy and precision, the rider being wholly dominant in regard to pace, approach and take-off, demanding and receiving complete obedience. They may not always be elegant horsemen, but they are effective. The method suits them and they carry it out with thoroughness and success.

The ideal of the horse moving and jumping in complete freedom, unhindered by the rider, is undoubtedly appealing, but it entails the possession of exceptional horses, expertly trained in the system, for it to be practised successfully.

Although the adherents of the pure forward seat will argue, admittedly with some logic, that the seat they advocate has every advantage, the average rider will not find it easy to maintain for anything but short periods, and the exclusion of the back and seat as aids limits the rider's conventional control to some degree.

In this country, and indeed elsewhere, we have taken a middle course between the two roads of complete dominance and complete freedom. Whether there is a recognisable British seat is doubtful, but, in general, with our background of the hunting field, we allow our horses to do a little thinking for themselves, and do not encourage them to place complete reliance on the rider. To my mind this is nearer to the ideal of a partnership and more acceptable than complete domination. Even so, opinions differ, sometimes considerably, as to the means used to attain the end.

Theory and Practice

It may well be asked why it is necessary to approach the business of riding in such painstaking fashion when there are numbers of men and women (there will be one or two in every hunt) who know nothing of the finer points of equitation and yet whose horses carry them well, and to all intents happily, for many seasons. The answer is that these men and women are brave, natural riders who, by experience, have found for themselves an effective method of crossing a country. How they do it is something of a closed book and, beyond remarking that it is as well to leave his head alone, they are usually hard put to explain their inherent prowess in the saddle.

Books on equitation are rarely perused by such people – there is after all no point in their attempting to change their seat, or to absorb new ideas, when they have evolved a perfectly effective method of their own.

I know of more than one eminent judge whose seat on a horse is an affront to the eyes, and, one would think, to the horse also. Yet I would that horses went as well for me as they do for these gentlemen.

They are, however, the exceptional horsemen – certainly not the average ones, who form the great majority of the riding public. In addition they are dangerous people to copy.

The less talented, among whom I include myself, must work that much harder, absorb a little theory by intelligent application, and then learn how to put it into practice if they are to get as much, and possibly more, satisfaction from their riding.

This is particularly the case for those who come to riding a little late in life. I am neither as brave nor as supple as I was 20 years ago (40 years ago?), but my horses probably go better, and I ride them more intelligently and considerately than I did in my extreme youth.

The Penalties of Limitation

In those days my ambition was to become a superlative horseman. I never achieved it because I had neither the means nor, in consequence, the time and I was not possessed of the necessary talent.

Once I had accepted my limitations in this latter respect I realised that if I was to be no more than a competent horseman and horsemaster, anything I did with horse would be the result of conscious study, planning and execution. Because of my lack of natural talent it is necessary for me first to define a final objective, possible of accomplishment on the part of both myself and the individual horse; secondly, to divide the road to this goal into a series of smaller objectives; and thirdly to formulate, by studying the characteristics of the horse, a method which will achieve each one of them. Finally when the operation is commenced I must never forget to make sure that each minor objective is made secure before I pass on to the next.

Three Factors in Riding and Training

The natural horseman will achieve his ends much quicker than people in my situation; that he may not know how he has done so, or why he carries out certain actions, is of no consequence to him.

The elementary analysis which follows will not help such men to improve themselves, it is given for the benefit of those whose gifts are not so great and then only as a tentative guide.

The objective I have referred to, that of producing a balanced, obedient horse, is certainly within the scope of any intelligent person willing to make the efforts of the sort I have indicated. The establishment of communication will, however, be made more quickly and more satisfactorily if the rider has an understanding of three factors:

(1) The mental make-up and characteristics of the horse

(2) The physical structure of the horse as it relates to movement and balance

(3) The elementary theory of riding

Obviously, the application of this knowledge will be dependent upon the physical ability of the rider to put it into practice, but even this facility can be acquired without too much difficulty by riders of normal physique who are not entirely without equestrian tact.

INSTINCT AND CHARACTERISTICS

Many of the methods employed in training the horse and reaching a state of communication with him arise from the animal's peculiar mental make-up. It is through our knowledge of these special traits that we are able to use them to our advantage and adapt them to our purpose.

The first quality to recognise in the horse is that of *gregariousness*. He is a herd animal and his instinct is always to remain with, or to return to, his own kind. Although it is an instinct which is overcome when the rider has gained a sufficiently advanced state of obedience (as when a

The Caprilli system in Italy, the country of its origin.

horse leaves his companions to jump in the show-ring on his own, or is turned aside from a line of horses in the hunting field to follow an independent route of his rider's choosing) it is never entirely eliminated.

On the other hand it is an instinct which can be exploited, and explains why a hunter will jump obstacles, which on his own he might well decline, when in the company of other horses or when, having become separated from his fellows, he is asked to return to them.

Complementary to this gregarious instinct is the question of *security* or, perhaps, the lack of security.

The horse in the wild state finds security in the company of his companions in the herd. Removal from the environment, by however many hundreds of years, and re-alignment of his sense of security to his altered circumstances, may well colour his whole outlook, and detract from this basic need. This is particularly the case when a horse is kept singly, and manifestations of insecurity are more likely to occur with such horses than with those in say a racing stable or riding school.

I have already mentioned that in the wild state the majority of horses submit happily enough to the discipline of the dominant stallion, the leader of the herd, and that in domestication it is possible for his human master to assume this function. This responsibility for leadership and security is one that the horse-owner must fulfil before he can hope to achieve communication or co-operation. An insecure horse is rarely a calm horse, and a horse that is not calm is never attentive or receptive.

It is this lack of security which makes a horse in new surroundings unwilling to leave his box or even to nap (i.e. refuse to go the way he is asked) when first ridden by a new owner. Should the rider not recognise this and, instead of encouraging the horse and allaying his fears, set about him, almost irreparable damage will be done to the relationship.

It should also be recognised that the horse associates, or should associate, his stable with security as well, of course, as the place where he is fed, a procedure which influences him not inconsiderably. The effect upon him will be the same as that produced by other horses and he will always go more willingly towards it than away from it. It is as well, therefore, when siting a schooling area to keep it away from the *immediate* proximity of the stable.

The *love of routine*, particularly with regard to feeding times and exercise periods, is closely connected with security and the latter will be affected if a routine is not maintained.

Work does not come naturally to a horse, even after centuries of subservience. By nature he is a *lazy*, tranquil creature and if left to his own devices is quite content to spend the time eating, sleeping and browsing. It is, therefore, quite beyond his comprehension as to why his master should want him to gallop across this field, trot down that lane or jump over a log, when he could more easily walk around it. Fortunately the horse is extremely *co-operative*, far more so than a dog, and is more than ready to fall in with his master's wishes, when, and this is the important part, he understands what those wishes are. This is rather remarkable when we consider how *nervous* the horse is. Essentially he is highly strung and very easily frightened, a sudden movement or a strange object on a familiar path will rouse his deepest instincts and his defence is to flee from this potential danger. One of the most important traits to appreciate is the extraordinary *sensitivity* of the horse. He is extremely sensitive to pain or the threat of pain.

The horse is not equipped to play an aggressive role, his safety lies in his ability to flee from danger and as a result his tolerance of pain is low.

Other four-footed animals of less strength, the dog is one of them, are not nearly so sensitive in this respect and will turn upon an aggressor – not so the horse – his defence is always in flight.

Horses that are said to *fight* the bit are not in fact doing so. The horse pulls against a rider whose uneducated hands act in a similar fashion, not in a spirit of opposition, but because he is trying to get away from the pain he experiences. It is this innate sensitivity, combined with his desire to please, that allows us to control the body of the horse by the indications of our legs, as for instance when we apply one leg to move the quarters. In this case the horse, unless physically unable to comply with our request or in a state of high excitement, moves *away* from the pressure.

In the green horse we may have to supplement the pressure of the leg by a tap with the whip and while the horse may not, or should not, consciously associate the tap with the fear of pain, subconsciously he will do so and will move away in consequence.

It is only when the horse is confused, excited, physically incapable of co-operation, or when the stronger instinct of self-preservation or the fear of experiencing greater pain assumes an ascendancy, that he resists the simple indications of his rider.

One of the more frustrating characteristics of the horse is his propensity to become *excited*. Other horses will produce this reaction, the tension of the rider can do so, and it is particularly apparent when he is asked to jump or do something a little out of his normal routine. This trait is hardly one that is helpful to the rider and, while no amount of training will eradicate it entirely, it should be a prime consideration to keep it within reasonable bounds. In all forms of schooling the aim must be to obtain the necessary responses in a state of calm. An excited horse is never attentive.

It may seem difficult to understand how this timorous, sensitive fellow can also have *courage*. And yet, paradoxically, most horses possess this quality in abundance. The horse will, if ridden by a firm, sensitive horseman, overcome his natural fears, and launch himself over strange obstacles. Tired, and without the stimulus of his fellows, he will battle on in response to the urging rider. He will cross marshy ground, although every wild instinct tells him that this is terrain which is dangerous and should be avoided.

It is true that he will do these things if the rider induces in him excitement, bordering on panic. A horse is often, and wrongly, made to jump in this way a fence he has constantly refused, instead of being taken back to jump lower and less difficult obstacles. To use such methods only results, however, in producing a horse that is ultimately so soured that he may become impossible.

Finally, and of great significance, is the *memory* of the horse, which is highly developed and very retentive. Once the animal has associated certain signals with certain movements he does not forget the lesson. Conversely, if he associates a movement or a particular place with discomfort or fear he does not forget this either and will evince excitement and resistance.

It is largely by our understanding this extraordinary capacity to remember and to associate various happenings with the memory of pleasure or discomfort that we are able to train the horse.

Reward and Punishment

As a result of our knowledge, rewards for co-operation will be frequent and punishment for disobedience very rare indeed. Always, in fact, the carrot – rarely the whip. The "carrot" need not necessarily be an edible one and, in fact, too many titbits can result in a horse becoming silly and in extreme cases something of a bully.

A horse can just as well be rewarded for good work by an encouraging vocal noise – I say noise because the horse does not understand words – only the tone of voice in which they are uttered. A horse will feel equally rewarded by being called "a b ... old b ... ", providing the tone of voice is of the right sort, as being addressed as "mummy's pet booflekins". In the same way a pat on the neck, or being allowed to stretch out his head and neck after a period of work asking for collection, is just as much a reward as one of a more material kind.

The edible reward should certainly be given, and sometimes it will prove to be a useful bribe, but it should be reserved for special occasions.

As an instance of the trouble that can be encountered by the indiscriminate use of titbits, I remember a horse I had who found lateral work (i.e. sidesteps) difficult. Very patiently I eventually obtained a couple of steps, then, without thinking, I took a piece of biscuit from my pocket and gave the horse his reward from the saddle. I found this worked so well that very soon I had obtained four sidesteps – and there it stopped. When the horse had completed just four steps he would halt and turn his head, waiting for his biscuit. I must confess I never had the heart to try and break him of this habit which he had acquired entirely from his master.

To overdo the reward is forgivable, but to do the same when it comes to punishment is both stupid and inexcusable. In almost every case where the horse resists there is a very good reason for him doing so.

There are, to my mind, three main reasons for resistance: when the horse is asked to do something beyond his physical and mental capacity; when it causes him pain to comply, because of an ill-fitting bit, a rank bad horseman, a strained muscle, an incorrectly made shoe or a painful back condition or when he becomes confused by the inability of the rider to convey his wishes clearly through the medium of the aids. In each of these instances the fault is not that of the horse, but of the rider.

Horses, like humans, however, are not all, or always, angels, even though they may be more fitted for Heaven than their masters. Occasionally we may find a horse who is deliberately disobedient and wilful. He must then be corrected firmly, but without anger. Even in these cases it is usually the fault of some previous owner who has provoked the initial resistance and we should be very wary lest the punishment is too severe in relation to the crime. The majority of horses are extremely susceptible to the voice and in the same way that the reward need not be a real carrot, so punishment is not necessarily the whip. A good growl is often sufficient to produce the required result.

If the whip has to be used a slap on the shoulder or a sharp tap to reinforce the leg is usually enough. I would only hit a horse hard if he persisted in running back, which is just too dangerous to be tolerated, and then I would hit him very sharply, once on either side, accompanied by a salutary dig with the spurs.

The important thing to remember is that punishment must be immediate if it is to be effective. This the horse understands and remembers.

To punish him five minutes after the event does no good at all, it only serves to confuse him, as he cannot understand why he is being punished. It is only when he associates immediate punishment with a particular resistance that he understands the cause and effect.

It is, of course, the height of stupidity to punish a horse who is frightened, as for instance when he shies or plays up in traffic. We are then only confirming and adding to the fear in his mind of the particular object which caused the trouble. Our purpose on these occasions is to demand his obedience and distract his attention away from the traffic or the flapping sack on the hedgerow.

Never should the horse be punished through the bit. It is permissible for the more experienced to resist, intermittently, a continued mouth resistance on the part of the horse and even to give a light upwards jerk, but no more than might cause a momentary discomfort. The bit is the most delicate of the lines of communication set up between horse and rider and if it is abused the structure of confidence collapses. It will take months of patient work to rebuild it.

Finally, the intelligent horseman will never allow himself to be put in a position where he is forced to punish the horse.

Does the Horse Think?

Whether this highly strung animal, who has the ability to evoke so great a fascination in us humans, is intelligent or not depends on one's interpretation of intelligence.

Many great horsemen have said that he is not intelligent, but is purely governed by his peculiar characteristics which the greater mental capacity of man has turned to his own ends. I would not deny the horse's inability to think in abstract terms, but thre are far too many instances which display equine intelligence for me to agree that he is unintelligent.

I am sure horses are intelligent, they vary in degree as do humans, and their intelligence is certainly not of the sort we easily recognise, but it is there if we, the masters, can develop it. This is the whole crux of the matter. Intelligence will be governed and developed by environment and by the ability and sensitivity of the human individual concerned.

The mistake is to try to humanise our animals and to endow them with the sort of understanding we would like them to have. Horses are not human, they are animal, in their own right and with their own dignity.

On the whole I find them as intelligent as, and often far more attractive than, many of my two-legged acquaintances.

The Physical Structure of a Horse

If it is important for us to understand the mental make-up of the horse it is just as essential that we should understand his physical anatomy as well.

In very simple terms we are confronted with a relatively rigid body mass supported by four pillars. The equilibrium of the mass is then adjusted by the agency of the head and neck acting as a sort of pendulum with a weight – the head – at one end.

The movement of this body mass is on an almost central point which is termed the centre of balance, or the centre of gravity. It is, in fact, rather like a see-saw which pivots on a central support.

In the horse at rest the centre of balance is determined as being at the intersection of two imaginary lines. The first is drawn vertically through the centre of the body, some ten inches behind the withers, and the second, horizontally, through the point of the shoulder to the buttock.

This can be proved quite conclusively by taking two large scales and persuading the horse to stand with his hindfeet on one scale and his forefeet on the other. The exact position of the balance will vary slightly according to the conformation of the subject but, all in all, the intersection point, which has been referred to, will be found to be more or less correct.

It was once assumed that a balanced horse distributed his weight equally over all four limbs. This is, in fact, a fallacy. The horse at rest, standing on all four feet, has a greater weight upon the forelegs than on the hindlegs, while in movement the balance of the horse and the distribution of weight shifts according to the posture of his body.

At speed the outline, or the posture, of the body is extended and to maintain its equilibrium the head and neck are stretched out. The centre of balance, following the extension of head and neck, then moves forward. Conversely if the head and neck are raised, lightening and raising the forehand, the horse, in order to remain balanced, lowers the quarters, engaging the hindlegs under the body, and in consequence the centre of his balance moves to the rear in accordance with his altered and shortened posture. Should the horse move laterally the centre of balance is shifted from the centre towards the direction of movement. Likewise a horse turning sharply at speed shifts his centre of balance inwards in accordance with the turn's direction.

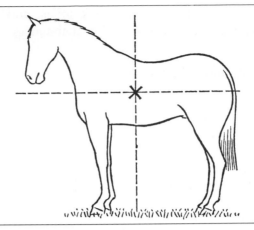

The centre of balance in the horse at halt.

A horse maintains equilibrium in movement by repeatedly losing and regaining his balance. If a leg or legs do not come to earth at precisely the correct moment he will experience a longer period of momentary equilibrium loss and will stumble. If the leg is unable to reach the ground in a certain time he will fall. In either case he will endeavour to maintain his balance by movements of his head and neck, which control the weighting of his limbs and the shifting of his point of equilibrium.

A horse, therefore, rarely distributes his weight evenly over the four pillars supporting his body mass. In extreme extension, as in the gallop of the racehorse, the horse may be balanced, but his weight is carried to a large extent on his forelegs. In extreme collection, as in the dressage horse, the weight is transferred to the hindlegs.

Unhampered by any weight upon his back, or by a hand imposing restraint upon the position of his head and neck, the horse can gallop over rough ground, adjusting his centre of balance by means of moving his head and neck, to suit the requirements of the particular terrain he is crossing. He stops and turns gracefully, easily and at will. But this is not the case when he is carrying a burden in the shape of a human being, who may weigh one-fifth of his total body weight. The retention of balance is then made more difficult because not only has he to cope with his own problem, but with an additional shifting body as well, having a centre of balance of its own.

One could quote the instance of a man being asked to run carrying an unevenly weighted knapsack slung from his shoulders, in such a way that it bumped his bottom as he ran, to illustrate the point. It must,

"In riding across country the rider . . . must align the body weight with that of the advancing and retreating centre of balance."

however, be obvious that just as the man will be able to run better with an evenly weighted knapsack, strapped securely, as high on his back as possible and, therefore, as near to his centre of balance (the true centre being the top of his head), as the limits of practicability allow, so it will be easier for the horse if his burden is sited over *his* centre of balance,

Cross-country jumping in excellent style (this and opposite page).

shifting in accordance with his movement and to all intents and purposes fused to his own body.

In riding across country, therefore, the rider, if he is to be the least possible encumbrance to his horse, and is to allow the animal to perform with maximum efficiency, must align his body weight with that of the advancing and retreating centre of balance of his mount.

As the movements of head and neck, by contracting and decontracting and by being raised and lowered, control the equilibrium of the horse it follows that, ideally, the rider should therefore not interfere or impose a head position, but that his hands should follow every movement of the head.

This would be acceptable to the pure, non-interference Caprilli school and possibly to many more of us if we had horses upon whom we could entirely rely. When, however, obstacles are to be surmounted the horse usually needs some assistance from the senior member of the partnership and we will, in fact, by the actions of our bodies impose a posture on the horse, asking him to shift his centre in accordance with the demands our actions make, although in the actual take off and in the flight over the fence we will revert to the policy of non-interference, positioning our bodies over and in line with the movement of the centre of balance.

Exemplary positions: (above) *riding downhill;* (opposite page, top) *riding over an obstacle;* (opposite page, bottom) *riding on the flat. Note in all three positions the rein contact.*

Surprisingly, to many, the horse is not by nature very well equipped to carry weight, and it is only by training him that he becomes conditioned to carry a rider and is physically able to answer the indications which ask him to shorten or lengthen his posture, and so to shift his centre of balance to comply with our requirements.

The rider can be said to be in balance with his horse when his body is weighted over the horse's pivoting point, the centre of balance, at all paces.

The horse, when ridden, is balanced when his weight distribution is such that he is able to shorten or lengthen his posture and, therefore, the line of his balance (the line of balance is upwards from rear to front in collection, when the forehand is lightened, and the opposite way round in extention, when the forehand is weighted) either in response to the indications of the rider or, in the absence of those indications, in accordance with the particular circumstances of the moment.

The propulsive power of the horse is, as we have seen and as most people are aware, contained in the quarters and hindlegs of the horse. What is perhaps not so readily appreciated is that the power which drives the body mass forwards is the same as that which powers the changes of direction made by the body mass. In the minds of a great many riders, I am sure, is the mistaken idea that the propulsive power, the engine of the horse, is connected from the pelvic structure, via the backbone, to the horse's head. This, of course, is not so. The quarters are connected to the *shoulders*, but the head and neck, as will be seen from a glance at the diagram of the skeleton, are free, flexible, and not influenced or connected to the movement of the quarters. Unless this is understood clearly we shall, and many people do, continue to ride thinking that the position of the head and neck, when bent laterally to one side or the other, governs the direction of movement of the body mass. We will, in fact, think that where the head is pointed the body will automatically follow.

Very often, of course, this is exactly what does happen, because the horse associates the bending of his head to left or right as an indication from the rider that that is the way he wishes to go. The green horse, or one that has decided that to turn left is not in accordance with his wishes, is quite able to turn to the right even though his head points in the opposite direction. In fact the more the head in these circumstances is inclined to the left the easier it becomes for the horse to move to the right.

The horse pushes his body round a corner by engaging the inside hindleg more strongly and further beneath his body. That is, in a turn to the left it is the left hindleg which is employed and vice versa. It is rather like a skater who in a similar fashion turns on his inside leg.

The change of direction is, therefore, initiated from the rear and it is the positioning of the shoulders, connected to the propelling force by the spine, which completes the turn. In the trained horse, accustomed to move under weight, the slight inclination of the head and neck in the direction of the turn acts in accordance with the movement of his centre of balance and follows the inclination of the shoulder. The movement is then from rear to front, not the opposite way about.

Most of us will have seen the recalcitrant pony with his nose pulled round almost to his rider's toe, persisting in moving in the opposite direction, despite the thumping legs and exhortations of his rider.

Apart from his obvious wilful intent, the extreme position of his head is placing his body in a position where he can best accomplish his disobedience. The inside shoulder is so completely restricted as to make movement in that direction impossible and, in addition, his *outside* hindleg will be engaged so far under him that it contributes materially to his intention to do the opposite to what is required by his rider.

The disposition of the head can be clearly seen when working a young horse on the lunge, particularly at the canter, where he will very often hold his head outside the circle rather than following a correct line. He is then using the head and neck as a balancer to counteract the inward movement of his gravitational centre, and freeing his inside shoulder to more easily cope with the movement. As his body becomes more supple and his balance improves he will not find it necessary to use his head and neck in this way, although when turning sharply at speed he may do so. Indeed, an experienced and skilful show-jumping rider may be seen to incline his horse's head outside the direction of movement when he is moving at speed in a restricted space within the confines of the arena and the various elements of the course.

It is because of the inflexibility of the spine combined, in the untrained horse, with stiff muscles on either side of the backbone and with the natural over-development of one side, that the horse experiences difficulty in making a true circle, i.e. one in which the track of the forelegs is exactly followed by that of the hindlegs.

The one-sided development of the horse, which is rather like humans being either right or left-handed, is usually on the right or offside. It commences with the curved position taken by the embryo within the womb, and is further encouraged by our handling youngstock from the nearside.

As a result untrained or partially trained animals will usually turn more easily to the left than to the right. Early training is, therefore, aimed at encouragement of *equal* muscular development on either side of the back: until this has been achieved the horse will ride "one-sided".

In the trained, supple and developed horse, working on a circle, a very little flexion takes place in the lumbar area, the head and neck are inclined on to the line of direction, the rib cage on the outside of the circle assumes a prominence, while that on the inside flattens, and the outside shoulder is pushed outwards and slightly in advance of the inside one. The *appearance* is then that of the horse being *bent round the rider's inside leg*.

The Mouth and Bitting

As the majority of riders are so greatly concerned, often to the point of obsession, with the horse's head and particularly his mouth, it seems reasonable that before inflicting various pieces of ironmongery upon this most sensitive part of the animal's anatomy we should understand something of its construction. Indeed, unless we inspect a horse's mouth and have a knowledge of the action of the various bits which are available I cannot see how a correct selection for a particular horse can be made.

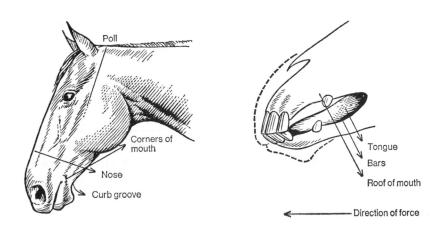

Parts of the head affected by the action of various bit groups.

Benjamin Latchford, the greatest of the 19th century loriners, once said that there was "a key to every horse's mouth". He also said that of every twenty bits he made "nineteen are for men's heads and one for the horse's"; be that as it may, it is surely advisable to have a look at the lock before selecting a key.

As we have already seen, each jaw, in a full mouth, contains six incisor and twelve molar teeth. We have also noted that the upper jaw is larger than the lower and that the upper molars grow down and outwards, while the lower ones behave in opposite fashion. It is not difficult to see that because of this arrangement the outside of the top molars and the inside of the lower ones will receive little wear. Unless, therefore, the teeth receive regular attention the enamel on these sides will become sharp and the cheeks or tongue, or both, will be in danger of laceration. Obviously there will be no key to a mouth in this condition. It may appear to be elementary to urge regular, daily inspection of the mouth and yet I wonder how frequently many horse-keepers do inspect their charges' mouths in the course of the year. Not very often I suspect.

An inspection of the mouth will reveal the *bars*, an area of gum between the incisor and molar teeth and the *tongue*. We shall also be able to see how thinly protected are the *corners of the mouth*.

In general the bars will be more or less sharply defined and shaped like an inverted V, or they will be broad, flat and fleshy. The former are usually found in Thoroughbred horses and the latter in those of more common descent. *Both in their virgin state are sensitive*, the first being more so than the second. Occasionally, and may we be forgiven, we shall see bars that are heavily calloused and even deformed by severe bitting and heavy hands.

It follows, therefore, that a mouth with sharply defined, thinly protected bars, will require the lightest (in reality the least severe) of bits and the most sensitive of hands if the horse is not to become demented by pain. Conversely, in extreme cases where the bars are unduly flat and heavily covered, it may be necessary to use a slightly sharper bit if we are to communicate our wishes satisfactorily.

All mouths are sensitive to a greater or lesser degree, but there are no hard-mouthed horses, only hard-handed riders.

In the same way there are no horses with one-sided mouths. It is possible, I suppose, for a horse's mouth to become less sensitive upon one side or the other if his rider persists in using one rein to the virtual exclusion of the other. The real trouble, though, in the one-sided horse is not in his mouth, but in the one-sided muscular development of his back and his inability to move straight, i.e. the hind feet following the track of the front ones.

The tongue, too, can cause bitting problems. Often, particularly in Thoroughbred horses, it appears almost too big for the mouth. As a result the organ tends to spread over the bars and so obstruct the direct action of the bit upon those parts and upon the lower jaw.

There is then the difference in the actual shape of the mouth, a blood horse usually having a long, thin structure and a common horse the reverse. The structure of the mouth in this respect is, therefore, a determining factor in the choice of bits other than those of the snaffle group. A Pelham bit, for instance, is just not suitable for a long mouth. If the mouthpiece is correctly adjusted to touch the corners of the lips the curb chain cannot fit into the curb groove, but will ride too high on the unprotected jaw bones, causing chafing, even ossification, and certainly unnecessary pain and discomfort. In some cases this can be partly overcome by using a vulcanite mouthpiece which, being as thick again as a metal one, allows the chain to take up a lower position.

On the other hand a Pelham bit may well suit a short mouth, which just will not comfortably accommodate a Weymouth bit and bradoon.

A cursory examination of the jaw bones will show how important it is for the curb chain to fit correctly. The curb groove at the base of the jaw bones is fairly heavily protected with gristle, but above this point the bones are covered only with skin and, therefore, are easily susceptible to injury.

Whatever the bit selected it should never be one of the pencil-thin variety. The bars and the corners of the mouth, upon which the bit acts, are composed of millions of sensory nerves. The narrower the bit the more confined is the area upon which it exerts pressure and the more quickly will that area become numb and insensitive. A broad bit, with a large, flat mouthpiece, is softer in its action as it spreads the pressure over a correspondingly larger area and affords greater comfort to the horse.

Horses, as we have seen, pull *against* pain in order to get away from it, and control is never obtained by its infliction.

The Five Bitting Groups and Their Action

Having gone so far this is probably an opportune time to study the action of bits and the various types which are commonly employed.

I have dealt with this subject in more detail in the book *Saddlery* (J.A. Allen), but as it is clearly necessary for the horseman to understand what the piece of metal at the end of his reins is doing it will be as well to recapitulate the main points.

Briefly, the object of the bit is to *assist* us in obtaining direction and regulating the pace. If we wish to enlarge that basic definition, we might say it is the means whereby we suggest a desirable head position, which makes it easy for the horse to co-operate with our indications in regard to pace and direction, and is also the means by which we influence the outline. Please note the inference that the bit is not a means of domination, nor is it a peremptory command, but rather *an invitation to co-operate.*

The principle involved is as follows: there are five main groups of bits, all of which, sometimes strengthened by the aid of auxiliaries such as nosebands and martingales, act upon one or more of seven parts of the horse's head. The parts involved are the *bars*, the *corners of the lips*, the *tongue*, the *curb groove*, the *poll*, sometimes the *nose* and occasionally the *roof of the mouth*.

The five bit groups are the *Snaffle*, the *Weymouth bit and bradoon*, the *Pelham*, the *Gag*, and the *Bitless* bridle, which may assume a variety of shapes, as indeed may some of the other groups.

The snaffle acts upwards on the corners of the lips when the head is held low, as might be the case with a young, green horse, or to the rear when the head is held higher and the nose retracted so that the bit acts across the lower jaw, involving an increased contact on the bars and rather less on the corners of the lips. The snaffle may be either jointed or have a mullen or half-moon shaped mouthpiece. The last named is the milder and becomes even more so when constructed not of metal, but of flexible rubber.

The bradoon part of the Weymouth combination acts in the same way as the snaffle, although, when used in conjunction with the curb, its function is more towards raising the head. The curb bit is vastly more complicated and acts upon a number of the specified parts of the head. It consists of a mouthpiece with a hump in the middle, known as the *tongue port*, to which are fitted cheeks of varying length, to the eye of which is fastened a curb chain.

The purpose of the port (the German word is *züngfreiheit*, meaning tongue freedom) is to allow the tongue to be accommodated within its shape and so prevent it from lying over the bars and obstructing the action of the mouthpiece's bearing surfaces. Upon the size and shape of the port depends the degree of accommodation for the tongue.

The mouthpiece, when the cheeks of the bit assume an angle of 45° or more in response to rein pressure, exerts a downward influence, and one which operates slightly to the rear, on the bars.

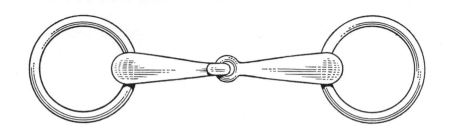

A good type of snaffle.

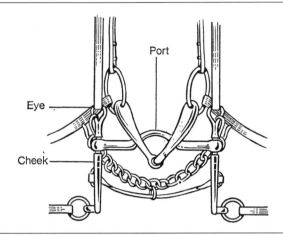

A Weymouth bit and bradoon.

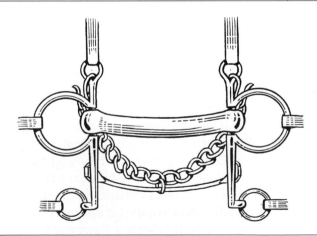

A Pelham.

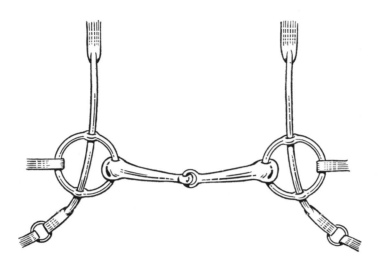

A gag snaffle.

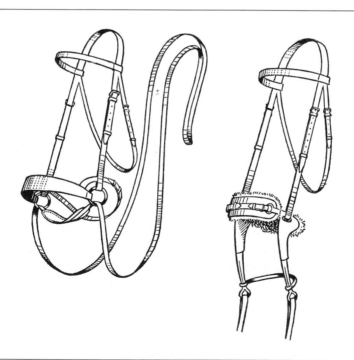

Two bitless bridles.

The downward movement is further accentuated by the forward movement of the eye, to which the cheek pieces of the bridle are attached. When the cheek is inclined at an angle out of the vertical it follows that the eye, by means of its attachment to the bridle cheek pieces, exerts a downward pressure on the poll.

There is then the additional restraint of the tightening curb chain on the curb groove encouraging the horse to give, or flex the lower jaw.

Only in bits with a tongue port of excessive height is pressure imposed upon the roof of the mouth. Such bits are not within the realm of civilised horsemanship.

The severity, or otherwise, of the bit depends upon the length of the cheek, greater leverage being obtained with a long cheek than with a short one.

Upon the length of cheek below the mouthpiece depends the pressure on the bars, whilst the length of cheek above the mouthpiece dictates the degree of pressure imposed upon the poll.

The action of the Weymouth, therefore, is highly sophisticated, allowing the rider to suggest a head position with great accuracy.

The Pelham which, admittedly, suits some mouths, is a hybrid attempting the impossible. It seeks to combine the action of snaffle and curb in one mouthpiece, an aim which cannot wholly succeed.

When the snaffle rein predominates the action is that of the snaffle, when the curb predominates that of the curb bit. With very skilful rein control it is just possible that some sort of combination of the two is possible, but it is rarely achieved.

Usually the mouthpiece does not have a port, but is of the half-moon variety, and when this is the case greater pressure is brought on the tongue and there is a less definite action on the bars.

The Gag snaffle, by passing the bridle cheek through holes in the bit rings, becomes an accentuation of the ordinary snaffle in its action. It can be regarded as raising the head by severe upward pressure against the corners of the mouth, although, in fact, it exerts an equal, if not so painful, pressure downwards on the poll.

Unless carefully handled it can result in an inflexible head carriage and restrict extension of the head and neck.

The last of the bit groups, the bitless bridle, operates purely on the nose, just above the base of the nasal bone. It can be used to restore the confidence of horses with badly bruised mouths and in its simplest form is the basis of training used on the Western horse.

I use it consistently in the schooling of young horses before the gradual introduction of a bit, and always when teaching jumping. I only wish more people would appreciate its efficacy.

The nose is also employed when a drop noseband is used with a snaffle. The noseband is useful in preventing evasions, such as sliding the bit across the mouth and out of its central position, evasion by excessive opening of the mouth and in restraining an over-impetuous animal by inducing him to lower his head and accept the action of the bit.

Martingales, never an end in themselves, reinforce or assist the bit action by restricting the upward movement of the head. I once used them extensively, appreciating the extra control they afforded and for the sake of the life-line provided in the shape of the neck strap. Nowadays, I consider them largely unnecessary, but retain the neck strap to preserve my seat and dignity in unforeseen eventualities.

No bit can possibly be effective unless properly fitted. The snaffle may project half an inch either side of the mouth, and should touch the corners of the lips. When a curb bit is used, as in the Weymouth, it should rest about halfway along the bars. Curb chains should not be used without lipstraps, which prevent their rising out of the curb groove.

When a drop noseband is fitted it must lie some three inches above the nostrils, which entails the *drop* part (i.e. the rear strap which fastens under the mouthpiece of the bit) being long enough to allow the nosepiece to assume this position.

There are hundreds of bits made in every form that man can devise, all of which are aimed at controlling the horse. Most of them can be ignored, and some should be condemned as monuments to ignorance. A competent horseman, given a horse that has not been entirely ruined, should need no more than a snaffle, possibly a drop-noseband, and a Weymouth bit and bradoon.

ELEMENTARY THEORY

Having absorbed this much it is now necessary to consider a little fundamental theory. This is not difficult in itself, the problem is putting it into practice, which requires a little more time, but is made easier if we know what we are trying to achieve.

The key to good riding is supremacy of leg over hand and it is, therefore, unfortunate that a fundamental requirement when teaching or learning to ride is that the beginner should have a leg on either side of the horse and sit facing the front end. The instinct of self-preservation is the strongest of all, and when the would-be horseman is placed on what is to him an insecure base it is not surprising that he should regard the reins placed in his hands as convenient lifelines.

Once he achieves a degree of security he may not be quite so reliant on the reins to preserve his balance, but he is still facing the front and is physically in connection with the horse's head, which he can see. He also knows that most horses will turn, after a fashion, if he pulls the necessary rein, and that if he pulls both simultaneously the horse may stop; again, after a fashion.

Many riders go no further than this and for the rest of their days ride their horses with their hands alone. They have become obsessed with the front end, by which means they seek to control and position their unfortunate animals. They may even decide to go in for a little dressage and will fly to the nearest saddler's shop for a Weymouth bit and bradoon, by which means they fondly imagine they will achieve "collection".

Oh! that they could all be turned round to face the horse's tail and become, if not obsessed, at least aware of the engine, the driving force, which is behind the saddle, and upon the proper control of which depends the posture and balance of the horse.

The Aid Combination

In equitation we have at our disposal certain aids, that is we communicate with the horse by using our voice and the various parts of our body. These are known as natural aids. Artificial, supplementary or auxiliary aids are the whip and the spurs.

I term these signals the Aid Combination and it is best explained by a diagram which, for obvious reasons, I call the Wheel of Equitation. The wheel has a central hub – the strong, supple and independent seat. It then has four spokes – the legs, the trunk, which includes the seat, the back and the disposition of weight, the hands and the head.

If one of these spokes is weak it cannot perform its function and the wheel collapses. If the wheel has no hub to which the spokes are connected we have no wheel at all.

First then, the independent seat, which can be defined as one having no dependence upon the reins for its security, and in which the limbs and body weight are in a state of physical freedom and are able to influence the horse according to the rider's wishes, while the rider remains *in balance* with the horse.

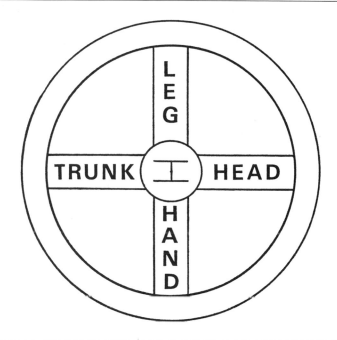

The Wheel of Equitation.

Upon this seat, the hub of the equitational wheel, depends the effectiveness of the aids. Without it the limbs are restricted in their movement, being more concerned with staying on than in communicating with the horse.

Similarly, each spoke is dependent upon its fellows and the aids they represent are only effective when used in combination, which does not mean they are necessarily used *simultaneously*.

We have already recognised as a fundamental fact that the horse is propelled forward by the engagement of his quarters and hindlegs, the source of his forward movement, and that his posture and balance are similarly controlled. We ride, therefore, from rear to front, the legs initiating movement and the hands directing, in part, and controlling the power created.

What then are the functions of the aids within the combination? Let us take first the head aid, as it is the first link in the chain. Without thought any subsequent action is likely to be abortive.

Before asking the horse to perform a movement, think first. this may sound so elementary as to be ludicrous, but unless one can ride intelligently, always asking of the horse a little less, rather than a little more, than he is capable of performing, the result can hardly be successful.

In very simple terms the function of the legs and trunk is to create energy behind the saddle. The horsy term is *impulsion*. In answer to the action of these aids the horse's quarters and hindlegs are brought under him to supply the necessary thrust for forward movement. The energy thus created is then either released or contained by the action of the hands connected by the rein to the bit.

The easiest way to understand this is to think of a horse as a length of spiral spring (a simile used by the late Lt.-Col. Jack Talbot-Ponsonby, which I acknowledge with thanks). When the legs and trunk push from the back and the hands restrain at the front then the spring is contained in compressed, or shortened, form between the two points. If the legs and trunk continue to push and the hands instead of restraining, open, then the spring will be elongated, or extended.

The hand controls the degree of compression created by the legs, but without the push from behind its actions are negated. In riding, true forward movement is impossible without the action of the aids creating the necessary thrust. The hand is, therefore, dependent upon the actions of the legs and trunk and can only operate on the horse effectively and correctly if energy behind the saddle has first been created and then maintained.

This is why the true art of horsemanship rests on the phrase, supremacy of leg over hand.

Remember, always, THOUGHT before ACTION, LEG before HAND.

When impulsion is created and maintained and the hand restrains, we shall, in the trained horse, achieve *collection.* That is a shortening of the outline of the horse by strong engagement of the hindlegs beneath the body, a withdrawal, raising and lightening of the forehand and a corresponding movement to the rear of the centre of balance. The stride then becomes shorter and more elevated and the pace slower.

Conversely, when the hands release the energy (the impulsion is never, in fact, entirely expended, the hands always retaining a portion) there will be a lengthening of the outline, which is *extension*. The head and neck will be lowered and stretched, the point of balance will move forward and the stride will be longer and lower.

The ability to shorten and extend the horse at will is necessary to achieve a balanced, obedient and supple horse. To a certain point it is fairly easily accomplished, but the extremes of collection require great skill on the part of the rider if the horse is not to lose the ability to extend. Extreme collection is not necessary in the average riding horse. It is sufficient to be able to vary the speed of the pace and to be able to obtain very brief periods of compression. I have said that the legs and the trunk create the power and the hands control the output, but it is clear how necessary it is for the aids to be used in combination.

The legs not only create power, but they also control the positioning of the quarters, while the hands, used in combination with the former, control the forehand.

Each leg and each hand is used in conjunction with its partner, the one directing, the other supporting. In almost every case the action of the legs precedes that of the hands.

The Function of the Aids

The three prime and elementary essentials of control are to go forward, to stop, or to go slower, and to turn to either right or left. While the application of the aids to produce certain movements is dealt with later in this section the principles involved in their use should be understood.

Pressure by both legs applied slightly to the rear of the girth induces the horse to move forward.

The application of one leg, a little further back, supported by a lighter application of the other, causes the horse to move his quarters away from the stronger leg. The function of the supporting leg is then to control the degree of movement. The rider's leg also controls the corresponding hindleg of the horse, i.e. the rider's left leg controls the horse's near hind and vice versa. Therefore, when riding a circle, when the horse is being *pushed* round the corner by his *inside* hindleg, it is the rider's inside leg, activating the corresponding hindleg, which provides the impulsion. The rider's outside leg, held a little behind the girth, is in support and controls the bend of the quarters, preventing them from moving outside the line of the circle.

The seat and back of a rider sitting as it were with open, spread seat bones and not on the tensed muscles of the buttocks, which would raise him out of the saddle and out of contact with the horse, are a powerful aid to forward movement and the energetic engagement of the hindquarters. Used in concert with the hands and the legs they assist in obtaining either extension or collection. The effect of a back braced and driving *forward*, not *downwards*, when used with the legs and a hand that restrains, is to achieve a shortening of the posture – a compression of the spring. Under the same circumstances, but with the hand releasing, the effect is to urge the horse into extension.

In collection the trunk, by inclining slightly to the rear, alters the weight distribution and induces the horse to further alter his posture by *imposing* upon him the necessity to move his centre of gravity to the rear in order to conform with the altered weight distribution of the rider. In lateral movements the weight of the rider, to remain in balance with the horse, will be placed correspondingly on the side towards which the horse is moving.

While, in general, the rule is for the rider to position his weight over the centre of gravity of the horse, there are occasions when the experienced rider can deliberately use the weight aid to assist the movement he asks of the horse, and to place the horse in a position where it is he who must alter his centre of gravity to conform with his rider's weight distribution.

With the application of the hand aids, the pattern of the aid combination is almost complete. The ideal to aim for is the elastic fingers and forearm connected to a rubber elbow joint. The action taken by the hand on a schooled horse, or on a horse that is being trained, is a closing of the fingers, possibly accompanied by a slight flexion of the wrist to restrain, and an opening of the fingers accompanied, possibly, by a forward movement to release and induce extension. The hand may close, it may open, it may move forwards, sideways, upwards or downwards, but never back. If it moves back it pulls, and it is pulling that provokes pulling on the part of the horse. The pulling hand not only encourages the horse to pull, but it also restricts the stride *and the essential forward movement.*

The demands made by the hand are always intermittent, never must they descend to a dead, maintained pressure. The hand asks and almost immediately yields. If the required action is not obtained it acts again and yields immediately it receives a response. It is the dead, unyielding pressure which causes a similar reaction in the horse.

To move forward the hand follows the indication of the legs by opening slightly. In movement it is the legs which *push* into accepting contact with the hand. The hand must never be allowed to make contact by withdrawing or pulling. *Always it is the last link in the chain, never the first.*

At the halt the horse is *pushed* by the legs to a hand which closes. The hand is in fact a sort of door which is opened to allow the horse to pass through, and closed, in varying degrees, to decrease the pace and to halt. It is unfortunate that we speak of "pulling up" a horse, which is what many of us, in fact, do, rather than *pushing up* to a halt. It is equally unfortunate that while we are told to "close the legs and feel the reins" when halting, we are not always told that there is a time to release the legs. Far too often the instruction is interpreted as a clamping of the legs on the horse coupled with a fairly hefty tug on the reins.

This is a total misconception. The action of the legs is to send the horse into contact with the hand, the moment this is accomplished the hand closes. The leg has now done its work and is then relaxed, and for a moment the hand predominates, while the legs are held in readiness to ensure that the quarters remain straight.

By my book and on my horses, if you go on pushing into a closed hand you are asking the horse to stand up on end.

In changing direction the two hands act in conjunction, just as the legs do. The inside hand indicates the direction, leading the horse through the bend, while the outside hand supports, preventing the horse falling in towards the centre.

The elementary way to turn a corner is by the use of what is called the direct rein. In turning to the left, the inside, left hand is turned finger nails uppermost, thumb pointing in the direction of the movement, and is carried slightly outwards.

The right hand, still having contact with the mouth and supporting its opposite number, moves slightly forward to allow the horse's head and neck to bend to the left. If this is not immediately effective the direct rein can be further strengthened by the supporting hand, held slightly forward, but pressing intermittently against the withers to push the shoulder in the required direction. The rein acts in the turn a split second following the increased pressure of the leg.

Later in the horse's training it will be sufficient, providing there is absolutely equal tension on both reins, to slightly release the tension on the outside rein, i.e. the right rein when turning to the left and vice versa.

Finally, when the horse is supple, balanced and very responsive, the inside hand will ask, by a brief squeeze of the rein, for a slight relaxation, a giving, of the inside jaw. In time the slight movement of the hands in the required direction will be sufficient to obtain the turn and an automatic relaxation. In all movement, with the exception of the trot where the centre of balance is relatively static, the hands follow the motion of the head. Failure of the hands to follow the motions made by the balancing agents results in restriction of movement.

In all cases, the efficiency of the hand depends on the impulsion created by the legs and follows their action.

Without this impulsion, the horse becomes like a becalmed boat. You may then turn the rudder as much as you like, but without the boat being in motion, it will remain becalmed and will turn neither to left nor right. The rider must therefore make the fullest use of his legs and very little of his hands.

Where resistance to the hand is met it can be countered by first using the legs, and possibly the back and seat, with even more energy and in certain cases by rather more active and sometimes seemingly unortho-dox rein aids.

The use, for instance, of an *intermediate*, opposing rein, is invaluable in obtaining a decrease of pace and a checking of over-enthusiastic impulsion should the horse resist the intermittent, direct action. The right hand, supported by a slightly raised left hand, is moved above the withers where it resists. The effect is to push the weight of the horse's body directly on to the line of this resisting rein. The position of the hand, either hand can be used, can be varied according to the variation in the direction of the thrust it seeks to oppose.

By experience, we shall find other uses of the rein to counteract resistances or to assist us in positioning. Benoist-Gironière, the French author and horseman, holds, for instance, that if we study the reaction of the horse to the action of the rider, we will often do what at first may seem to have quite the opposite effect on the horse. If, for instance, the horse persists in raising his head unduly we only increase his resistance by dropping the hands. The answer is to raise the hands, whereupon the horse reacts by dropping his head; the opposite is the case when the horse refuses to raise his head.

This may at first sound anything but logical, but it does work if employed with tact by a skilled horseman. In much the same way it does not take one long when training a young horse to discover that the quick application of the opposite aids will often achieve the result wanted without provoking resistance to the point where we must enter into a battle.

The last of the natural aids is the voice, the use of which in certain circles is regarded with disfavour, which is a pity, as it can be so effective. As I teach obedience to the voice in the early stages of lungeing, I see no reason why I should not continue to use it in mounted training to reinforce, or to let the horse more easily understand, the application of the other aids. If I give the horse the aids to halt and he does not at first respond, what is more easy, or effective, with a horse who is already accustomed to obeying the voice, than to say "whoa". If he then stops I have achieved my object without upsetting him and in a little while he will obey the aids without the addition of my "whoa".

A horse is so easily soothed or encouraged by the voice that I see no reason why he should be deprived of something which he enjoys and to which he responds.

The artificial aids of the whip and spurs are used purely to reinforce the leg. The former can be tapped behind the rider's leg if no response is received when the leg is applied, and the latter, far from being cruel, allows the experienced horseman to make even finer and lighter indications of his wishes.

These then are the aids, the means of communication, but as we have seen they cannot be put to use unless the rider has first obtained a secure seat. It is only out of security that we are able to achieve control.

The Rider's Seat

First let us consider how the rider should sit and secondly, how he can maintain this seat when the horse is in motion.

Clearly, as we are all different in make and shape, it is impossible to lay down a fixed position which will suit us all. What we must do is to adapt our conformation so that the seat employed is the one in which we can most effectively remain in balance with the horse and apply the aids freely and effectively.

To remain in balance it will be necessary for us to sit in the deepest part of the saddle. The leathers can then be adjusted to suit our length of leg, neither too short, which would have a tendency to push our seats towards the cantle and reduce its effectiveness, nor too long, which would affect our security and leave our feet continually reaching for the irons.

The lower leg is then drawn back with the heel lowered, but only very slightly, and the toe raised in corresponding measure. In this position the thigh and half way down the calf is in contact with the barrel of the horse and readily available to apply the aids. The knee is then flat on the saddle flap and pointed to the front. If then, with the iron on the ball of the foot, the toe is inclined slightly outwards, the heel pushed even further down and the weight placed more on the inside of the iron, so that the outside of the boot sole is raised, the knee and thigh are pressed even closer to the saddle. It is not necessary in the slower paces to adopt this locking position of the leg, but it gives greater security at the faster paces and when crossing a country, when the seat is raised from the saddle.

The mistake made by beginners is to grip – grip is only necessary in emergencies and is achieved by pushing the heel down as described.

Continual efforts to grip only raise the rider from the saddle, instead

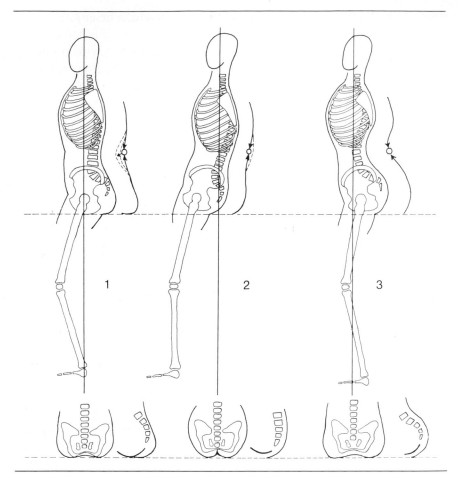

The rider's seat: 1 = right; 2 and 3 = wrong.

of encouraging him to sit with an open seat pushing the flesh of the buttocks behind him and sitting on the seat bones.

The trunk and head are held erect, but not stiff. The head is important, if it is allowed to drop down it affects not only the back, which rounds, but also the security of the seat. The ideal is for shoulder, hip and heel to lie in a vertical line.

The arms are held naturally at the side. Keep your elbows in by all means, but don't clamp them to your body. The hand is held, following the line of the forearm, slightly curved, with the thumb uppermost. The rein should form a straight line between bit and elbow, which precludes this wretched habit of fixing the hands on the withers. Most important is that the two hands should be held the width of the bit apart. Hands clasped together and held in the pit of the stomach are useless. For some reason I cannot explain, the horse, as it were, passes up into contact with the bit through the hands and if these are held together the passing up process stops there. Never carry the hands as though on the handlebars of a bicycle. They become immediately inflexible and insensitive because of the tensing of the muscles of the forearm.

The length of the rein is largely dictated by the conformation of the horse and the position of his head. Too long reins cause the hands to move back in order to effect control. Reins held too short disturb the weight positioning of the rider and are usually too tight. The rein, therefore, should be only as long as is practicable – and this is a few inches longer than most of us think. In this position the rider has virtually anchored the lower half of his body, but without conscious effort and without rigidity.

However, a warning note needs to be sounded about the ineffectual use of the rein. It needs to be held and used in a positive way. There is really no point in pushing the horse forward from the legs without there being a controlling contact at the other end. Early on in the horse's training we have to ask, little by little, for him to work within a frame imposed by the legs at one end and the bit at the other. If we fail to do so later efforts to put the horse on the bit will always meet with resistance. After all, if the horse has been allowed to slop along with his nose poked out anyhow it will be difficult for him to understand (and to comply physically) with legs and hands which suddenly demand that he should not only engage his quarters and round his back but must also drop and retract his nose.

(A horse is "on the bit" when the face is held in the vertical plane, with flexion at the poll and in the lower jaw. The mouth is then held below the level of the rider's hands, a position in which the latter has maximum control.

A horse is "above the bit" when the face is held forward of the vertical plane and the mouth approaches the point where it is above the hands.

A horse is "behind the bit" – an equally uncomfortable sensation – when his nose is tucked into his chest behind the vertical plane.)

In the full seat, that is when sitting in the saddle at either walk, trot or canter, the body remains upright, the spine undulating with the movement. When the half, or jumping, seat is employed, the rider maintains the same anchoring leg position, but with shorter leathers, inclines his trunk forward without rounding the back, and raises his buttocks out of the saddle while maintaining a contact with his fork.

(Opposite page, top) *Sian Thomas BHSII working on the lunge with the author.
There is no substitute for these regular lunge lessons which are an essential in the
development of the seat.*

(Opposite page, bottom) *An exercise which corrects stiffness in the upper body,
particularly round the shoulders and neck muscles.*

(Above) *The work at canter with Sian sitting deep into the saddle. The horse,
Merlin, is a five-year-old Continental warm-blood, a Danish Sports horse with a
predominant Trakehner background. The strong, very correct limbs are
particularly noticeable.*

The weight is then taken on the pivot of his knee and upon the heel. To
post at the trot a slight forward inclination of the trunk is all that is
necessary, and the seat bones need only rise an inch or two from the
saddle.

If the knee and the lower leg maintain their position the rider, with
some practise, will not find it difficult to remain in balance. Once,
however, the knee straightens, and the lower leg goes forward in
advance of the vertical line formed by head, knee and toe, balance is lost
and the rider is behind the movement of the horse. In recent years there

A commendably relaxed horse and rider demonstrating half-pass to the right. Sian is riding her Palomino horse Taurus, a Thoroughbred/Welsh Cob cross bred at the Dwyfor Ranch Stud, Gwynedd.

has been a tendency towards taking the lower leg too far to the rear, which is just as bad. The rider is then tipped on the front of the seat bones and on the fork, a position which is inhibiting so far as balance and any proper application of the aids is concerned. This particular problem arises, I think, because of the instructors' imperfect understanding of what may be termed a "dressage seat" and the very poor design of the majority of dressage saddles. As a result riders are forced into an entirely unnatural position. The thigh is encouraged to be held vertically with the lower leg drawn back and in consequence the rider is tipped forward and out of balance with the seat largely out of contact.

The problem, of course, is to be able to maintain this seat and the only way is to practise on a horse, preferable on the lunge, without reins and with an instructor correcting the position.

There are numerous exercises which are helpful, but the real answer to the development of this deep seat is work on the lunge with guidance from the ground.

It is well worthwhile going to a good instructor to develop this basis of equitation. Practising on your own is all very well, but you cannot see your own faults and you are likely to get into bad habits which will be almost impossible to eradicate later on.

Work on the lunge on a schooled horse is, I am convinced, essential. Certainly the work should be carried out without reins but not, initially, without irons for too long a period.

At a later stage, jumping without reins over low fences in an enclosed lane is an excellent exercise for balance and security. Again there is no need to dispense with the irons all the time, nor do I believe in pupils being made to fold their arms, stretch their arms over their heads or thumb their noses. One does not perform these antics when jumping with reins, so why do them when the reins are removed? It is not helpful to the balance and it is, therefore, much better to encourage the pupil to push his arms forward on either side of the withers in a line with the horse's mouth. This at least is something like following the movement of the head, whereas I can think of no occasion when it would be necessary to jump a fence with the reins held in the arms outstretched above the head. On the other hand stretching the arms sideways and backwards, thus opening the chest, is helpful in correcting a rounding back and lowered head position.

For the young and agile any sort of activity work, such as vaulting, jumping facing the tail or anything else you like, is good for balance and confidence.

The Saddle

Finally, although a properly designed saddle will not teach anyone to ride, it goes a long way to helping the rider sit correctly.

The modern all-purpose or general-purpose saddle is made so that the rider, with the minimum of effort and the maximum comfort and security, is placed over the horse's centre of balance. It achieves this object by having, amongst other features, a dipped seat and the stirrup bars positioned forward. At the same time it allows the rider to sit in the closest contact with his horse and in no way hinders the application of the aids.

Some of the more old-fashioned saddles, of pre-war vintage, seem to have been made in deliberate defiance of present day equestrian practice. The seats were flat, the head or pommel stood rather higher than the cantle, the waist was so wide as to spread the thighs and the bars were positioned so far to the rear as to ensure that the rider could only sit behind the movement. In addition, they were uncomfortable.

The modern saddle is a real help to the rider and an essential part of his equipment. As Lt.-Col. Frank Weldon wrote in the foreword to my

Careful fitting of the saddle is essential if it is to contribute to the performance of horse and rider and be entirely comfortable for both. This saddle is ideal for this young horse. It is not unduly dipped in the seat neither is it exaggerated in the cut of panel and flap.

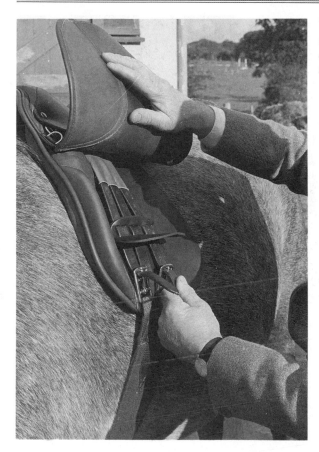

With the girth in position the panel lies flat and snug, following the shape of the back.

book, *Saddlery*, "not only does it put the rider willy-nilly into the most convenient position for the horse to bear his weight and understand his signals, but it is infinitely more comfortable to sit in, and above all, almost impossible to fall out of. I would no more dream of using a conventional hunting saddle in preference to a modern general purpose one for hacking, hunting or cross-country riding than I would pick a kitchen stool rather than a well-upholstered armchair for a Sunday afternoon nap."

I agree with every word – or almost. There are some of us who could fall out of anything.

(Since these words were written the design of English saddles has deteriorated significantly and even the very expensive and well marketed German saddles are by no means without their faults.

From the rear the saddle sits squarely on the back, the channel being sufficiently wide to obviate the possibility of any pressure bearing on the spinal vertebrae.

It is just as important to fit the bridle to the head. The throatlatch must be sufficiently loose to allow the insertion of the fingers. If it is too tight it will inhibit proper flexion at the poll.

For comfort the noseband must lie below the prominent facial bones.

The young horse bridled and under saddle. Both bridle and saddle are neat, unobtrusive and fit very well indeed.

The worst examples are, without doubt, the dressage saddles, many of which ignore a basic principle by having the stirrup bars placed too far forward. This positioning, in conjunction with too short and too dipped a seat results in the rider being tipped on the fork. The bars in a dressage saddle should be "extended", that is, they must be of a design which allows the leathers to be placed further to the rear so that the rider can retain the leg position whilst sitting squarely on the seat bones.

The fault in the general-purpose saddle is concerned largely with the flap and panel being cut too far forward and the tree having an exaggerated dip. The result is that the rider is compelled to sit out of balance; his weight becomes concentrated over too small an area; the free movement of the horse is prevented and there is a real possibility of the back being injured.

Fortunately, a "zephyr" of change is now becoming evident.

Within a few years saddles which can be adjusted to fit any back, fitted with stirrup bars which allow adjustment for any length of leg or leg position and which put the rider even closer to the horse than before, but without risk of injury to the horse's back, will be almost commonplace. One can only hope that far more emphasis is given to the subject of saddle construction and fitting in our training syllabi.)

CHAPTER 10

Preparing the Horse

Before proceeding to the various ridden movements I have included this section on lungeing, loose schooling and the use of long reins.

Lungeing, in particular, is a subject which appears to be neglected or misunderstood by far too many horse-keepers. There are even people who look upon it as a sort of equine treadmill and label it as a cruel practice. In cases where a horse is chased round in a small circle the condemnation may be justified, but this sort of thing is very far removed from the proper purpose of the exercise.

All horses and ponies young or old, benefit from work on the lunge.

Lungeing, in its simplest form, is getting the horse to work round the trainer in a circle to either hand, the horse being controlled by means of a line from the trainer's hand to a cavesson (a special type of head-collar), by the voice and by the trainer's long whip.

There is no *mystique* connected with the exercise; anybody, even a child, can acquire the simple technique and its value is inestimable.

The objects of lungeing are these:

(1) To teach a young horse to go forward freely

(2) To improve the balance of all horses

(3) To build up and make supple the muscles naturally, without their being formed in opposition to the rider's weight

(4) To encourage lateral flexion

(5) To encourage equal muscle development on both sides of the horse

(6) To condition young or weak animals before subjecting them to the rider's weight

(7) To exercise animals who for some reason cannot be ridden

(8) To make calm an over-fresh horse before riding him

(9) To accustom the horse to this work so that he can be safely ridden on the lunge, without reins, for the purpose of developing the strength and security of the rider's seat

(10) To teach the horse acceptance of discipline, and the habit of obedience

(11) As a means of introducing the horse to jumping

A number of the objectives may need little further explanation, but it is as well to consider the principal ones in more detail.

The natural balance is improved, and consequently the quality of the individual paces, by this work on circles, which encourages the horse to use his hindlegs. As we have seen, in order for the horse to turn correctly and easily, he brings his inside hindleg further under him so as to push himself round the corner. Properly worked on the lunge the hindlegs are constantly engaged, and in the latter stages of the exercise we shall discern a marked improvement in the head carriage as a result of the lightened forehand induced by the activity of the hindlegs under the horse.

Because the backbone is capable of little if any flexion the horse finds difficulty in making a true circle: a difficulty which is increased by stiff muscles on either side of the spine and by the natural over-development of one side.

This natural disposition to one-sidedness is further encouraged by our handling horses almost entirely from the near side. It is, for instance, particularly noticeable when young stock are led out in hand. In early training not only does the horse prefer to go on a certain rein, generally the left one, but the trainer finds it easier as well, and if he is unwise tends to give too little work, instead of rather more, on the opposite rein. The result is for the horse to avoid working on the rein which causes him physical discomfort and on which he has difficulty in adjusting his centre of balance. Very often he is then dubbed as having a one-sided mouth. By this time he may have, but the primary reason for his resistance is not that his mouth is insensitive, but that his bodily development is unequal. Without equality of development he will be unable to engage, on a circle, the inside hindleg and will be driven into making a resistance.

Finally, on the lunge, there will be no restriction in the development of the back muscles, which might well occur under saddle when the immature muscle may stiffen in opposition to the weight.

It should be clear from the foregoing how necessary it is to condition the horse before riding him. Nothing is more dangerous than to ride a young or weak horse before his back muscles are strong enough to take the weight. At best the horse will hollow the back to avoid discomfort, and it is more than likely that he will become sour and unco-operative. In addition it is possible to do lasting damage to the spinal vertebrae. Horses with sore backs (quite unforgivable in any stable) can be exercised on the lunge and parents will find it useful in conditioning ponies before their riders return for the holidays.

It is not just a question of discretion being the better part of valour that prompts me to advise the lungeing of over-fresh horses before they are ridden. It is just sound common sense. There is really no point in getting up on a mad fresh horse bursting with oats and *joie-de-vivre*. It may please you to "master" him, that is if you don't finish up flat on your back, but in the process there has probably been a certain amount of rough handling and the whole procedure is hardly conducive to a sympathetic partnership. It is far better that the horse should expend his high spirits, quite harmlessly, on the end of a lunge and be ridden when he has regained a calm and receptive frame of mind. Lastly, the great value of the lunge is in teaching obedience and discipline. These habits once implanted greatly facilitate future training. Their inculcation is, in fact, the basis of training.

Of equal importance is the opportunity given by the exercise in developing the trainer's sympathy with his pupil and enlarging his understanding of the horse's mental and physical capacities. It is indeed quite surprising how the mental affinity between horse and rider can grow under the conditions that pertain during lungeing. Our own Welsh pony is a remarkable example of the partnership that can be attained and besides carrying out transitions both on the lunge and loose can be controlled, if only for a matter of minutes, by my "thinking" commands at him. I do not claim that this is in any way thought transference, because it is possible that he perceives subliminal movements on my part, but it shows to what extent a mutual understanding can be achieved. (The Welsh Mountain pony referred to died very recently in his paddock. He taught me a very great deal but more importantly he taught the children of five families, his last young rider being our latest god-child.)

While lungeing is easy to understand and is enjoyable for the horse who, in general, like to be under discipline and takes pleasure in co-operating, it is fairly hard physical work, particularly in the early stages. Ten or fifteen minutes are quite enough for the early lessons and 40 minutes are the very maximum for a fit, trained animal. Periods of 20 to 30 minutes are usually as much as the average horse can manage without losing his concentration. Long periods on the lunge for young or older animals will impose far too great a strain on the body structure.

Facilities and Equipment

These items are neither complicated, nor difficult to obtain.

Ideally an enclosed flat *manège* is the most suitable, and for the later training a piece of undulating ground which can be roped-off, or otherwise enclosed, is very useful. The purpose of lungeing over an uneven surface is to improve further the balance of the horse by accustoming him to making more frequent adjustments to his centre of gravity.

Any patch of ground, a corner of a field is convenient, will do in the absence of a school and a temporary enclosure is easily made with stakes and a few lengths of rope. It is, however, important that the area should be enclosed in some way, as in the open a horse has too much to distract his attention from the job in hand.

The essential equipment required comprises a lunge cavesson, that is, a stout sort of head collar which has a padded nosepiece which fits snugly and which is equipped with three rings, set on swivels; one in the centre and one on either side. In addition one needs a lunge rein and a long whip.

I also like to have two further dees set at the rear of the cavesson nosepiece, on either side, for fitting side-reins when the time comes. When buying a cavesson choose one of light, modern design and discard anything which does not fit perfectly.

The lunge rein is usually of web, which has the advantage of not burning the hand should the pupil become playful. It should again be as light as possible and can fasten to the cavesson ring by either a swivel mounted hook, or a strap and buckle set on a swivel mounting. Without these swivels, which, incidentally, need to be kept well-greased, the rein very quickly gets twisted and tangled.

The whip, equipped with a long thong and lash, is useless if it is not properly balanced and light. I use one made entirely of nylon, which is as near perfect as I require.

I have termed these three items "essential", which in essence they are, but much can be done with a headcollar, a piece of rope and a long switch from the hedge.

Side-reins and a roller fitted with a crupper are additional items of equipment. Over the years I have come to make increasing use of them to obtain an overall carriage by "suggestion". Nothing is ever adjusted tightly but the presence of the crupper and of the side-reins, too, does have the effect of "bringing the horse together".

Some years ago I advocated the use of side-reins in which a piece of elastic or a rubber ring was inserted. I now believe this to be wrong as the elastic, although it gives to the movement of the head, exerts too constant a restraint, which the horse avoids by withdrawing his head and possibly becoming overbent. My side-reins are, therefore, now made of plain leather about half an inch wide.

Young horses, or horses unaccustomed to the exercise, are prone to knocking their legs about when working on a circle and, therefore, polo boots or exercise bandages over cotton wool are a necessary protection.

The fitting of the cavesson is very important; the nosepiece should fit fairly tightly, well above the nostrils, and the jowl strap will need to be reasonably tight if the headpiece is not to pull forward over the outside eye.

I usually fasten the lunge rein to the central nose ring where it gives more control, but others attach it to the inside ring. I have occasionally had horses who threw their heads about when the lunge was fixed in the first fashion but went well when it was fastened on the inside ring. In much the same way I have found horses carrying their heads too much towards the centre when the inside ring was used, and who went better when it was on the nose. It, therefore, depends upon the individual.

I should say that the late Henry Wynmalen, for whom I had the highest regard, advocated the lunge being attached to a ring at the back of the cavesson, behind the jaw bones. I have never tried this method, but I would not presume to disagree with so great an authority.

Method

The first stage in teaching the exercise requires an assistant to lead the horse round the trainer. I like my assistant on the outside of the animal, not on the inside. My reason for this is that I find the horse is more likely to come into the centre (which he must not do) when the assistant, placed on the inside, eventually moves away from him. In addition, I want the horse to concentrate his attention upon me, and this is more difficult for him to do if I am shielded by the body of the assistant.

The trainer stands in the centre with the rein in the leading hand, that is the left hand when the horse circles on the left rein and vice versa, the spare end of the rein is passed across the body and held in loops in the other hand. It is important not to have the rein hanging round one's feet – it is only too easy to become up-ended should the horse try to get away. The whip is held, point to the rear and resting on the ground, by the trainer's free hand, i.e. the right hand for the left rein and the opposite for the right.

At this stage the trainer should position himself in what I term the "Triangle of Control".

He places his body facing, and slightly to the rear of, the animal's hip, he is then *behind* the horse and able to encourage him forward, if necessary with a slight movement of the whip.

Should the trainer position himself in advance of this position, nearer or opposite the horse's shoulder, the horse will endeavour to turn away from him, or even turn round, and control will be lost. Correct positioning is almost the whole secret of successful lungeing.

To commence the horse is led round the trainer by the assistant until he accepts the situation calmly and goes quietly on both reins, carrying the weight of the lunge line, which should be rather less than taut.

Once this is achieved the first words of command can be taught. This is the halt from the walk. Again it is not what you say, but the way that you say it. I use the word "whoa" and the tone should be low and drawn out, as in all commands asking for a decrease in pace. For those asking for upward transitions, i.e. walk to trot, trot to canter, the command is divided into a preparatory drawn-out note and a sharp executive snap, as in "CAANN-TER!" The voice need not be loud, but it should be clear and incisive and the tone and words used always remain the same.

On the trainer giving the command "whoa" (I introduce a personal and entirely irrelevant *tremolo* into the word) he will immediately follow the command with a tightening of the fingers on the rein. The assistant, who has been holding the cavesson very lightly, now brings the horse to a halt, immediately making him stand squarely on all four legs.

The trainer than walks *out* to the horse and rewards him. Don't let the

First lessons on the lunge: (opposite page) *not quite sure what is required of him the young horse is initially hesitant;* (above) *a moment later he begins to settle down. The trainer is positioned opposite the hip so that she can send her pupil forward from behind;* (below) *he is still a bit wide-eyed and a little unco ordinated but a* rapport *between pupil and trainer is becoming evident.*

assistant perform this task – the relationship that is being built is between horse and trainer and nothing must obtrude upon it.

I always go out to the horse to reward, *never* do I ask him to come in to me. If he is encouraged to come in at this or any other stage he will continue to do so, and you will never get a proper halt.

The horse will very quickly understand the meaning of "whoa" and will associate it with being rewarded. It will not be long before one can dispense with both the tightening of the rein and the assistant's help in obtaining a halt.

I continue to use an assistant until the horse has learnt the transitions from halt to trot and from trot to halt, and obeys my voice at once. This may take three or four lessons and during this time I accustom the animal to accepting the movement of the whip when he is asked to go forward; this is a sweeping movement with the point still resting on the ground. He is also taught to move away from the whip when it is pointed at his shoulder as an indication that he should move outwards and not fall in towards the centre.

By the fourth lesson, sometimes earlier, I have the assistant walking on the outside of the horse some six feet from his head, and in the following lesson dispense with her services altogether.

Now I must concentrate on maintaining my triangle of control, keeping always behind the animal and urging him forward. It is at this stage that one encounters the occasional disobedience.

The horse, if he has never been brought to the centre, will not usually try to come in to the trainer, but if he does one must alter one's position to get in line with his hip and drive him forward. A flip on the lunge rein, and the resultant smack as the ripple finishes on the nose, will usually be sufficient to make him stay out. He may, too, try to make off. Under no circumstances should the trainer then dig his heels in and pull the horse round on his forehand. This is most dangerous and can cause serious strains. The way to cope with the predicament is to go with the horse, checking him by intermittent jerks on the rein. The same thing can happen if the trainer urges the horse forward too strongly, but in this case even greater tact is required. The fault in this instance is that of the trainer, whose urgings the horse has obeyed. The horse must not, therefore, be punished. The trainer must go with him and restrain him very gently.

In these early lessons I am more concerned with the horse going forward than his making a perfect circle and I, therefore, move about fairly freely on something resembling a circle within the track made by the horse. I concentrate on keeping the rein not quite taut and, of course, I change the rein, i.e. the direction, very frequently, giving rather more work on the stiff side than on the other.

There is a school of thought which insists that the trainer pivots on his heel and forces the horse to accept the circle. I am not in favour of this method as it encourages the horse to hang against the rein and to take his quarters outside the track of the forefeet.

To change the rein I again use a simple method which I find more satisfactory than threatening the poor animal with the whip and chasing him round on the opposite rein. I halt the horse, walk out to him and lead him across the school, where I halt him facing the opposite direction. I then move away from him, having reversed the whip and rein in my hands, and ask him to walk-on or trot as the case may be.

If the horse bucks or plunges on the rein I allow him to do so until I think he has done enough, when a sharp word will bring him back to the job in hand.

The next stage is to insist, gradually, on a proper circle. When this is established I teach, by judicious slackening and tightening of the rein, which will in time give way to my voice alone, the variations in pace at walk and trot. I ask, and receive very quickly, a free extended walk and trot and the same paces in something of a more collected fashion with a more energetic engagement of the hindlegs.

Throughout this initial training it is essential to teach one lesson at a time, recapitulating at the beginning of the next session to make sure that the lesson has been properly learnt.

The whip is used only to indicate the trainer's wishes, a week or two's work is lost if the animal is struck with it and learns to regard it as something to be feared instead of respected.

Once I have established the trot, with no straining at the rein, I urge the horse into the canter. If after an enlarged circle or two (the first ones may be a little exuberant) I find he is pulling on the rein I have started too early and must go back to more work on the trot. Circling at the canter is difficult and hard work for the horse. It should not, therefore, be overdone. Should the horse strike off with the wrong leg (i.e. he should lead with his left fore on a circle to the left and vice versa) bring him back to halt and start again. Continue this until he automatically strikes off correctly on the word of command.

The final stage in this work on the flat is reached when the horse goes through the upward and downward transitions, including the variations, such as canter from halt, halt from canter, etc., and is able to vary the pace of each gait at word of command. By this time the head will have been persuaded to follow the track and not be held to the outside of it.

The horse will have been worked over rough ground as well as on the flat surface of the school and will have become pretty well balanced.

Use of the Side-Reins

Initially, I attach the side-reins to the rear rings of the cavesson. I attach them so that they are of exactly equal length on either side, tightening the inside side-rein is a pernicious philosophy attended by all sorts of evils – the horse carries the quarters outside the track and he learns to hang on one side of the mouth. The reins are fitted loose enough so that they just begin to loop when the nose is withdrawn and the head raised.

If the reins are too tight the head will become overbent to avoid their restriction, the neck and back stiffen and the fluidity of the movement will be lost.

When the horse is used to the weight of the rein and responds by producing an improved carriage I fit the reins to the snaffle bit, which will be worn under the cavesson.

Using the reins from the bit introduces a new element, providing us with the means to encourage the horse to make contact with the bit. To begin with, therefore, I fit the reins very long and work the horse over a pole-grid laid on the ground. To cross the grid the horse must lower the neck and stretch out his nose. This not only encourages, particularly at trot, the desirable rounding of the back and the increased engagement

The effect of the side-reins and tackle: (opposite page) *working the horse in the side-reins produces a noticeably improved carriage. The horse "comes together";* (above) *a balanced trot on the circle right. Note the adjustment of the side-reins;* (below) *a really lovely extension at trot obtained by an expert and sympathetic trainer.*

of the hindlegs but it must also send the horse into contact with his bit as his outstretched neck takes up the slack in the rein.

Thereafter, I adjust the reins for working on the flat, fitting them somewhat shorter, but never tightly. Gradually, therefore, I am imposing a frame within which the horse will work. I obtain it by pushing the quarters up to the head, the position of the latter being governed, in perfection, by a slightly looping rein. And that is what I shall be trying to do from the saddle, sending the horse from my legs into my governing hand which then takes the place of the side-rein. There will be no great difficulty about obtaining the carriage within the frame imposed because the horse has already accepted the latter in the course of his lunge work.

Jumping on the Lunge

Following this the horse can be introduced to jumping, first by walking, and then trotting, over spaced poles, between 4–5 ft apart, along the side of the school. The trainer should by this time experience little difficulty in positioning himself to allow the animal to negotiate the poles in a straight line. These poles, once the horse accepts them calmly, are later replaced by low cavalletti, over which the horse is asked to trot.

(Opposite page) *The horse reaching forward into contact with his bit on long side-reins. The outline at this stage and the engagement of the limbs is exactly what is required; (above) crossing an improvised grid with great activity, a good outline and manifest forward movement; (below) a beautiful jump in excellent style over an improvised obstacle. Note the handling of the rein in all three pictures.*

Any tendency to rush is checked by the voice and the trainer concentrates on getting the horse to drop his head, round his back, and pick up all four feet energetically and with rhythm.

Following this, the same procedure, starting with the poles, can be carried out on a circle. This is much more difficult and takes a little time to perform correctly. Later the horse, now quite accustomed to jumping and full of confidence, can be lunged over a variety of low fences at trot and at canter, the approach being controlled by the voice.

Under no circumstances should the horse ever be lunged off the bit. The risk of damaging the mouth, and the confidence of the horse in the trainer, is too great.

Loose Schooling

As the ultimate test of obedience I remove the lunge rein and work the horse in the school loose. I do, however, leave the cavesson on. It is probably unnecessary, but the horse associates the wearing of it with work and discipline and so it remains. I carry out all the movements described, including jumping, purely on the word of command, assisted by the strategic positioning of my body a little to the rear of the horse.

Once again there is no *mystique*, and this stage of training and obedience is easily taught by a person of average sensitivity, intelligence and competence.

Should the horse be disobedient when loose, particularly regarding the halt, it is best to ignore him and urge him on. He will soon settle and be glad to stop when asked. It is possible, and is sometimes recommended, that a horse who will not stop on the lunge or loose, should be driven against the corner of the school. I have no doubt it is effective, but it won't exactly cement the understanding we are trying to achieve. If the training is carried out on the lines indicated the matter should never arise, or at any rate assume such proportions as to warrant a rather drastic though effective remedy.

Initially one may have to do rather more than walking about when the horse is loose to keep him on the outside track, but never having been brought into the centre he will soon stay out of his own accord.

There are people who disapprove of loose jumping and attribute all sorts of evils to the practice. To my mind there is no better way of teaching jumping. The horse, completely free, works out the approach and judges the distance for himself, and if he is not overfaced rarely makes a mistake. It is also an excellent study for the rider, who observes at close quarters the exact movements of the horse when jumping, and is made to realise the importance of the animal being completely unrestricted in his execution of the leap.

Most loose jumping is carried out in an enclosed jumping lane. I do not possess one, and so have to make do with solidly erected fences in my small outdoor school, in reality a not too well-drained sand ring. I may have to work harder, but my animals jump fences without wings, low but solid, and as yet have no idea of running out.

Any horse, of any age, benefits from schooling of this sort and it lays a very firm foundation for future mounted work, as well as creating close bonds of understanding and trust between pupil and master.

Long Reins

For many years I made little or no use of the long reins, persuading myself that the simpler movements could best be taught from the saddle. I say "persuaded" because when this book was first published in 1969 I was not very expert at the exercise, although I did long-rein ponies. Today, I am a little more adept and feel justified in saying that in skilled hands, or just educated ones, there are advantages in long-reining to further the "mouthing" of the horse, to teach obedience to the indications of the rein and very particularly to develop the carriage, balance and paces without the inhibiting weight of the rider. For ponies there are even more advantages, since few small children are capable of schooling a young pony effectively and good, lightweight adults with experience are always at a premium.

There are four methods of long-reining. There is the Danish system, derived from the Neapolitan style of the Renaissance, perfected by Colonel Egede Lunde and pracised most expertly in Britain by the late Einar Schmit-Jensen and his pupil Miss Sylvia Stanier. In this the horse wears a driving pad, the reins passing from the mouth to the hand via the terrets on the pad. The French use a harness collar from which the rein passes downwards through a ring fixed low on the roller and thence to the hand.

In Vienna, the long reins are used to show off a trained horse and are therefore not relevant to our needs, whilst both Danish and French methods, though enormously productive are rather too specialist for most of us.

The so-called English method differs from others in that the outside rein passes round the quarters.

The late Einar Schmit-Jensen (above) demonstrating the Danish method, the reins passing through the terrets, across the back to the hand; the "improved" English method using dees on the roller (opposite page, top), the reins in this early lesson are attached to the cavesson rings; (opposite page, bottom) the classical method of long-reining which shows off the paces of the advanced horse.

Done badly, as it often is, it is worse than useless. Done well, using a roller, rather than the rough and ready method of passing the reins through run-up stirrup irons, the results can be astonishingly good and I commend the practice wholeheartedly, although I do not say that the end product will be any better than that obtained by an educated rider from the saddle.

To begin with the long reins are attached to the outside rings of the cavesson, the horse or pony wearing loose side-reins to the bit, a roller and crupper. Only when the trainer and the horse are well-accustomed to the work are the reins attached directly to the bit.

If an assistant is available to lead the horse both reins can be passed at the outset through the rings of the roller; if not, the inside rein comes directly to the hand as in lungeing, with the outside one passing through

Long reins: (above) *nothing is left to chance during this first lesson, the horse being allowed plenty of time to get used to the idea;* (below) *the horse being driven off the bit with the outside rein passing round the quarters.*

the roller ring and round the quarters. Should the horse object, then the outside rein can in an emergency be dropped and control maintained through the direct, inside lunge rein.

If the horse or pony has learnt to listen to the voice and to trust it the whole thing is simplified, for it is through the voice that the trainer reassures his pupil.

All is usually well so long as the horse can see his trainer, as when the latter is in the optimum position of control three-quarters-on to his rear. He loses confidence and becomes reluctant to advance forward freely when the trainer is directly behind and thus almost entirely out of his vision.

The presence of an assistant helps to overcome the problem materially and her help is also needed in making the first changes in direction on a simple S-bend.

The secret of the directional changes is to begin at walk on large circles, the horse being made to pass in front of the trainer when the latter wishes to change the rein. But all the time communication must be maintained by the reassuring voice as well as by the gentle, guiding hands.

The work really begins when forward movement is established and the horse can be driven at walk, trot and canter from the bit. Changes of direction and pace can all be practised for short periods. But beware, tight circles, as on the lunge, can be very damaging to the limbs and inhibiting to the freedom of movement. It is just as valuable, if not more so, to drive the horse through fields and on quiet tracks and, if you can find them, over small banks and ditches. It does wonders for developing his confidence and initiative.

The essential element, of course, is concerned with the hands at the end of the long reins. Indeed, were I to have the training of young horse-people the ability to long-rein would be high on the list of my priorities. If you can develop light, sympathetic hands with reins 18–20 ft away from the horse's mouth you will have no difficulty in maintaining the "gossamer" contact from the saddle.

(Unhappily, "good hands" today are not given anything like the emphasis devoted to them even 20–30 years ago. The "hands", or lack of them, displayed by some of the top, modern dressage riders, for example, would not have been acceptable when I was a boy. Had I dared to ride with those twang-taut reins I would have been termed a "butcher-boy" and advised to take up a more appropriate sporting pastime – like bending iron bars or weight-lifting. Similarly, there is in our training systems insufficient recognition of how to "make a mouth".

This is the first time that Alison McInerney got on to Bandook's back.

Our forebears understood the art very well – it is a pity that our horse-world, with the exception of some of the professional showing men, has almost lost sight of the art.)

In the long reins the hands, as when the rider is mounted, must never *pull*, but they do, if they are to be positive, have to take up any slackness which arises.

The inside rein produces flexion (obtained by a gentle *vibrato* action of the fingers), the outer one contributes to the maintenance of balance.

Ideally, the fingers need to work the reins in time with the fall of the hindlegs. It is easier, however, to look at the forelegs, taking contact through the rein in rhythm with the movement, the fingers squeezing as the corresponding foreleg is raised.

To change direction it is only necessary to ease the *outside* rein in accordance with the classical precept. It is inhibiting if one descends to pulling with the *inside* one and it only causes a shortening of the stride and a departure of the quarters to the outside of the track being followed by the forelegs.

We need also to drive the horse forward into an increased contact with his bit and, hopefully, into an improved carriage, by working from directly behind the quarters. But you need a wall or hedge to help keep him straight.

The next stage is to practise assiduously the transitions from halt to walk to trot and back again until the horse is foot-perfect. Then the rein-back can be attempted. For the most part, the rein-back, which in my book is a relatively advanced movement if properly executed, is rarely done well nor sufficiently understood. I never can understand why it should be thought to be within the accomplishment of small children riding at gymkhana level, when it can, indeed, be an excruciating sight to witness.

Teaching the horse to rein-back in the long reins, if properly done, simplifies the movement under the saddle beyond belief.

The rein-back is obtained from a *balanced halt, with the horse being happily on the bit, by asking him to go forward.* As he responds and begins to move forward, the hands, instead of following the mouth and allowing the movement, close on the rein in time with the movement of legs. That is, the right hand acts as the right leg rises and vice versa. If the action is continued in conjunction with the encouragement of the forward movement the horse will step backwards in balance and in two-time. There will be no suggestion of his having been pulled backwards.

It is helpful when teaching the movement to have the support of rails or a hedge on one side of the horse. Thereafter ask for one step at a time and when you can obtain four clearly defined steps be content. If the horse does not understand that he is being asked to move back, or if you feel in danger of pulling him back, have the assistant tap his foreleg with a cane or even tread on his toe.

The moment the horse has made the number of steps required urge him forward again. Teaching a horse to go backwards always has an element of danger, lest he should discover that by continuing his backward progression he can put the rider at a disadvantage. For this reason he must always, and immediately, go forward following steps to the rear.

It is possible for the very skilful to go further, teaching flying changes

Just over 18 months later Bandook (above and opposite page) was competing successfully in Riding Club one-day events.

at canter, and even one-time changes, doing lateral work etc. Most of us should be well content if we can change the leg at canter on a figure of eight, the horse being brought back to trot for a few strides before being asked to strike off on the opposite leg. We may also attempt the half turn on the forehand and quarters. They are not very difficult to achieve but they are not that easy either and the novice would be well-advised to leave them alone.

CHAPTER 11

Teaching Paces, Movements and Jumping

Facilities

In order to improve the paces and obedience of the horse under saddle we require similar facilities as we need for lungeing him, viz. an enclosed space. Few of us will be able to afford the luxury of a covered school, but an outside ring on level ground, perhaps in the corner of a paddock with the unfenced sides either railed or roped off, is almost as good, if not so comfortable. The surface must, however, be suitable and the going good.

Ground having a subsoil of gravel, chalk or sand provides the best surface because it will be naturally well drained. Clay land is not nearly so good, either in summer or winter.

If one has the space, and is prepared to expend a little money, a very good outdoor ring can be constructed by removing the topsoil to a depth of from six to eight inches, levelling the surface and then laying four inches of broken brick rubble well rolled in with a heavy roller. On top of this a further three inches of small clinker can be laid and rolled in. A two or three inch top dressing of rough sand, or a mixture of tan and sawdust, laid on top, then gives a good rideable surface in all weathers. Today, however, there are a dozen or more companies specialising in arena construction who will do the job for you from start to finish.

The size of the school depends upon the area you have available, ideally it would be approximately 180 feet × 60 feet, but one can manage quite well in smaller spaces.

We shall also need half a dozen stout poles and at least three cavalletti. The dimensions of a cavalletto are given later in this section and they are not difficult to construct from straight pine poles. They can, of course, be obtained ready-made from a number of firms specialising in the making of jump equipment.

Fences, for jumping schooling, can be improvised very satisfactorily with straw bales, petrol cans, brush and gorse, railway sleepers, etc.

Objectives

Overall objectives will naturally differ according to the needs and ambitions of the individual and depend very much upon the latter's conception of an ideal, or even suitable, riding horse.

Indeed, if one has never ridden anything but a riding school horse round the same interminable lanes it is unlikely that one will have the slightest idea of the pleasure to be obtained from riding a schooled horse. On the other hand there are numerous hunting people, owning potentially good horses, who are not much wiser.

The extent to which a horse can be improved by training depends to a considerable degree upon his conformation, but whatever his shape he will certainly be a better, more comfortable and valuable horse for a little intelligent and simple schooling.

To own an unschooled horse and to make no effort to improve him is rather like owning a boat fitted with a motor, and then spend all your time rowing the thing.

For the average horseman, owning a horse with no major deficiencies of conformation, it is not difficult to produce a balanced, responsive animal obedient to the indications of leg and hand. Such a horse, in my view, should be smooth to ride at all paces, able to vary the speed within the gaits, capable of moving backwards and sideways for a few steps, of turning on his forehand and quarters and jumping reasonable obstacles calmly and safely.

This is surely not expecting too much. One cannot, of course, hope to have a horse who is always one hundred per cent obedient and responsive. He would be a very dull fellow if he was. He is after all an animal and, like us, he will have his off days, times when he is non-co-operative and occasions when he will depart from the straight and narrow path to assert himself as an individual, or just give rein to his sense of humour.

In order, however, to produce this near-paragon it is necessary to spend a little time on the consideration of ways and means, and rather more time putting them into effect.

One of the objectives in lungeing the horse was the improvement in fluid balance and the greater part of his subsequent schooling is directed to furthering this end.

No horse can be pleasant to ride or be handy in his movements unless he is capable of impulsion. We have already seen that it is impossible to achieve any degree of extension, collection or even forward movement without this quality. Impulsion is the bedrock of riding and impulsion is only obtained from balance. Upon the improvement and perfection of balance depends the successful outcome of schooling.

Before, however, we can begin schooling from the saddle the horse must be sufficiently muscled to be capable of the work he has to do. If the lungeing programme has been carried out properly and has been alternated with gentle, straightforward hacking much of the ground-work will have been completed, and the horse will be physically and mentally equipped to proceed to work in the school. The rider, too, must be in reasonable physical shape and must prepare himself for the role of instructor.

Good teachers spend more time preparing their lessons than giving them – indeed preparation is the secret of instruction and each lesson should be planned well before riding into the school. This is not to say that one's programme must be inflexible. It must, in fact, be very flexible. Some days everything will go well, on others you will seem to have achieved nothing.

However it goes, the one *inflexible* rule is never to teach a movement before the previous one has been completely assimilated. If the horse finds a lesson difficult and you are not getting anywhere, go back to the previous, and easier, lesson and then think, when he is put back in his box, in no way upset or confused, whether it was not your fault. In most cases you will find it probably was, so you must work out another line of approach.

Never put a horse into his stable in other than a happy frame of mind. If you do he broods and goes sulky. Never try to teach anything if your temper is becoming frayed. None of us is infallible and we all get agitated, tense or just plain angry sometimes. In this state we can teach nothing. The answer is to get off the horse, walk round the school, or recite the longest poem you know by heart, until your temper is very well under control. Then carry out a simple movement which the horse enjoys doing, reward him and finish the lesson there.

The Four Gaits

Before considering the exercises and movements which can be practised in the school we should look at the way the horse moves at the various gaits. The four natural gaits of the horse are: Walk, Trot, Canter and Gallop.

The walk is a pace of four separate beats marked by the successive placing of each lateral pair. The sequence of the footfalls when the walk starts on the left leg is: left hind, left fore, right hind, right fore.

The trot is a pace of two beats, the horse placing one pair of diagonal legs on the ground and springing, following a moment of suspension, on to the other diagonal. One beat is heard as the left hind and the right fore touch the ground simultaneously and one, after the briefest interval, as the opposite diagonal touches the ground.

In the canter three beats can, or should, be heard if the horse is cantering correctly. The horse may canter either with the right fore leading (the right lead), or with the left fore (the left lead). In fact, of course, the leading leg is not the first in the sequence of the beats, but the last. On the right lead the sequence is left hindleg, then, simultaneously, the left diagonal, left fore and right hind, and lastly the leading leg, the right fore, then a period of suspension before the next stride is taken.

The canter in the school or on a circle is correct when the right lead is employed on a right-handed circle and left lead on a circle on the left rein. It is a false lead, known as cantering on the wrong leg, when the left lead is used on the right rein and vice versa. It is, however, easy for the rider to feel when he is on the incorrect leg as he receives a fairly violent jolt under the outside of his seat and his outside shoulder will be thrown forward. Counter canter, which though it involves moving on the "incorrect" lead, is something quite different, being a fairly advanced exercise carried out in the interests of improved balance.

The gallop, the fastest pace, which is not used in school work, becomes a four beat pace (i.e. with the off-fore leading: near-hind, off-hind, near-fore, off-fore, followed by a moment of suspension), but has considerable variation in the sequence of movements according to the speed.

With conscious effort and attention the rider should be able not only to hear the footfalls, but to feel which foot is coming to the ground. When he does he will find, particularly in the canter, how much more effectively and precisely he can apply the aids.

To start the school work first commit to memory the various school figures which are illustrated. These are designed to improve suppleness and balance by asking for continual directional changes and consequently changes in the shifting centre of balance.

Starting the Exercises

Commence work, for short periods only, at the walk round the school, crossing the arena diagonally when you wish to change the rein. At this early stage do not bother about the head position, but concentrate on riding into each corner with active legs, the inside one pushing the horse forward, the outside preventing the quarters swinging out.

As a second stage pick up the reins and push the horse forward until you feel him making contact with the bit. Now you can commence the smaller circles, more frequent changes of direction and some curves and serpentines. Check the efficiency of your leg aids by riding the *inside* track occasionally, i.e. about nine feet from the wall or rail of the school. Very often you will find your horse tends to go to pieces when divorced from the guiding wall.

Check, too, the strength of the aids. After a very few lessons it should be possible by a very slight movement of the legs to obtain a turn. If the horse does not immediately respond, reinforce the aid with a tap from the long whip, held in the inside hand, just behind the girth. With a long whip there is no need to remove the hands from the rein and this tap will be sufficient to send the horse on. Under no circumstances strengthen the leg aid or let it degenerate into a kick, otherwise all future aids asking for greater impulsion will have to be correspondingly stronger in comparison.

In all movements concentrate on keeping the horse straight and only

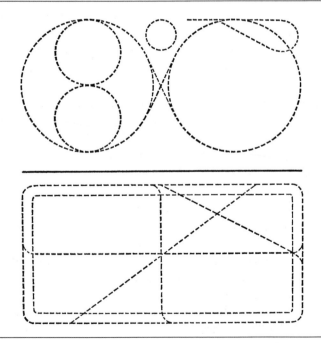

School figures: (above) *the variety of school circles and changes of hand;* (below) *the various changes of hand possible in the school. The inside dotted line indicates the inside track.*

allowing the quarters to follow the track of the forehand.

Straightening the horse is not, of course, quite so easy as it sounds and every horse will have a stiff side, which is why they become more or less unstraight. Suppling exercises, like the shoulder-in, are a way to achieving straightness but much can be done before reaching that stage if we are constantly aware of the necessity to keep the horse straight and work intelligently towards that end.

The horse, as we know, is considered to be straight when the hindfeet follow directly the track made by the forefeet. For the most part, he experiences difficulty in going straight on account of his off-side hindleg.

Almost every horse has more difficulty in engaging and flexing that leg than its opposite number. As a result the foot may be compelled to be put down outside of the track made by the corresponding foreleg and so, willy-nilly, the horse becomes crooked and stiff on that side, leaning on the left rein and against the rider's leg on that side.

It might be thought that to counter the problem one should work hard at making the horse bend more satisfactorily on his stiff side but that, I assure you, just doesn't work. Instead, the discomfort he feels is met by increased and understandable resistance.

The way to go about it is from the trot pace, which is the most valuable in all our schooling of the horse. Work at a good, active trot, giving and taking the rein on the stiff side by means of a strong squeezing action of the hand. Any tendency toward pulling the rein will be immediately counter-productive.

The opposite rein is held quietly in support and the right leg acts in continuing nudges to encourage the engagement of the horse's off-hindleg.

It can be taken a stage further by working on turns and circles. The hand then acts to open the rein on the stiff side, directing it towards the hip whilst riding the circle. The contact has then to be exactly equal, which needs thinking about, and the horse is asked to describe the circle in the *wrong* bend. (Heresy? Not at all – read Benoist-Gironière or Museler or Handler, Decarpentry *et alia*.)

It is, of course, uncomfortable for the horse and for that reason must not be over-done but in a very short time he will begin slowly to accept the outside rein and give on the stiff side.

It is part of school riding to straighten the horse, or to check for straightness, after passing through the corners. It is done by keeping the shoulder somewhat away from the wall or the edge of the arena. How? Simply by moving the inside hand to the side by a very little and laying the outside rein lightly on the neck.

The Walk

The three school paces are the walk, trot and canter, and all three are further sub-divided in relation to the modern dressage requirement.

There are four sub-divisions of the walk: *medium, collected, extended* and *free*.

Medium walk is a free, unconstrained movement of moderate extension. The steps should be even and distinct with the hindfeet touching the ground *in front* of the prints made by the forefeet.

Collected walk will not be attained until the horse is at a relatively advanced stage of training but that is no reason why we should not work towards it.

In collection the horse moves resolutely forward with the head in a near-vertical position and the neck raised and arched. The hindlegs, flexing strongly at the hocks, are actively engaged under the body in response to the increased power of the driving aids. The seat and the small of the back push forward and upward with each stride while the legs act in intermittent squeezes. They are never applied in a dead, continuous, clamping motion. The greater engagement results in increased

(Below) Sian Thomas and Taurus at medium walk; (opposite page, top) still at walk and entering the corner. Note the good acceptance of the rein and leg aids; (opposite page, bottom) the horse reaching down in the walk on the long rein, the rider's hands encouraging the stretching movement whilst maintaining contact.

impulsion and if the hands close slightly on the reins the energy generated will be contained within the framework imposed by legs and hands.

The steps are more elevated and shorter than at medium walk because of the greater flexion of the joints and the hindfeet touch the ground *behind* the prints of the forefeet.

In *extended* walk the horse covers as much ground as possible with each stride but without losing the essential regularity of the four-beat pace. The head and neck extend and the hindfeet touch the ground *well in front* of the prints of the forefeet.

In *free* walk the horse is in an extended outline with complete freedom of head and neck. Essentially it is a rest pace which we use following a period of shortening in our approach to collection.

To start with our efforts at collection or shortening will be hardly perceptible and once we feel the horse shortening we should, after insisting on a few properly executed strides, reward him by letting him go on in extended walk, which is so much less demanding of him.

This stage will not, however, be reached for some time and should not be attempted until the work at the trot is becoming established. If in the early lessons we can obtain a good free medium walk alternating with an energetic free or extended walk this is sufficient.

Moving Off and The Halt

We can, however, perfect the move-off and the halt, and we can begin asking for those relaxations of the lower jaw mentioned previously.

No horse will move off alertly and in balanced fashion unless he is first brought to attention.

Start by mounting the horse, insisting on his remaining still while you do so. If he moves off before you are ready, place him in a corner of the school facing the wall or fence and spend ten minutes getting up and down. If he moves as you are half way up, come down again and make a fresh start.

Most horses get into the habit of moving off as soon as the rider puts a toe in the iron because they are well aware that the same toe will, within seconds, be dug into their ribs. If you cannot mount from the ground unassisted have someone give you a leg up or use a mounting block. It is more dignified, less exhausting and does not exasperate the horse by pulling him off balance and subjecting him to the discomfort of a shifted saddle.

Pause a moment, to settle yourself in the saddle, before picking up the reins. Pick them up quietly and gently to give the horse no opportunity to anticipate the command to move off. Now bring him to attention by a momentary, and very slight, application of both legs pushing him up to hands which, again momentarily, squeeze the reins. Now apply the legs again and open the hand slightly to allow the horse to move forward.

In a similar way the horse must be given a warning of your intention to halt and he must be in contact with the hand before he can do so. The aids to halt commence with a stretching of the back and loins (but not a leaning back of the trunk, which would impose greater weight on the quarters and encourage the horse to lean on the bit), increased pressure from the seat bones and a slightly increased drive from the legs sending the horse up to a hand which closes. Initially we may have to repeat the hand aid before the horse understands, but the moment he obeys the hand must yield. Once the legs have acted, and the horse has shortened his posture to conform with the closing hand, the leg must revert to a passive state, being held ready to control any deviation of the quarters from the straight line. Within a short time the horse will stop immediately from the walk, but at first he may need to take a step or two before he can halt entirely.

Relaxation

At the halt, practise immobility for a few seconds before moving off again and when this is easily obtained ask for the relaxation of the lower jaw. The hand works in the same way as on the long reins, the fingers vibrating gently on the required side, the other hand supporting.

It is possible that you will find the horse relaxes the jaw quite easily on one side, but resists on the other, for reasons already explained. Usually it will be on the right side to which he objects and we can overcome this, getting him to lower his head and relax the jaw, by walking him off on the left rein with the fingers closing slightly on this side as we proceed down the long side of the school. We will vibrate the fingers on the right rein, at the same time using the right leg rather more strongly to push him up to the right rein, while maintaining the light contact on the left one. Gradually we shall get the required relaxation at walk and trot, and also at the halt. Once this is achieved equally on both sides, a simultaneous action of the two hands will produce a full and equal relaxation of the jaw and a slight lowering of the head.

The Trot

Now we can introduce the same school figures at the trot, which is the most valuable of the schooling paces.

The trot, like the walk, varies in its form and is obtained by a slightly stronger action of both legs, first from the walk and later from the halt. In this last named case the horse is helped to differentiate between the two pressures involved by the rider applying the trot aid from the halt a little further to the rear than the momentary squeeze asking for walk from halt.

As with the walk there are four sub-divisions of trot: *working, medium, collected, extended.*

Working trot, a most productive pace, lies between *medium* and *collected*, being inclined more towards the latter than otherwise. It is employed as an approach to full collection for horses not yet capable of the latter.

Medium trot is between extension and collection, inclining towards the former. It is rounder than the extended trot but with good engagement nonetheless, the hindfeet touching down *in* the prints of the forefeet.

(Below) *working trot with good hindleg engagement;* (opposite page, top) *Taurus about to extend the trot across the arena;* (opposite page, bottom) *and in extension – with Sian concentrating very hard!*

In *collection* the stride shortens and becomes more elevated, the hindfeet prints falling behind those of the forefeet.

The *extended* trot asks the horse to cover as much ground as possible with a lengthened stride – it is not a matter of going faster!

The neck extends and the impulsion from the quarters causes the shoulders to be used more actively so as to cover more ground without the action becoming elevated.

In the spectrum of the trot paces the extremes are collection and extension. Working trot is positioned slightly to the collected side of the centre line, whilst medium trot can be placed fairly close to extension.

The most common failing in the trot is for riders to go too fast. Go slow so as to obtain an increase in rhythm and impulsion.

As far as the rider is concerned there are two variants of his position within the gait. He may either execute a *rising*, or posting, trot, that is he raises his seat *slightly* out of the saddle so that he rests in the saddle on alternate beats only, or he may maintain a "full seat", *sitting* trot, throughout the movement.

In the sitting trot the rider sits, as it were, with an open, relaxed seat absorbing the shock through a supple and erect back which *undulates* with the movement of the horse. The critical portion is the small of the back which is the connecting link between the trunk and the lower body.

This is what should happen, that it rarely does is because the sitting trot is used too soon in the horse's training and is not used sufficiently in the early training of the rider, who is always taught to post before learning how to sit in the gait. It is easy enough to sit in balance, i.e. with the rider's weight over the centre of balance of the horse, when the horse is sufficiently balanced and his back muscles are properly developed. Until, however, this is achieved, and it will only be so when the horse is capable of a certain degree of shortening within the pace, more harm than good will be done.

If the horse is not well-balanced the effect of the sitting trot will be to over-burden the quarters, as the rider moves *behind* the centre of balance, which will hinder impulsion and the engagement of the hindlegs. The very opposite is what we are trying to achieve. If, in addition, the rider's hands are asking for a retraction of the head, the horse's back will hollow and his head will be pulled upwards to a degree where it will become "above the bit", that is, where the nose is carried upwards and the neck bends upwards from its lower third.

The sitting trot is used in the *collected* pace as a further inducement to full engagement of the quarters and because it is the only position in which the rider can be *in balance* when the horse assumes this posture; if however it is consistently employed, before the horse is ready, the result will be to produce a rough uneven pace and resistance throughout.

For short periods it is permissible to use this seat, which greatly facilitates the action of the legs, when we are asking for a shortening of the stride or for any transition in pace, but each short period must be followed by a longer one permitting complete relaxation.

I am quite convinced that much of the criticism levelled at horses and riders when executing even the simplest tests of training, or dressage if you like, has its roots in too great a use of the hand and too early an employment of the sitting trot so far as the horse is concerned and perhaps the rider, too.

There then remains the question of the diagonal when rising at the trot in the execution of a circle.

As might be expected there are three schools of thought. One says the rider should rise on the inside foreleg, and consequently the outside hindleg; that is, he is sitting as the inside hindleg advances and is therefore better positioned to use his own leg to drive this hindleg further forward, i.e. on a circle to the right he rides the left diagonal and vice versa, a second says the opposite and a third could not care less which diagonal you use.

The first argument would seem to be more logical and is the one I endeavour to practise, but the important thing is to change the diagonal when the rein changes.

(*Where the terms left rein and right rein are used they mean a circle to the left and right respectively. The use of "inside" and "outside", whether applied to the limbs of either horse or rider, or to the reins, means that limb or rein on the inside or the outside of the circle respectively.*)

Poles on the Ground

It is during the work at walk and trot that poles laid on the ground, followed later by cavalletti proper at the trot pace, can be introduced.

The poles, spaced at about four to five feet apart, according to the length of the individual animal's stride, and up to five in number, are first laid out on the long side of the school. The horse is first asked to walk over these and later, when he accepts them as commonplace, to trot over them.

He should be allowed to cross the poles with a free head and neck, but without losing the rhythm of his stride. Never allow him to go too fast or to rush at them, much less to attempt to jump them. The object is to help the horse in becoming supple, to improve his balance and outline by the rounding of the back and the greater flexion demanded in the hocks, and to lay a sound foundation for jumping.

At the trot the rider can best assist the horse by following and encouraging the outward stretching of the head and neck with the hands and by leaning slightly forward with the seat a fraction off the saddle.

As the horse becomes proficient the poles can be laid around the circumference of a 20-metre circle, when the rider must insist upon the horse following the correct track, so that the poles are negotiated at the proper distance apart. The centre of the poles should lie on the required track and the work done equally on either rein. The use of the cavalletti in detail is dealt with later in this section.

The Canter

The canter is the most difficult pace for the horse to perform correctly and should not be attempted in the school until the work at walk and trot is established and the horse's balance at those paces is controlled and fluid.

As in the trot the variation is between *collected, working, medium* and *extended*, and the same criteria apply, but there is the additional complication of teaching the horse to strike off on the correct leg, i.e. inside foreleg leading.

The horse will have already learnt on the lunge, and perhaps in the long reins, how to canter on a circle on the correct lead, but without the burden of a rider to upset his balance. Now he must learn to canter a circle under the rider and to vary the speed, with the consequent shortening and lengthening of his body and the shifting of his centre of balance that this will demand.

He will have been prepared for the work during his ordinary hacking, first by being urged into a canter from a trot, to get him used to the pace, and then by the rider positioning him and applying the aids in such a way as to get him to lead off with one leg or the other.

Positioning the horse previous to a movement is all important in the canter, just as it is when we give notice to him of our intention to make a transition from one pace to another.

The horse is best able to make the transition from trot to canter when he is slightly bent towards the direction of the movement. If, therefore, we want him to lead with the right foreleg, i.e. to circle to the right, the

Working canter, active and in balance and with the rider deep in the saddle.

Extended canter, the rider driving more actively.

The half-halt, the hands momentarily resisting the leg action to reimpose the balance by raising the forehand.

transition is best taught, initially, at a corner of a field. As the horse approaches the corner at the ordinary trot, on the right rein, the rider sits in the saddle, which he will always do when asking for any transition from one pace to another, and brings the horse to attention by pushing him up to the hands (a minimal half-halt in fact).

He then bends the head slightly to the right, to a point where the eye can just be seen, maintaining support on the left rein to prevent any deviation from the track. At the same time he sits slightly more strongly on the right seat bone and applies his right leg on the girth and the left leg behind the girth.

The supporting rein, apart from maintaining the track, when combined with the push from the rider's seat, prevents the horse altering the rhythm and accelerating.

The alteration in the distribution of the rider's weight is in accordance with the shift of the centre of balance towards the inside, caused by the flexion of the horse's body, and is practised in all circles and turns. The degree to which the rider displaces his weight is dependent upon the degree of flexion of the horse and to some extent upon the speed, when the action of centrifugal force is involved. In time

The horse bent correctly on the arc of the circle with the inside hindleg fully engaged under the body.

the rider will be able to feel the extent to which the aid should be used as he becomes more finely attuned to the horse's movements.

The seat bone on either side is weighted *not* by collapsing the inside hip, or by pushing forward the corresponding shoulder. The rider leans the upper part of his body sideways very slightly and *stretches* his inside leg. The most common fault is to exaggerate the sideways inclination, to the point of bending at the waist. When this occurs the rider will upset the balance of the horse, provoking a natural, defensive resistance in the opposite direction.

In the canter to the right, the inside, right, leg will be the stronger, as its purpose is to drive forward, and underneath the horse, the right hindleg. The other leg, in its supporting role, controls the bend and will prevent the outward movement of the quarters as well as assisting the movement forward.

How strong these aids should be, and how much stronger the inside than the outside leg, depends on the stage of training. As before, the lighter the aid the better. Should the horse lose his quarters to the outside, or have them moved too much to the inside, the movement is lost, and the fault lies with either too little or too much pressure from the outside leg.

The last factor in the canter aid sequence is the immediate yielding of the hands to allow the horse's head and neck to extend forward as he enters the first canter stride.

When we first commence the exercise in the open we shall, however, be content if the horse strikes off correctly, and we will not bother him by insisting on a perfection of movement which at present he is not capable of performing.

Beyond asking him to go calmly, occasionally to extend in response to the legs, seat and advancing hand, and to come back to the hand when it seeks to check the pace, we need not concern ourselves in these early days with more advanced niceties.

If the horse, despite the aids, strikes off incorrectly, stop him and start again. If he displays excitement and attempts to go faster and faster, bring him to a halt, trot one or two small circles on either hand asking for variations in the pace and for one or two relaxations of the lower jaw to either rein, before trying once more. This has the effect of reminding him that obedience is expected whilst imposing a little discipline.

If, of course, the horse is fresh and mad keen for a gallop it is best to let him get the itch out of his heels, after which he will be in a more co-operative frame of mind.

In the more confined area of the school the horse is positioned in exactly the same way, but it is best to ask for only a few canter strides to start with and then to bring the horse back to the trot.

Once the horse strikes off easily on either rein and is able to canter round the school, varying the pace as he is asked, we can make the rectangle smaller by riding the inside track, which will also remove his reliance on the wall, and then attempt smaller circles, using half the school. If the horse finds these small circles difficult you have gone too fast and must do more suppling work at trot and in larger circles at the canter.

Gradually we can ask for the canter stride at increasing distances and away the supporting corner, until we can obtain the correct strike off in the centre of the long side of the school, or in the middle of the arena on either leg.

Quite early in the training at canter in the school the horse can be taught the canter from the walk, which is, in fact, easier for him, as the pattern of footfalls at the walk is more closely related to those of the canter than the footfalls of the trot.

Later he will be able to canter from halt, which is an excellent balancing exercise and should be practised as soon as the work at canter is performed smoothly, without loss of rhythm and with good balance.

The Half-Halt

The *half-halt*, within any gait, is generally understood to be a means of producing a downward transition, i.e. from canter to trot, trot to walk, or for checking the rhythm of a particular gait by shortening the horse. At the canter, particularly, it is also a balancing exercise asking for immediate displacement of the centre of balance to the rear.

In trot or canter the half-halt, used as a balancing exercise or, in reality, as a means of re-imposing balance, is achieved by the rider sitting firmly in the saddle, using both legs actively behind the girth, to further engage the quarters, while effecting an immediate closing and raising of both hands – but very lightly please.

The result is an immediate compression of the horse towards his centre without breaking the gait.

This, however, is not quite the case in the canter pace, when we ask for a transition to trot or walk, or for the full halt from canter.

These movements are more easily accomplished if the closing of the inside hand (i.e. right at the canter on the right lead and vice versa) fractionally precedes that of the outside hand, the former closing as the inside foreleg comes to the ground. These actions interrupt the sequence of footfalls and the moment of suspension is lost. The outside rein is in fact operating as the outside hindleg touches the ground when the halt will be easily achieved.

To shorten the stride at canter, checking the impulsion, the use of the inside hand, inclining the head towards the leading leg, will slightly close the inside shoulder thus restricting the extent of the stride.

Half-turn on the forehand, the horse pivoting on the inside foreleg.

Half-turn on the quarters.

Conversely, the use of the outside hand to straighten the head gives greater freedom to the leading shoulder and extends the pace.

Change of Leg at the Canter

Figures of eight, serpentines, etc., will call for the horse to change the leading leg in accordance with the change of direction, and while the skilled horseman will in time obtain a flying change (i.e. a change of lead in the air – the rider changes the canter position at the moment immediately prior to suspension) the average rider will not find this movement necessary.

It will be sufficient, by means of the half-halt, to bring the horse back to trot for a few strides at the centre of the figure of eight, to re-position him and then to strike off with the opposite leg.

Should the horse be reluctant to strike into the canter stride within the school at the commencement of the schooling at this pace he will be encouraged to do so by using a cavalletto at its lowest height. The horse will at this stage be conversant with the poles on the ground and work over cavalletti. If three poles are laid out some six feet apart, followed after an interval of nine or ten feet by a cavalletto at the approach to the corner the horse will usually go into canter to jump the last obstacle.

While the turns and circles involved in school work assist in the improvement of balance and increase the suppleness of the horse their value is lost if they are not performed correctly. On the turns the horse's quarters must follow the track made by the forelegs, the horse giving the appearance of being flexed around the rider's inside leg, and being straightened by leg and hand when the turn is completed. Any falling in towards the centre at the turn must be opposed by the supporting leg, hand and weight aids, applied momentarily as the horse attempts to shorten the corner.

The circles, too, must be absolutely true ones, obliging the horse to maintain a sustained bend with increased activity and engagement of the inside hindleg. A common fault is for the horse to slow down on entering the turn, which must be combated by increasingly active leg aids.

Turns at the Halt

The two turns from the halt are those executed on the forehand, when

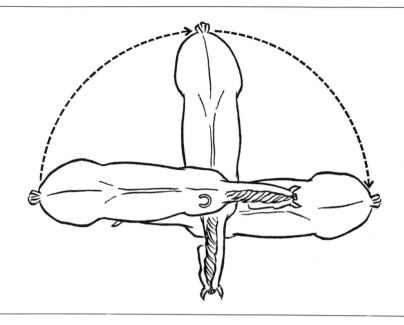

Turn on the forehand.

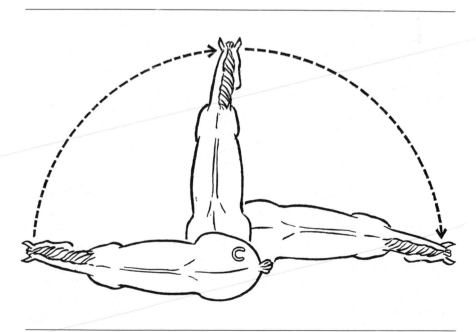

Turn on the quarters.

the quarters are moved round the pivot of the inside foreleg, and those on the quarters, when the forehand moves round the pivot of the inside hindleg. Both can encompass a full turn (360 degrees), a half turn (180 degrees), or for practical purposes even less.

The turn on the forehand teaches the horse obedience to the lateral action of the leg, after he has learnt the forward and retarding actions, and is usefully employed when opening a gate.

The turn is best taught, at first, in a corner of the school and in a turn to the right the horse would have the wall or fence upon his right side with the joining fence in front of him. In a turn to the right it is the head which moves in that direction, while the body goes to the left. The opposite being the case in a turn to the left.

The aids are simple, and when used in conjunction with the corner of the school are usually easily understood.

First the horse is brought to a balanced halt. The head is then inclined to the right to a point when half the eye can be seen by the rider. It is important that the horse should be pushed well up to his bit as this movement takes place, but not so much that he moves forward.

The right leg now acts a good hand's breadth behind the girth, if

The halt in balance, the rider bringing the shoulders a shade behind the hips.

necessary reinforced by a tap from the long whip held in the right hand, to move the quarters, a step at a time, to the left. The left leg, behind the girth, controls the steps. The left rein supports the right, preventing any outward movement of the shoulder. One or two steps is enough to start with, and they can be increased in number as the horse gets the idea.

The horse is easily prepared for this turn by its being practised in the box, when the trainer, standing to the front of the horse, inclines his head with one hand and taps his flank with the whip in the other. The turn is never attempted while in movement.

The turn on the quarters is just as useful, as it is the prelude to the horse taking side steps (it, too, is used in opening a gate, or rather when moving away from it when it has been opened and closed).

Again the rider for a turn to the right inclines the horse's head in that direction, but at the same time he now weights his right seat-bone. The rein, supported by its companion, is now beginning the movement, while the left leg, a hand's width behind the girth, prevents the quarters moving outwards and controls the turn step by step. The right leg remains in support to prevent the movement of the inside hind which forms the pivot of the turn.

Again a corner of the school can be used with advantage and a tap on the shoulder with the whip, held in the left hand, can be helpful. In both cases the opposite aids apply for turns to the left.

The Rein-Back

I have always regarded this as an advanced movement, only capable of execution by a balanced, trained horse and a rider who has acquired a deep sympathy and understanding of the aids. It is, however, asked for at various riding club tests. I recently judged one where the horse was asked to rein-back between bales of straw which involved at least ten steps, and I have even seen it attempted at Pony Club rallies.

Not surprisingly these efforts, not understood by either horse or rider, result in a complete travesty of the movement and considerable discomfort for the horse.

The rein-back is a pace of two time with the impulsion initiated by the forelegs. and the legs are moved in diagonal pairs.

As in all movements success depends upon correct pre-positioning of the horse. The rider must obtain, before asking for the rein-back, a balanced halt, with the horse in a shortened attitude, by pushing forward from back, seat and legs into the restraining hands. In theory, and in practice also, if the rider continues to apply these aids properly

The rein-back with excellent, light contact on the rein and the seat skilfully lightened to free the back.

after the halt has been obtained the horse must move backwards, although an improper use of the aids with too great a pressure from leg and hand, might well result in the horse rearing.

However, the horse will better understand this if the rider urges him back through alternate closing pressures on either rein, persuading the corresponding foreleg and then the diagonal hindleg to move to the rear.

Just prior to the rein action the legs can become passive, being held in readiness to counteract any swinging off a straight line by the quarters, or any tendency to take more than one step at a time and run backwards.

Two steps are quite sufficient and three or four, clearly defined, are as much as will ever be needed.

Side-Steps

For most riders this work appears to have no immediate practical purpose beyond developing the horse, making him supple and flexible and increasing the rider's sense of the aids. The side-steps, however,

Leg-yielding to the left. Note the position of the off-hindleg.

teach increased obedience to the leg and give to the rider a far greater degree of control over his horse. As such they are valuable and worth persevering with.

In its very advanced form perfection in work on two tracks is not easily achieved, but it is possible to obtain simple side-steps without too much difficulty.

In lateral movement the horse is bent in the direction of movement with the forehand always in advance of the quarters, the fore- and hindlegs always moving on two distinct tracks. The two principal movements are the *half-pass* and the *full-pass*. In the former the horse moves sideways and forwards, in the latter he moves sideways without advancing to his front. In both cases the outside legs are crossed over and pass in front of the inside ones with the horse's head flexed in the direction he is going.

The turns at the halt will have already prepared the animal for side-steps and we can go a stage further by teaching him, for very short periods only, the suppling movement known as *shoulder-in*.

This is best started in the trot pace, immediately after leaving a corner of the school, before the horse has quite straightened out of the turn, although initially trial runs can be practised at walk. The right rein (if on a circle to the right) directs the head, asking for flexions on that side and in that direction, and is supported by the left hand. Too much rein at this stage closes the shoulder and obviates the movement.

The hand has now moved the forehand over towards the inside track of the school and the right leg, behind the girth, urges the horse forward and engages the right hindleg. The outside rein, however, must support this action, otherwise the horse just goes into another turn. Equally important is the action of the left leg, behind the girth, which encourages and controls the apparent bend of the horse round its opposite number. If impulsion begins to fall the outside leg must move forward on to the girth to assist its partner and provoke increased forward movement. The rider slightly stretches his inside leg to place a little more weight on the inside seat-bone.

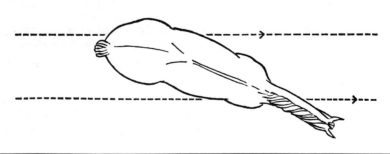

Shoulder-in.

Shoulder-in, well-executed in a good overall bend.

The horse should now be bent away from the direction in which he is going, and the forehand should describe a track inside that of the quarters.

This is a difficult exercise for the horse and, again, one or two steps are enough on either rein and should be immediately followed by allowing the horse to move on following the arc of the circle and to do so freely and vigorously.

The half-pass itself is most easily introduced away from the school when riding along a quiet road or track. If one is on the left side and wishes to move to the right, the head is again inclined in that direction very slightly, the right seat-bone is weighted, the left leg, a hand's width behind the girth pushes the quarters across, while the right limits their movement and maintains the impulsion if necessary. The supporting left hand can assist further by being pressed against the wither intermittently to encourage the lateral movement of the shoulder.

This is easily achieved under these circumstances and leads to obtaining the same steps, and possibly one or two at the full-pass later on if they are required.

The practical application of the side-steps, apart from the obvious advantages, can be exploited when riding in traffic or when asking the horse to pass some unusual or frightening object.

Being able to position the horse and to obtain the attention necessary for one or two steps at the shoulder-in is an ideal way of imposing a little discipline and of distracting his mind from the object in question.

Leg-yielding is really a follow-on from the turn on the forehand. It is regarded as the first of the suppling movements and it is very easy for the horse to perform since no real bend is required.

The exercise begins in walk, the rider taking the inside track. In this position the horse is always willing and almost anxious to return to the familiar outside track. If we wish to move to the left we apply the right leg, flat behind the girth and pushing inwards. The right rein is applied (in front of the wither and towards the rider's left hip) to obtain a slight bend of the head to the right (just enough to see his eye) and the left hand is opened outwards to indicate still more clearly the sideways movement required. The use of the left leg is important. It must act to maintain the forward movement. Whatever you do, avoid exaggeration which would turn the movement into a sort of travesty of shoulder-in. The lighter the aids the more easily the movement is accomplished – and that is true in everything.

Bits Used in Schooling

All the work described can be carried out in a snaffle, with or without the assistance of a drop-noseband, but the change from snaffle to bit and bradoon should not be unduly delayed.

The more sophisticated bridle can be introduced once the school movements can be executed at a canter. Not only does the bit and bradoon assist the flexions, but it encourages a raising of the head and is less likely to have the horse hanging on it, as can happen with the snaffle alone.

The majority of horses go very kindly in this combination, provided that the rider is sufficiently skilled to use it judiciously.

I do not advise the intermediate use of a Pelham, or its use at all, unless the horse's mouth is so constructed as to make the double bridle a permanent impossibility.

The Use of the Cavalletti

Throughout the horse's training use will have been made of poles and cavalletti and it is as well to study the value of the latter in some detail.

It is most unfortunate that the cavalletti training system, well-proven over more than eighty years, should have been subjected to criticism, much of it misinformed, in recent years. In fact, although the British Horse Society continues to sell Dr Reiner Klimke's valuable little book *Cavalletti* (J.A. Allen), it has stated that their use is no longer recommended. There is a danger, which I acknowledge, in piling cavalletti one on top of the other to make a fence, but otherwise there can be no valid criticism of this versatile system as a whole and I, as well as a great many more experienced horsemen than myself (including the Olympic gold medallist Dr Klimke), will continue to use it effectively and as safely as anything else in this equestrian vale of tears.

Indeed, one of the greatest experts on cavalletti usage is Lt-Col J.D. Crawford, formerly Chairman of the Training Committee and a Fellow of the Society.

The principal benefits of cavalletti are directed towards the training of horse and rider for jumping, which requires a horse to be balanced, supple, calm and obedient and their use is, therefore, complementary at all points in the schooling programme and for all purposes. It can, therefore, be introduced at an early stage.

Once the horse has been lunged over obstacles and accepts jumping as part of his ordinary routine he progresses, under the saddle, to the crossing of spaced poles on the ground, which can then be followed by the cavalletti.

The cavalletti are first laid out at their lowest height between four and a half and five feet (which can later be increased to six feet) apart and the horse is made to approach at the trot out of a large circle. He should cross the cavalletti maintaining impulsion and rhythm, rounding his back and being allowed to stretch out the head and neck.

If one can run to five cavalletti, three should be used initially and then increased to five when the horse negotiates them calmly on either rein.

A diagram is given of the suggested dimensions of a cavalletto and it is important that all five should be of the same length and have the same height variations. The horse is now ready for the introduction of a small jump, which is made by moving cavalletto four up to cavalletto five.

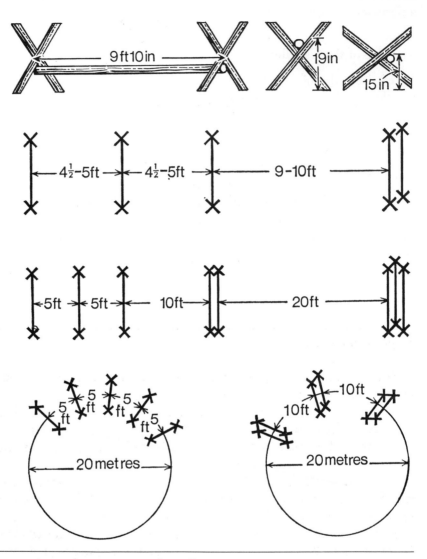

Construction and arrangement of cavalletti.

(*a*) Dimensions

(*b*) The first arrangement of cavalletti so that the final element becomes a jump

(*c*) A further variation in the arrangement of cavalletti

(*d*) (*Left*) The disposition of cavalletti on a 20 metre circle for the trot pace

    (*Right*) for the canter stride

(*It is not recommended that cavalletti should be piled as in the final element of fig. (c). It would be better to construct a small fence. It is quite permissible to use two cavalletti side by side to form a small spread fence.*)

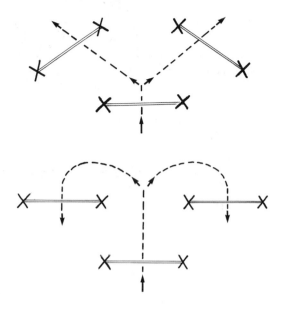

Simple cavelletti exercises.

You may now, exactly as before, trot over the first three and still in the same pace jump the last element.

If one has a sufficiency of cavalletti numerous variations in the distance can be made, but it is important not to exceed the lowest height at the trot, otherwise a hop develops which obviates the benefit of the exercise.

Cavalletti work can also be carried out at the canter, starting again with poles, but now spaced 20 ft apart, so that the horse is not tempted to jump two in one stride. Once this is established cavalletti can be substituted at the 10 in height, which can be gradually raised to first 15 in, and then to 19 in, and the distance apart reduced to 10 ft.

Balance is further improved by altering the distances, in multiples of 10 between the cavalletti and introducing cavalletti at different heights and spreads.

Finally, and I am indebted to Lt-Col J.D. Crawford, F.B.H.S., for this more advanced exercise, cavalletti can be used on a 20-metre circle after the horse has become accustomed to poles on the ground on a circle of the same diameter.

The canter sequence of cavalletti should be approached on the arc of

Trotting over low cavalletti in line.

Trotting over cavalletti set on a 20 metre ride.

Cantering over a cavalletti placed on a circle.

Jumping in an easily-constructed jumping lane.

the circle at the trot with the horse correctly bent, quarters following the track of the forehand, and going into the first stride of the canter to jump the first cavalletto. Still maintaining the bend he should complete the remainder at canter and then quietly be brought back to trot.

Should the horse become excited at any stage always go back to lower cavalletti at a slower pace.

During all work on the circle the rider must insist on the correct bend being kept and the track being maintained.

These exercises are of enormous value but, as in all things, progress must be gradual, the horse never being hurried into a more advanced lesson until he has fully assimilated the previous ones.

Jumping

Success at jumping comes from work on the flat, which produces a calm, obedient, supple and balanced horse. If the work described so far has been carried out properly the jumping of small obstacles will be a natural progression of the training, which the horse will accept with confidence and equanimity.

Showjumping is a specialist art, demanding a horse of exceptional talent, but any reasonably schooled horse should have no difficulty in jumping fences of up to 4 ft.

A very active trot over the pole grid, the rider is in an exemplary jumping seat and maintaining a perfect contact with the mouth.

A straightforward schooling fence jumped confidently. The rider's position is excellent.

First phase in the approach to a parallel. The rider maintains a driving seat.

Second phase in the approach, immediately prior to take-off. The rider raises the seat and the weight goes into the heel.

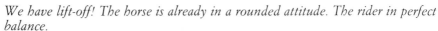

We have lift-off! The horse is already in a rounded attitude. The rider in perfect balance.

The angle of the knee closes, the hands follow the mouth allowing the rounded flight phase but the body is maintained in line with the movement not in front of it!

The landing, the horse taking his weight on the near foreleg. The rider's seat has returned to the saddle, the leg is strengthened by the raising of the outside of the foot and the hands, fingers open, are in line and in contact with the mouth.

Initially the fences in the jumping area should be very low, not more than 2 ft 6 in in height or 4 ft in width. They should, however, be numerous and varied; but this does not mean the outlay of large sums on expensive fences, but rather an outlay of ingenuity and powers of improvisation.

Poles, some of them coloured, sheep hurdles, straw bales, oil drums, brush and railway sleepers can all be pressed into service to make jumps posing different problems of approach and execution. Spread fences are necessary, pyramids, staircases and, if possible, some sort of bank and ditch that involves jumping from one level to another, as well as an in and out.

Practise jumping these fences, altering their layout as often as possible, until the horse can pop over from any angle without excitement.

Gradually the height and spread can be increased and also the distance between fences. As a general rule, allowing for the horse's stride varying between eight and 20 ft, the following distances are applicable between individual fences:

1 stride	22 feet
2 strides	35 feet
3 strides	47 feet
4 strides	59 feet
5 strides	71 feet and so on

Fences, however, should not be placed at these distances until the horse and rider have accumulated a little experience. Proper education on the flat, whereby the horse can be shortened and lengthened at will and jumps out of a state of balance will, however, go a long way towards solving problems of distance and approach.

Allow always at least 2 ft more space between fences for upright jumps and shorten the distances in front of inclined fences.

However confidently the horse jumps at home he needs outside experience (when to start with he may not go so freely) at small shows, club hunter trials, etc., and the more he has the better and the safer jumper he will become.

The Horse Jumping

If we have observed the horse jumping loose we will have noted three main phases, *the take-off, the flight* and *the landing* and we will have realised that his centre of balance alters considerably during the jump.

In the *take-off*, depending upon the height of the fence and the speed at which it is approached, the hindlegs are brought under the body, the horse then pushes his forehand off the ground with the forelegs and raises his head and neck; the quarters, hindlegs and the back then thrust upwards suddenly, and as the horse enters the *flight* phase he stretches out his head and neck. He then folds the legs and describes an arc over the obstacle with rounded back and with head and neck outstretched.

As he comes in to make the *landing* the horse stretches out his forelegs, placing first one and then the other on the ground. In order at this moment to adjust his balance and decrease the weight carried by the forehand, he then raises head and neck. Then the hindlegs come to the ground, behind the forefeet, the head is accordingly lowered and the horse enters into the canter stride.

We shall also see that an upright obstacle is approached at a relatively slow speed and in this case the quarters are very strongly engaged, whereas the forehand is not so much so. The opposite is the case when the obstacle is low and wide. The speed is greater and it is the forehand which is used to a greater extent.

Individual horses, according to their conformation, will also have discovered at which speed they jump best and it is a wise rider who takes mental note of this characteristic.

Position of the Rider

From the foregoing it will be seen that the rider, if he is to allow his horse to jump to the best advantage, should understand the motions made by the horse if he is to remain in balance during the jump, and if he is not to interfere with its effectiveness by disturbing the important balancing motions of the head.

To do so his approach to the fence will be made in his jumping position, i.e. body inclined forward, seat just resting in the saddle, legs drawn slightly back in a driving position and heels well down to secure the lower half of the body. On a free jumping horse, the position over a low fence remains the same throughout the three phases of the jump, the rider's hands only moving forward to follow the movement of the head.

Should the horse not be going forward freely then the rider will have to use the additional power of his back and seat to drive him on and must then sit in the saddle, timing the forward inclination of his body with the exact moment of take-off, which is not quite so easy at first. It becomes even more difficult when the fence has to be approached slowly. The usual mistake is for the rider to be left behind the movement, when one can but slip the reins and grasp a neck-strap, or even the mane to avoid making matters worse by denying the horse freedom of his head. It is possible to get in advance of the movement, when the upward thrust of the forehand will be correspondingly overweighted and the success of the whole jump will be in jeopardy.

Practise, however, makes perfect, or nearly so, and if the rider jumps as many low fences as possible he will very quickly get the feel of the jump and be able to adjust his balance accordingly. To overjump the horse would, of course, be foolish, but if the fences are *low* there is no reason why 20–30 should not be jumped in the course of an hour or more's schooling.

During the jump, as we have seen, non-interference by the hand is of paramount importance. This will not be achieved unless the rider holds his hands the width of the bit apart and moves them forward, below the withers, to follow the motion of the head. Initially, it is better to push the hands too far forward and lose contact, rather than to risk interference with the mouth. If contact is lost it should be replaced as soon as possible, as the horse uses the rein for additional support on landing.

Work on the lunge over low fences with the rider concentrating on the jumping position, head straight and looking beyond the obstacle, back straight, knees pointed and low, lower leg flat and heel down, is the best basis for a jumping seat.

During the landing, particularly over fences involving a steep descent, the rider will find that to remain in balance his trunk must incline more to the vertical and will be less forward. The landing shock, however, will be absorbed and the rider able to resume his jumping seat if the knee remains bent and the leg position unaltered.

While schooling, either on the flat or over fences, is a fascinating occupation it has the same effect upon horses as an overdose of work had upon Jack, who, as will be remembered, became a dull boy.

It is a means to an end – not an end in itself. If we are to keep the horse interested and happy he requires periods of relaxation between the times spent on school work.

Allow him days when he does nothing more than hack gently through the countryside. Take him out to rallies, enter him in hunter trials and take him hunting as much as you can. After all, these are the things that are the reason for schooling, and he will learn more during a day's hunting than during a week in the school.

Using a distance fence to obtain the correct approach to a larger obstacle.

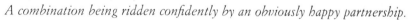

A combination being ridden confidently by an obviously happy partnership.

CHILDREN'S PONIES

The training of ponies and their riders presents a far larger problem than can be explained adequately here, but in general, will follow the same principles, even if it does not encompass the same movements.

Once the pony is obedient on the lunge, and paces have been established and the pony is jumping freely, one has an opportunity of strengthening and correcting the rider's seat by working in this medium, and it will be easy to teach both pony and rider the aids.

The aids can be explained to the child and then she can be asked to apply them at a certain point in the school. If the pony is slow to react, or does not understand, the child's aid is reinforced with the spoken, and already learnt, command, *trot, canter* or *whoa*, as it may be. Very quickly the pony will learn what the action of his rider's legs and hands means and will obey them without the additional incentive of the voice.

Jumping starts again over poles on the ground and progresses to cavalletti and finally, to small, wingless fences of every possible variety.

If the child begins jumping in the school, and on the lunge, reins can be dispensed with, a neck-strap being provided as a help to balance. The pony, who has learnt to jump freely without the rider, will not have his confidence impaired by the fear of having his mouth hurt.

Later the child can jump by having the reins fastened to the rear rings of the cavesson and, finally, when the seat is secure, with reins to the bit. If the pony has been properly educated on the lunge and a little further simple schooling has been done on long reins the child should experience little difficulty in learning control.

Progressive training of the pony obviates the senseless leg thumping, stick whacking and mouth pulling which weakens the rider's security and is too often seen. Badly schooled ponies only encourage rough handling by the child and can hardly contribute to his or her enjoyment.

It is unlikely that one will ever find what current advertisements term a "bomb-proof" pony, but certainly something approaching this description is conducive to peace of mind. For this reason the introduction into school work of the "nuisance game" is both useful and great fun for everybody.

I start by walking with the pony down the drive or round the yard while numerous small helpers bounce balls, under supervision, at a respectable distance. Gradually larger balls are used and the bouncers come nearer to the pony until eventually balls and running children are ignored. The same thing is done with flapping towels, handkerchiefs and newspapers. Finally the pony will work loose in the school to the accompaniment of transistor radios and clapping children, whilst balls can be bounced off his back and flags waved round his head without his batting an eyelid.

Ponies, and horses too, often have an aversion to water and nothing is more annoying, or for a child more unseating, than the animal who dances round every puddle in the road.

The aversion is easily enough overcome by standing the pony, securely tethered, in a yard with a haynet to keep him occupied. A hosepipe can then be turned on at the other end of the yard and left running. Eventually, and inevitably, the pony will be standing in a pool of water which has crept up on him so gradually that he will have hardly noticed it. Water can then be splashed on his legs and it will not be long before he permits with equanimity the hosepipe to be played over his limbs without raising objections.

Traffic is, of course, a major concern in these days and again it pays to walk a pony round farm machinery and to accustom him to moving vehicles in his own surroundings. Once he accepts these he can be taken out on the roads on the inside of a steady horse until he is ready to face traffic on his own. In this regard it is better, and safer, to let the pony face traffic on his own when going back to his stable. He is far less likely to play up at this stage of the ride than when going out.

It should not be too difficult to teach children road sense when riding and to demand their ponies' attention in much the same manner as that already described. Similarly, it is not too much to expect parents to teach, by precept and example, ordinary good manners. The majority of car- and lorry-drivers will slow down on meeting a pony or horse. Their courtesy should be acknowledged.

Ponies and children soon become bored and too much serious school work does them no good. School work is best absorbed when disguised as a game. Bending poles are useful in this respect as are the various Pony Club mounted games. In addition let the pony and child go hacking for the fun of it as much as possible, without worrying about head positions, heels down, elbows in and all the rest of it.

If one has a suitable horse to accompany the child work out a little cross-country jolly involving the jumping of a low log, a small ditch and other little obstacles.

A gallop across a field of stubble, particularly if it is at all undulating, does more for balance and confidence than a month of school exercises.

Lastly, a warning. It is all too easy for a situation to arise where a pony becomes over-reliant on its adult trainer and as a result plays the fool when removed from his immediate control.

The adult should be a background "father figure". His job is to start the pony on the right lines, then teach the child how to continue with the training. Once he has laid the foundations of a successful partnership he must then relegate himself to the role of adviser to both sides.

CHAPTER 12

Trailer Drill

Entering a box or a trailer without fuss was an essential requirement of the domestic horse 20 years ago, along with being steady to shoe and clip and being quiet in traffic.

It is certainly not less so today but I have the impression that a lot more horses are given little schooling in trailer drill, which is why, I suppose, one sees protracted battles between a posse of exasperated people (more than two and the battle is probably lost anyway) and one recalcitrant equine on every showground in the country. For that reason I have included this short chapter in this revision.

If a horse has never had a bad travelling experience and has been properly brought up to lead in hand there should never be any trouble about loading. In the past 20 years I have had one horse (not my own) who was difficult to box and she was cured in one week and without whips. (Admittedly, she had a trailer drill session twice and sometimes three times a day. Sometimes the operation qualified for danger money but at the end of the week she walked in and out without being led and in response to a slap on the rump.)

The late Col Joe Hume-Dudgeon, who was one of the best half-dozen teachers I have encountered in my lifetime, used to exhort his pupils to "make it easy for the horse". Easter, that is, for him to do what is wanted than to do otherwise.

It has to be the best sort of advice but in the loading of horses into trailers or boxes, and often when actually riding, there are people who seem to go out of their way to make it anything but easy for the horse to comply with their wishes.

So long as the horse has been taught to lead in hand, going boldly forward on his own account, the rest, for the most part, is a matter of taking sensible precautions.

If the trailer is placed against a wall so as to provide at least one "wing" the danger of a run-out is reduced by 50 per cent. Horses do not like a shaky footing under them, so put down the stabilisers so that the ramp remains firm.

Park the trailer with the front open and the ramp facing towards the

Trailer drill: (this page, top) *a trailer sensibly sited against a wall and with the stabilisers down to give a firm foothold;* (above) *no problems here;* (opposite page, top) *using a lunge rein to encourage the horse to load;* (opposite page, bottom) *well, the broom might just be necessary one day!*

sun, otherwise the interior resembles nothing more than a black hole, in which, so far as the horse knows, all sorts of unpleasant things may lurk. Move the central partition over to make the entrance wider and more inviting.

When beginning trailer drill, again leave nothing to chance. Let the training session commence *after* the horse has worked and has got the itch out of his heels.

Take a feed bowl in one hand and circle the horse in front of the box at a good ongoing walk. Make the circle to the left if the left side of the box is against the wall and vice versa.

It is then possible to make the approach from a somewhat oblique angle, which in itself reduces the possibility of a run-out.

Loading is, indeed, not dissimilar in basic technique to jumping, so far as the approach is concerned. Very often we make the approach to a fence off a circle and, as we should remind ourselves at every opportunity, the half of successful jumping is in the approach – the other half has to do with rider determination, and you can substitute handler for rider in the context of loading horses.

Make the approach off the circle so as to meet the ramp at a slight angle. Let the horse see the feed bowl as he puts a foot on the ramp and have a cheerful assistant walk up briskly behind him.

Once in the box, reward the horse, make much of him, and after a few moments at halt walk him quietly out down the front ramp.

If there is no front ramp, he has to back out, but he must do so one step at a time and on command. Follow the sequence: move back, halt, make much of him and then repeat it over again. Have an assistant at the side of the ramp who can guide the horse's quarters and ensure that he does not put a foot over the side.

The exercise can be repeated over a number of days, the reward being reduced on each occasion until it is no more than a carrot or a few nuts. You won't always have a bowl of oats handy.

When that is established start putting on the breeching strap and closing up the ramp, letting the handler remain with the horse while holding him up against the breast bar.

When the horse loads without hesitation, move the trailer about until he will enter it when it is parked in the middle of the yard.

However, even the best of horses may occasionally need a little in the way of encouragement for one reason or another. Always, therefore, have a lunge rein to hand, or even two of them. The rein can be attached to the trailer and then passed round the quarters by the assistant to give just that extra incentive.

The combination of two people with two lunge lines which can be crossed behind the horse is almost irresistible.

But what happens when one has no assistant? That is when you make use of "Professor" Sydney Galvayne's leading harness. Galvayne of the Groove, whose real name was Osborne, was a skilful trainer of horses, particularly of problem horses, and his simple harness is an invaluable loading aid.

In a simple form it is no more than a loop of soft, strong rope passed round the quarters and then up towards the wither. It is kept in place there by a breast rope. The ends of the rope are continued forward either through the rings of the bit or the headcollar. A pull on the ropes at the front end results in a tightening of the loop round the quarters at the other end, a matter guaranteed to cause some puzzlement in equine minds and one which in my experience ensures immediate compliance with the request to enter the container. I would no sooner take my good horse hunting without this useful piece of equipment than go without my own hard hat.

I read only last week in my Sunday paper R.W.F. Poole's account of being asked to assist with a loading problem at a Pony Club rally.

The instructress and I suppose half-a-dozen wide-eyed children were patting, cajoling, giving tit-bits and getting nowhere.

Poole, anxious to impress, took a yard broom, drove it at the pony's rear and the culprit "exoceted up the ramp into the trailer".

Alas, the instructress was hardly grateful, "Now that," she said, "is totally the wrong way to get a horse to load." She wasn't right, of course, because it was "a way" to load a horse and it worked. A triumph you might think of positive action.

There are times when horses, out of a probably perverted sense of humour, seem to be playing up for no very good reason. On those occasions a little muscular Christianity, as exemplified by Poole's yard brush, will not come amiss.

List of Suggested Reading

Crossley, Anthony, *Dressage, The Seat, Aids and Exercises* (Pelham Books)

—— *Training the Young Horse* (Stanley Paul)

Diggle, Martin, *Riding Over Jumps* (J.A. Allen)

—— *Riding Cross-Country* (J.A. Allen)

Foster, Carol, *The Athletic Horse* (Crowood)

Hartley Edwards, Elwyn, *Saddlery* (J.A. Allen)

—— *Horses, Their Role in the History of Man* (Collins)

—— *Manual of Horse Training and Management* (Unwin Hyman)

—— *Buying Horses and Ponies* (Pelham Books)

Klimke, Reiner, *Cavalletti* (J.A. Allen)

Podhajsky, Alois, *The Complete Training of Horse and Rider* (Harrap)

Serth, G.W., *Horse Owner's Guide to Common Ailments* (Pelham Books)

Thelwall, Jane, *The Less Than Perfect Horse* (Methuen)

Wynmalen, Henry, *Dressage* (A. and C. Black)

Pony Club Publication, *The Foot and Shoeing*

Index

Page numbers in *italics* indicate illustrations. Book titles and horses' names are also in *italics*.